Palgrave Macmillan Studies in Banking and Financial Institutions
Series Editor: **Professor Philip Molyneux**

The Palgrave Macmillan Studies in Banking and Financial Institutions are international in orientation and include studies of banking within particular countries or regions, and studies of particular themes such as Corporate Banking, Risk Management, Mergers and Acquisitions, etc. The books' focus is on research and practice, and they include up-to-date and innovative studies on contemporary topics in banking that will have global impact and influence.

Titles include:

Steffen E. Andersen
THE EVOLUTION OF NORDIC FINANCE

Mario Anolli, Elena Beccalli and Tommaso Giordani (*editors*)
RETAIL CREDIT RISK MANAGEMENT

Seth Apati
THE NIGERIAN BANKING SECTOR REFORMS
Power and Politics

Caner Bakir
BANK BEHAVIOUR AND RESILIENCE
The Effect of Structures, Institutions and Agents

Dimitris N. Chorafas
BASEL III, THE DEVIL AND GLOBAL BANKING

Dimitris N. Chorafas
HOUSEHOLD FINANCE
Adrift in a Sea of Red Ink

Dimitris N. Chorafas
SOVEREIGN DEBT CRISIS
The New Normal and the Newly Poor

Stefano Cosma and Elisabetta Gualandri (*editors*)
THE ITALIAN BANKING SYSTEM
Impact of the Crisis and Future Perspectives

Violaine Cousin
BANKING IN CHINA

Peter Falush and Robert L. Carter OBE
THE BRITISH INSURANCE INDUSTRY SINCE 1900
The Era of Transformation

Juan Fernández de Guevara Radoselovics and José Pastor Monsálvez (*editors*)
CRISIS, RISK AND STABILITY IN FINANCIAL MARKETS

Juan Fernández de Guevara Radoselovics and José Pastor Monsálvez (*editors*)
MODERN BANK BEHAVIOUR

Franco Fiordelisi and Ornella Ricci (*editors*)
BANCASSURANCE IN EUROPE
Past, Present and Future

Franco Fiordelisi, Philip Molyneux and Daniele Previati (*editors*)
NEW ISSUES IN FINANCIAL AND CREDIT MARKETS

Franco Fiordelisi, Philip Molyneux and Daniele Previati (*editors*)
NEW ISSUES IN FINANCIAL INSTITUTIONS MANAGEMENT

Kim Hawtrey
AFFORDABLE HOUSING FINANCE

Jill M. Hendrickson
FINANCIAL CRISIS
The United States in the Early Twenty-First Century

Jill M. Hendrickson
REGULATION AND INSTABILITY IN U.S. COMMERCIAL BANKING
A History of Crises

Otto Hieronymi and Constantine Stephanou (*editors*)
INTERNATIONAL DEBT
Economic, Financial, Monetary, Political and Regulatory Aspects

Paola Leone and Gianfranco A. Vento (*editors*)
CREDIT GUARANTEE INSTITUTIONS AND SME FINANCE

Caterina Lucarelli and Gianni Brighetti (*editors*)
RISK TOLERANCE IN FINANCIAL DECISION MAKING

Roman Matousek (*editor*)
MONEY, BANKING AND FINANCIAL MARKETS IN CENTRAL AND EASTERN EUROPE
20 Years of Transition

Gianluca Mattarocci and Alessandro Carretta (*editors*)
ASSET PRICING, REAL ESTATE AND PUBLIC FINANCE OVER THE CRISIS

Philip Molyneux (*editor*)
BANK PERFORMANCE, RISK AND FIRM FINANCING

Philip Molyneux (*editor*)
BANK STRATEGY, GOVERNANCE AND RATINGS

Imad A. Moosa
THE MYTH OF TOO BIG TO FAIL

Simon Mouatt and Carl Adams (*editors*)
CORPORATE AND SOCIAL TRANSFORMATION OF MONEY AND BANKING
Breaking the Serfdom

Victor Murinde (*editor*)
BANK REGULATORY REFORMS IN AFRICA

Bernardo Nicoletti
CLOUD COMPUTING IN FINANCIAL SERVICES

Anders Ögren (*editor*)
THE SWEDISH FINANCIAL REVOLUTION

Özlem Olgu
EUROPEAN BANKING
Enlargement, Structural Changes and Recent Developments

Fotios Pasiouras
GREEK BANKING
From the Pre-Euro Reforms to the Financial Crisis and Beyond

Daniela Pîrvu
CORPORATE INCOME TAX HARMONIZATION IN THE EUROPEAN UNION

Ramkishen S. Rajan
EMERGING ASIA
Essays on Crises, Capital Flows, FDI and Exchange Rate

Allesandro Roselli
FINANCIAL STRUCTURES AND REGULATION
A Comparison of Crises in the UK, USA and Italy

Yasushi Suzuki
JAPAN'S FINANCIAL SLUMP
Collapse of the Monitoring System under Institutional and Transition Failures

Ruth Wandhöfer
EU PAYMENTS INTEGRATION
The Tale of SEPA, PSD and Other Milestones Along the Road

The full list of titles available is on the website:
www.palgrave.com/finance/sbfi.asp

Palgrave Macmillan Studies in Banking and Financial Institutions
Series Standing Order ISBN 978–1–403–94872–4

You can receive future titles in this series as they are published by placing a standing order. Please contact your bookseller or, in case of difficulty, write to us at the address below with your name and address, the title of the series and the ISBN quoted above.

Customer Services Department, Macmillan Distribution Ltd, Houndmills, Basingstoke, Hampshire RG21 6XS, England, UK

Household Finance

Adrift in a Sea of Red Ink

Dimitris N. Chorafas

palgrave
macmillan

First published 2013 by
PALGRAVE MACMILLAN

Palgrave Macmillan in the UK is an imprint of Macmillan Publishers Limited, registered in England, company number 785998, of Houndmills, Basingstoke, Hampshire RG21 6XS.

Palgrave Macmillan in the US is a division of St Martin's Press LLC, 175 Fifth Avenue, New York, NY 10010.

Palgrave Macmillan is the global academic imprint of the above companies and has companies and representatives throughout the world.

Palgrave® and Macmillan® are registered trademarks in the United States, the United Kingdom, Europe and other countries.

ISBN 978–1–137–29944–4

This book is printed on paper suitable for recycling and made from fully managed and sustained forest sources. Logging, pulping and manufacturing processes are expected to conform to the environmental regulations of the country of origin.

A catalogue record for this book is available from the British Library.

A catalog record for this book is available from the Library of Congress.

10 9 8 7 6 5 4 3 2 1
22 21 20 19 18 17 16 15 14 13

Printed and bound in Great Britain by
CPI Antony Rowe, Chippenham and Eastbourne

Contents

List of Tables

Acknowledgements

I am indebted to a long list of knowledgeable people and organizations for their contribution to the research which has made this book feasible. I would also like to thank several senior executives and experts for constructive criticism during the preparation of the manuscript. Dr Heinrich Steinmann, Dr Nelson Mohler and Eva Maria Binder have, as always, made a significant contribution.

Let me take this opportunity to thank Peter Baker for suggesting this project, for seeing it all the way to publication, and for the editing work. Thanks also to Nick Fox for the copy-editing, David Jon Beverley for his contribution to checking style and spelling, and Keith Povey for overall coordination on the book's production.

Dimitris N. Chorafas

Introduction: Reasons for a Unified Approach to Economic Theory

Written for professionals, academics and researchers, this book addresses two of the most important political, economic and household problems faced by our society at this very moment. These are symbiotic themes defining, among themselves, the social and financial environment in which we live.

The first of these two themes is the *stress* which, from the viewpoint of the wider economy, characterizes social and financial issues – particularly in Western countries which have lost their empires. Taxes, pensions, health care and education are massive subjects which, by becoming entitlements, have not only restricted our freedom to use our economic resources, but have also affected our culture by driving the work ethic away and by creating the illusion that one can continue living in permanent debt.

The second theme is the entrenched trend towards the *debt abyss*. This used to be a Third World impediment, but now it brands the First World's status from sovereigns to households who, by default or deliberately, have taken residence in the middle of a sea of red ink.

Clear-eyed economists long ago warned against this; but it went unheeded. Back in 1958, in his book *The Affluent Society*, John Kenneth Galbraith rang the alarm bell. In the chapter entitled "The Bill Collector Cometh", he clearly stated that debt was no social solution: "consumer demand ... comes to depend more and more on the ability and willingness of consumers to incur debt ... There has been an inexplicable but very real retreat from the Puritan canon that required an individual to save first and enjoy later."[1]

It is not just my opinion but also that of many other people that the two themes – *stress in the wider economy* and *the sea of red ink* in which households are adrift – correlate. The first provides the broader economic and financial background, the second focuses on one specific area of the disaster: households in whose life government – and its twenty-first-century monster, the *state supermarket* – plays so large a role and which results in the following:

- By living beyond their means, common citizens and households have sold their souls to the devil;[2]
- The devil's priests are the bureaucrats: the more bureaucratic an organization becomes the greater the extent to which *useless* work tends to displace *useful* work;
- The most galling loss is that individual freedoms have been taken over by the all-mighty sovereign, with a loss of democracy and virtue with it.

The world is made of hay

As Lord Byron had it: "the world is made of hay which both men and asses fight to possess".[3] The hay of modern society is paper money serving as legal tender but having no prudential limits and no inherent value. Central banks and their sovereigns can print as much of it, and as fast, as their hearts desire.[4]

Of course, central bankers who want to be ahead of the curve pay lip service to the risk of inflation and try to forecast it, but this is not done in a pragmatic way, free of bias. It is utterly wrong to take inflationary effects lightly, because this leads to ill-advised monetary policies, illustrated by the fact that, over the twentieth century, the US dollar lost about 95 per cent of its spending power as a result of inflation.

Indeed, there is no better answer to the different "inflation is good for you" arguments than the one John Maynard Keynes (then at the British Treasury) gave to David Lloyd George, then chancellor of the exchequer (minister of finance), and shortly thereafter to be the prime minister: "with the utmost respect, I must, if asked my opinion, tell you that I regard your account as rubbish".[5] Allow me to ask you neo-Keynesians whether you have heard that message which comes straight from Keynes's brilliant mind. It takes both brains and guts to tell the boss that he is nuts.

Spending money beyond one's means as compensation for the fact that a run-down economy is not able to support a decent living, let alone to solve the country's important structural problems, is a wrong way risk. This failure of judgement is not limited to Western society. It has been copied and applied by countries still in the process of development. South Africa's growth potential, for instance, remains constrained by:

- High structural unemployment;
- Inadequate skills because of lack of focused training;
- High household debt – believe it or not.[6]

Whether in Europe, in America or in developing countries "spend now, earn later" puts pressure not just on the family budget but also on government finances – in the short, medium and longer term. It is a double whammy with mountains of debt that disorients the common citizen and corrupts those who govern.

Political and bureaucratic meddling is a third disaster. It comes therefore as no surprise that in Western nations public health care and pensions systems are in a mess, with trillions of unfunded liabilities. The maths looks truly alarming, particularly given the gridlock characterizing the political machine and the intensive lobbying by embedded interests for Byron's "the world is made of hay".

Choice of topics

The topics which I address have been deliberately chosen to provide a comprehensive and provocative analysis to scholarly and career people. Practical examples like education, jobs, the middle class, the IOU abyss and Galbraith's warning have been used to explain how we managed to reach such a low point in Western economies.

Other constructive, albeit critical, examples have been included with the aim of educating heads of families on how to avoid another meltdown of their finances like the one they so recently went through. At first glance, the readers to whom the first and second group of studies (Parts I and II) appeal look distinct from one another. But practically they are not, and this for two reasons. First, what has happened to the Western economy, from sovereigns to companies and households in 2007 and subsequent years, neither has a precedent nor is it limited to some social groups. Therefore, the neo-Keynesians, the monetarists and the Austrian school disciples have no theoretical answers to present-day problems. By contrast, much can be learned through the analysis of recent real life cases which provide the bridge from macro to microeconomics, and vice versa. This is precisely what I offer in this book.

Second, though the division into macroeconomics and microeconomics is accepted and practised by the majority of economists and political scientists, I do not believe in it. It is totally artificial. Scientists, too, look at the forces of nature on a departmental basis: as gravity, electricity, magnetism, and the weak and strong nuclear forces. In 1865, however, James Clark Maxwell succeeded in unifying two of them by combining electricity and magnetism. Today scores of physicists are at work trying to combine electromagnetism with the weak and strong nuclear forces – and eventually with gravity.[7]

Modern research in science looks at the whole spectrum from the very small to the very big. There is a continuum between studies of the atom and astrophysics. Why should it be that economics is studied in silos? The division of macroeconomics and microeconomics is a fictitious one which mostly, but not wholly, dates back to Wassily Leontief and Paul A. Samuelson.[8]

In a way not too different from the approach taken by Maxwell in the late nineteenth century, Vilfredo Pareto, after whom the famous law was named, made no distinction between macro and microeconomics.[9] Pareto, who was professor of mathematics and economics at the University of Lausanne, is also credited with the development of analytics more than half a century prior to Samuelson. A silo approach to economics makes no sense. It is time to unify the micro and macrodisciplines.[10]

In addition, theories in economics and other sciences are not forever. Often they are undone by a new nasty fact, while real life cases are cast in stone. The inclusion of practical examples should always be welcome, because changes necessary for an increased efficiency in education will not come about by their own will. As the large majority of educators appreciates, teaching needs to bring forward no-nonsense, down-to-earth examples in order to:

- Explain the issues;
- Document the thesis;
- Convince the audience.

Leadership by example

Real life case studies are akin to leadership by example, and this is so much more effective than managing by command, which has led to an over-governed society. The late Walter Lippmann diagnosed that "by command" there is a trend away from freedom of expression, characterized as an exercise of unlimited power by men with limited minds and self-regarding prejudices.[11]

Leadership by example is also the best possible way to reform, always keeping in mind that there is no new structure or policy which does not encounter resistance. To ease the way in which the blending of higher level concepts and practical cases can be brought to the reader's attention, each chapter in this book includes three types of issues which largely interact with one another. First is the *strategic*, mainly the metalevel thinking derived from the financial meltdown and absence of a dynamic economic recovery afterwards. "This is the worst recovery in history," said a former senior White House advisor.[12]

Second is the *tactical*, with plenty of examples of households under stress, enriched by advice on how to manage more effectively household finances. Household (and business) budgeting and cash flow projection are tactical tools. But the decision to apply them is strategic.

Third are the *metaphors*, incorporated as reference(s) to an important precedent, and aimed at expanding the reader's background or to avoid repeating points of contention.[13]

Examples of strategic issues included in this book are: Pericles 2013 (spending other people's money has consequences) and the growing gap in wealth and income; rent-seeking; "financialization"; Galbraith's warning; the middle class; pensions; health care; the talent gap; democratization of credit; socialization of risk; household leveraging; "your home is your castle"; subdued ethics; and the mammoth state supermarket.

The reader will find in this text plenty of references to tactical issues. These include the "Occupy Wall Street" movement; the different half-baked reincarnations of publicly supported health care (Clinton Care, Obama Care); the price and strategic content of education; reasons for high structural unemployment; and the task of restoring confidence – both publicly and within the realm of an individual family.

Examples of metaphors in the realm of our discussion are "paper oil" and "paper ships". Both provide a perspective on the evolution of derivative instruments all the way to "paper houses" – which the reader will be well advised to avoid. Paper houses is a new financial instrument addressed to house owners, particularly retirees, and on their social acceptance academia has not yet taken a position.[14]

It has been a deliberate choice to treat issues connected to home ownership, including the question of "shelter or burden", as a metaphor rather than as a tactical issue (house ownership, per se, is strategic). Another metaphor is the difference in the law of the land in the US and Canada, regarding home ownership. And another is the risks associated with a home investment, including price risk and foreclosure risk.

A formidable metaphor in leadership by example is "entitlements". When large, powerful issues like taxes and entitlements are being raised, the decision-makers (politicians, legislators and bureaucrats) should be forced to take account of feedback effects. The reactions of other players in the system, as well as the system's ability to sustain the surcharges, should be anticipated and studied. That does not come naturally to politicians and bureaucrats; yet it is cardinal.

A painful misconception

Since World War II households have been wrong in placing a huge amount of dependence on entitlements; they should have known better: Western states are more or less bankrupt. They were also imprudent to bet on over-indebtedness in order to enjoy the "good life". This has led to the IOU abyss and from there (for the majority of families) to having to navigate a sea of red ink.

As, nowadays, life is fraught with risks and uncertainty, the better way out for households is to get their act together by:

- Being proactive in finding work;
- Appreciating once again the value of money;
- Managing in an able manner their wealth;
- Looking at their homes as their castles, not as another speculation.

As far as the macroeconomy is concerned, has this descent to the abyss by a large part of the population been unavoidable? According to some economists, the answer is "yes" because the good times lasted too long. Thinking that adversity belongs to the past, we become overspenders, sluggish, myopic and unproductive. Complacent life styles had become so widespread that we did not realize we were drifting into a crisis.

This was a painful misconception, promoted not only by the business of spend, spend and spend, but also by some academics who preached that a sophisticated person leverages him or herself. He or she spends now and earns later or lets somebody else – for instance the taxpayer – pick up the bill. This shows no personal discipline (aside from the fact it lacks morals). People and households who follow this credo are simply straying, and since organizations are made up of people the state also is adrift.

If, and *only if*, our society returns to the basic principles which over five centuries underpinned the rise of Western civilization, will future historians *then* say that the deep economic crisis we are in led to the West's renaissance. The past offers paradigms. In the mid-nineteenth century Giuseppe Garibaldi, the general who practically single-handedly led Italy's unification, advised his followers on the economy and savings: "Who has ten spends nine; who spends twenty goes straight to ruin."[15]

Great lessons can also be learned from recent years. Caught by a bad surprise in one of his post-World War II projects, Konosuke Matsushita, who built the electrical engineering empire bearing his name, decided that what his company urgently needed was to develop quickly a thorough understanding of the problem. He personally led this effort by:

- Setting out to find what the causes were;
- Re-examining everything inside and out;
- Coming up with a well-founded solution.[16]

How successful households will be in redressing their balance sheets and in taking hold of their own future is going to be measured not by words but by results; results which, after years of drifting, they owe to themselves and to society. Endeavours which led to fruition have been often ascribed qualities that may or may not have been there. At the end of the day, however, nothing succeeds like success. The task is huge, which is precisely what a household's leader should want – and what he or she needs.

For political leaders in whose hands rests the future of the wider economy, the message brought by this book is that truly able people don't let the difficulties get the better of them. They confront their salient problem with the conviction that it can be solved, rather than wasting their energy worrying about difficulties which always show up in the way. This is the attitude which characterizes a leader, and it is also the spirit this book conveys. *"Glory follows those for whom it does not have enough dignity to guide"*, says an ancient proverb.

Part I
Society is Under Stress All Over the Western World

1
Our Society Has to Review its Business Model

1.1 Pericles 2013

In the first year of the Peloponnesian War each side's successes were few and equally distributed. But a pestilence decimated the population of ancient Athens and the citizens' morale dropped to a low point – many spoke against Pericles, the city-state's leader, who was personally responsible for the devastating war. The Athenians condemned him for breaking the peaceful coexistence with the Spartans, and attributed to him the miseries that the hostilities had brought.

To defend himself, Pericles used his skills as an orator, answering back that the citizen of a republic, brought up as a free citizen, must accept the greatest adversity when it comes. They should not lose view of their destiny. (I would advise Greeks, Italians, French, Spanish and Portuguese citizens to take good notice of this dictum.) Forget your personal miseries, Pericles said, in order to have no other thought than the public good. This is the argument Western governments are using today when people complain of:

- Unemployment;
- Austerity measures;
- The difficulty to make ends meet;
- The dismantling of the welfare state which has grown into a *state supermarket* (see Chapter 4).

The welfare state and its *entitlements* (see Chapter 2) were intended to be a display of the West's superior economic power. As President

Lyndon Johnson had it, rich countries could afford anything – war and social goodies at the same time.[1] But as entitlements grew they became unaffordable and unsustainable, ending as one more piece of evidence that no social theory lasts forever. Eventually it is undone by its own errors and abuses.

Invented in the twentieth century by William Beveridge, the British public servant, the *welfare state* has drifted off the rails, and it will remain a failure because its philosophy is that of spending not of producing. Part of the problem lies in a misunderstanding of the notion of "affordability". Thinking that everything is possible no matter how high its price may be distorts the relationship between means and ends. Political decisions turn on their heads because those making them (from voters to legislators and chiefs of state) have an imperfect appreciation of a modern economy's opaque forces and twists, and the mix of old political ideas and present day conflicts of interest make small game of analytics provided by macroeconomic models.[2]

Over the last four decades Western societies have been living in a sort of mirage about their wealth and the power of democracy. Myths led them to spend well beyond their means and the economy's ability to support the social net. With mountains of debt still rising, Western people and their politicians continue to believe that their country is "rich", and because it is rich it can afford every folly.

This is the modern version of Pericles' business model, which eventually destroyed ancient Athens. When the Athenians got into the habit of taking out of the common purse more than they had put in it, their city-state started to decline. Eventually its wealth collapsed, its defences crumbled and its citizens as well as their descendants lived under the yoke of Macedonians, Romans, Byzantines and Turks.

Spending beyond one's means at sovereign, corporate and household levels is exactly the kind of thing our society does not need – but ironically that's precisely what it gets. The tragedy of Western nations today is not that they have become poor (though this is the case) but that they think they are rich. It's an illusion which can best be labelled "Pericles 2013".

The (wrongly) celebrated father of democracy had come to the conclusion that votes can be bought by distributing entitlement, and that if need be force is right. Getting the money by force from other members of the Athenian alliance ignited the 30-years Peloponnesian War which destroyed ancient Greece. Then as now big spenders of unearned wealth don't understand that throwing money at the problem leads to policies which are wasteful and inconsistent, and so long as spending goes on unabated, the foundations of government will continue to crumble.

The theory behind this illusion is that the people and their sovereigns can spend, and somebody else will foot the bill. As a model, it mixes candour and a pathetic naivety. "Do not misunderstand me, I am your friend and protector," Pericles said to the members of the Athenian alliance (read: empire) who were asked to pay for the spend and spend policies of the metropolis. The city-states of the empire, too, initially thought Pericles was their friend; but they did wake up, and the next act was civil war.

There is a moral lesson to be learned from the decay of ancient Athens. Confronted with a growing roster of unsustainable entitlements (see Chapter 2) granted for political reasons by weak governments (without accounting for the consequences), sovereigns sink deeper and deeper into debt. By living beyond their means, the common citizens do likewise; then they fall into despair.

"I ... place economy among the first and most important of republican virtues, and public debt as the greatest of the dangers to be feared", wrote Thomas Jefferson in a letter to William Plumer on 21 July 1816 – but times have changed. The perverse logic of those who today govern the future of Western nations is: bet on debt. What has remained invariant from old times is that somebody has to pay.

Thomas Clausen, a former president of the World Bank and of Bank of America, said that the poorest nations and poorest people will be penalized most. André Tardieu, a former radical, socialist prime minister of France, said that we have to tax the poor, they are the most numerous. This is precisely what is taking place.

To understand the background reasons for *déclinisme* (decline), the reader should appreciate that a debt-laden society has no claim to wealth. Wealth is the stock of assets one has accumulated minus one's debts. Because some people are savers and others are big spenders, wealth is shared much less equitably than income. Plenty of people in poor countries have next-to-nothing. But quite a lot of people in rich countries have even less than that, because their liabilities exceed their assets.

Hard work creates wealth when husbanded by business opportunity and a benign environment promoted by a frugal (i.e. careful and economic) government and an economy characterized by the rule of law, good education, low taxes, high savings and plenty of investments. Wealth is not created, indeed it is destroyed, by distributing in small amounts what exists to everybody – like watering the garden.

1.2 The growing gap in wealth and income

From heads of state to common citizens, those who think of themselves as being more intelligent than others tend to ignore the economic realities, on the basis that for decades prior to 2007, though the debt bubble had got bigger, it had not burst. This created a desire to continue with accumulation and the trading of debt, on the belief that there will always be a greater sucker to pass the buck on to. This might work in the short run, but in the longer term it erodes the economy.

Examples are the fate of communism in the Soviet Union and of socialism in France and Sweden. The bottom *half* of Swedes have a collective net worth of less than zero.[3] This, however, does not mean that reckless inequalities and misleading slogans about laissez-faire are the best solution. Without firm regulation, not only the markets but also the whole of Western society bet their future on the "Greater Fool Theory".

The Great Fool Theory is a dangerous misconception. The French socialists say: "The rich should pay!". But who are the rich? And are they ready to act as paymasters? Those who have more money also have more sway. The fact that the pyramid of wealth distribution has a very wide base and a sharp point induced Vilfredo Pareto to make Pareto's Law. Today:

- The richest 1 per cent control 43 per cent of the world's assets;
- The wealthiest 10 per cent control 83 per cent
- The bottom 50 per cent have only a mere 2 per cent.

In India, a nation of 1.2 billion people, the 100 richest people own assets equivalent to a quarter of gross domestic product. And there are also some US figures worthy of the reader's attention. There has been a 300 per cent rise in the real incomes of the richest 1 per cent of Americans in the past 30 years, versus a mere 40 per cent rise in the median household income for the same period.[4]

According to the US Congressional Budget Office, between 1979 and 2007, in a little less than three decades, *after-tax income* grew by 62 per cent for all households, but for the top 1 per cent of earners the growth has been 275 per cent. This top 1 per cent of income earners controlled more than 20 per cent of total national income in 2007, double their share in 1979.

The top 1 per cent and bottom 30 per cent (or even 50 per cent) point to a huge discrepancy in wealth, but also a great disparity in terms of political influence which typically comes hand in glove with control of the world's capital. Not all politicians are smart, but the majority can read numbers and the numbers tell a lot about the impact of money, which rests on two legs: accumulated wealth and annual income.

According to the US Internal Revenue Service, those in the 1 per cent bracket make $960,000 or more per year – round it to $1 million – in annual income. Not everybody, however, is in accord with this definition. According to *The Economist*, the average US household income in 2008 was $1.2 million, but the 1 per cent began at $380,000 because the average was skewed by the super-rich. In 2007, the Congressional Budget Office put the cut-off at $347,000. Measured not by income but by net worth, in 2009 the top 1 per cent in the US started at $6.9 million.[5]

By some magic, the richer people also pay less in taxes. The Obamas, the current occupants of the White House, paid 20.5 per cent on their 2011 income of $789,000.[6] At that level, Barack and Michelle Obama are in the top 1 per cent of US income earners according to both the Congressional Budget Office and *The Economist* definitions. Mitt Romney, the Republican challenger in the November 2012 elections, also paid 20 per cent in taxes even though his annual income is some $20 million.[7]

"Million" is becoming a rather obsolete unit of income and wealth measurement. "Billion" (one thousand million) is today's metric. At the end of the twentieth century, near the peak of the dot.com stock market, there were world-wide about 200 billionaires, the largest number in America and in Europe, but also many in Asia. A decade or so later, in 2010, there were nearly one thousand billionaires: over 400 in the US and Canada; 230 in Europe; 120 in Asia (other than China and India); and nearly 200 in the so-called BRICS: Brazil, Russia, India and China – a 500 per cent increase.[8]

These statistics provide an impressive pattern of the concentration of wealth, but one should also account for its high volatility. Vast fortunes have come and gone. Typically, big fortunes took a generation or two to make, but did not last longer than the next two generations. Today large fortunes are made and lost at higher speed thanks to the growing *financialization* of wealth (see section 1.7) promoted by novel, volatile and risky instruments.

There has been no time in human history when wealth was distributed in an even way in spite of all the "isms" such as socialism, fascism, Nazism and communism. But as long as there were jobs, and therefore income, differences in wealth were not brought under the magnifying glass. "Treasure the things that are difficult to attain," urges a Chinese motto. In America "riches" were the goal of most young people starting their careers.

Misery, by contrast, is not characterized by volatility. It has the nasty habit of staying around and spreading. In 2010, in America, 46.2 million people fell below the poverty line, calculated as an annual income of $22,300 for a family of four and $11,140 for an individual. This increase lifted the poverty rate to more than 15 per cent of the US population, the highest in 50 years.

The averages also suffered. The median household income which stood at $52,500 in 2000 dropped to below $49,500 in 2010. Such a drop becomes more significant if inflation in the first decade of this century is accounted for. Moreover, the aftermath of the recession has seen to it that the reduction of income is skewed towards the financially weaker members of society.

This is not the only bad news. Given the widely accepted projections that both shorter term and longer term unemployment will continue at high rates, economists do not predict a turnaround in household incomes any time soon. Instead, they expect the current pattern to continue for several years. Analysts underscore the difficulties facing the federal and state governments as they seek at the same time to reduce deficits and help growing numbers of those worse off.

The increase in poverty among the working age population is a new phenomenon in Western countries. The late 2011 data laid bare the damage created by the deep economic and financial crisis which started in 2007 with the banking crisis. Not only were jobs massively lost and the number of unemployed soared, particularly the longer term unemployed, but the collapse in real estate prices in America, Britain and Spain set those countries back by a decade in real estate net wealth.

Wealth and income of course is not the same thing, but they do correlate. Income is more important than wealth, and the latter is created by the former if expenses are kept under lock and key.[9] The salient problem for the new generation is work and income, rather than inherited wealth.[10] Inherited wealth eventually destroys the person or household receiving it, because it incites the using of money without any consideration on how to rebuild the wealth and it affects a person's work habits. The same is true with easy money. The job environment, however, has deteriorated. Jobs which were there for the asking after World War II are gone because:

- Globalization (see section 1.6) eliminated a lot of opportunities for work in Western countries, particularly in manufacturing;
- Wrong career planning turned many youngsters into being unemployable (more on this in Chapter 3);
- Stiff labour laws permitted those who have a job to take those who don't as hostages. As it is not possible to hire and fire, or that such would entail heavy penalties, poorly performing persons cannot be weeded out. They continue occupying jobs which become unavailable to those from outside the closed labour system, who are actually seeking employment;
- The welfare state's heavy economic burden, which particularly fell on manufacturing, made Western products uncompetitive in a globalized economy.

Economists speak of a two-speed recovery for Americans: the wealthiest maintain their spending habits and lifestyles, while a large number of low-income citizens are mired in poverty. An example is child poverty which, since the mid-1960s when the federal "War on Poverty" was launched by President Johnson, in 2010 was the fourth highest recorded level. In nearly five decades of its existence, the "War on Poverty" has failed to deliver.

1.3 The standard of living and rent seeking

It needs no explaining that mounting inequality nurtures a sense of injustice, particularly in Western countries where year-on-year growing prosperity was believed to be another entitlement. This is not so in other parts of the world where free thinkers are few and the rule is for leading by command. Nothing had prepared the Western citizen for the loss of this growing prosperity which they considered as being due to them (see Chapter 2).

The trend towards a greater inequality started in the 1980s, well before the recent economic and banking crisis and the bursting of the biggest bubble in history. In US residential real estate, for example, never before had house prices risen so fast over a few years. This also happened in many other countries. Even if the bust has been less widespread than the boom, home prices tumbled a great deal in America, Spain and Ireland, which has decimated:

- The living standard of leveraged households;
- The capital of banks who had recklessly fed the real estate boom;
- The treasuries of sovereigns who imprudently added the banks red ink to that of their own, by trying to rescue them.

Employment has also been a victim and is another sensitive area where macroeconomics and microeconomics meet. The particular victim here has been youth unemployment which grew to 50 per cent in Spain and 30 per cent in Italy, Greece, Portugal, Ireland and Slovakia (see Chapter 3). There is something else embarrassing about this macro/microeconomic conjunction. Critics say that the young generation today may make pleasant company, but that they lack ambition. They seems happiest when doing comparatively little, but with this sort of spirit they are preparing for themselves a bleak future.

If this thinking of "doing less and asking for more" becomes ingrained, it will lead to disaster. Waiting for the state to find a job and to provide food and housing is a path which unequivocally leads to a lower standard of living, stress, unhappiness, wide-spread poverty and unavoidable decline. It creates a sort of a morose society, split between the haves and the have-nots, in which the options are limited to either being one of the poor living at the expense of the state or to being rich and overtaxed – anything in-between, essentially the whole middle class which provided the foundations of Western prosperity and democracy, is crushed.

According to Moisés Naim, the political scientist, "In 2012, peaceful coexistence with inequality will end and demands and promises to fight it will become fiercer and more widespread than they have been".[11] But so far, with the exception of the "Occupy Wall Street" movement (see section 1.4) which by April 2012 had fizzled out, this has not yet materialized.

Instead, evidence points to the fact that inequalities are increasing worldwide, and not only in the West. The annual rate at which richest Chinese saw their wealth grow is 18 per cent, according to a McKinsey report.[12] In the US, Ray Dalio, head of Bridgewater, the world's largest hedge fund, personally made $3.9 billion in 2011. On the other hand, the world's richest lost $9 billion with the market slump.[13]

Mounting inequality is not only a serious issue, but is also a complex one because in a democracy prosperity correlates with personal effort. It is very difficult to decide on a person-by-person, or household-by-household, basis who has worked hard to succeed – but has still not made it – and who has been loafing around waiting for the nanny state to pay the rent. What should be guaranteed is Napoleon's policy of *the career open to talent*. This is precisely what the featherbedding labour unions oppose.

In his aforementioned article, Naim points out another problem: the challenge of lowering inequality without harming other socially acceptable (and necessary) goals, such as investment, innovation, risk-taking and hard work. Some social scientists also add to this list the fact that countless alternative social systems have resulted in even more inequality, along with the loss of freedom (see section 1.2).

An example of the social distortion created by the nanny state is that of so-called "opportunity youths" – a curious label considering what it means in terms of content. Coined in America, it identifies 16-year-old dropouts who, in today's US society, constitute a depressing 17 per cent of the youth population. The way it is described in the financial newspapers in the US, in January 2012 the country was confronted with 6.7 million opportunity youths (essentially rent seekers) – each costing the public purse $750,000 over a lifetime.[14] With manna from heaven, individual initiative is wanting. "People create problems by not trusting their own judgment. By creating a committee. By constantly needing validation", said Pat Farrah, of Home Depot, to his employees. "You guys are empowered. You can find 99 per cent of the answers in the aisles, where the customers are."[15]

Individual initiative has fallen by the wayside because the nanny state is supposed to provide everything: money for ever increasing spending "needs", employment for all, free education, free housing (at least in France), good food, plenty of health care and good pensions. The state must not only find jobs for people unable or unwilling to search for employment, but these should also be well-paid. Everybody has *rights* but nobody has responsibilities.

One of the most labyrinthine problems confronted by governments in helping their citizens through adversity is how to differentiate between those who want to work but find no jobs and those who are simply *seeking rent.*[16] The dividing line has become blurred because in the welfare state the standard of living is more often determined by government subsidies, taxes (including negative taxes) and regulations – not by managerial and entrepreneurial activity. Even in ordinary business huge profits depend on whether companies:

- Have political friends;
- Win government contracts;
- Receive subsidies;
- Are protected by tariffs and quotas;
- Succeed at getting inhibiting regulations eased.

As I wrote in my book *Education and Employment in the European Union,*[17] a growing army of rent seekers have learned from older rent seekers how to earn money by doing nothing. The more this practice spreads, the greater are the abuses of the social safety net, while the effort to put the house in order (if and when there is such an effort) becomes less and less effective. The welfare state's "easy money for all" has contaminated the working population, starting at an early age, by teaching people how to live on rent and how to load oneself with debt.

One of rent seeking's results is that bribes grease the wheels of politics and ease the task of overcoming government controls. Corruption always emerges wherever bureaucrats have a major impact on economic conditions (with or without the so-called "fakelakia", a word widely used in Greece to mean envelopes containing money pushed under the table to buy the conscience of the receiver) and whenever a government gets outside its role as regulator of the economy and guarantor of financial stability (which is by far the no. 1 objective of central banks, rather than trying to solve single-handedly the economic crisis). One of the many types of rent seeking is compensating for imaginary ills. In October 2011 Long Island railway New Yorkers were claiming $1 billion in compensation for fake liabilities.[18]

In conclusion, society – particularly Western society – has too many "1 per centers", rent seekers, manipulators of imaginary ills and endowments which have largely been the outcome of a hasty populism. The time has come for a new departure which does not put its faith in the (imaginary) perfection of human nature but comes up with clear, pragmatic principles as to how best to go forwards. Maybe, but only maybe, movements like Occupy Wall Street can then contribute to a greater awareness by the general public.

1.4 "Occupy Wall Street"

Mid-September 2011 started in New York City as what first seemed a rally by many hundreds and then thousands of young Americans marching or camping out in Liberty Park in Manhattan's financial district.[19] Before too long, this rally expanded globally to become the Occupy Wall Street (OWS) movement which, in the short time of two months, spread to more than 900 cities worldwide. As one poll suggested, in America it won the support of a quarter of the electorate.

At first, both common people and political analysts did not have an easy time in understanding OWS's background and reasons, since they tried to judge the action by the demonstrator's slogans, placards and websites, becoming bewildered by the diversity of the messages. Then came the "Declaration of the Occupation of New York City" which summoned all those who felt "wronged by the corporate forces of the world" – a vast and vague wording.

According to many sociologists, the OWS movement is not a revolution; it's a reaction against the existing order. The motivation comes from the young people who decided they would not pay for their elders' errors. By contrast, a revolution is not so much against the existing order, as the setting up of a new order (at least on the surface) that opposes the traditional one. Examples are the popular outburst of the French Revolution and the well-organized takeover of Russia by Trotsky and Lenin.

What a popular youth movement and a revolution have in common is that their fruits take time to mature. The French Revolution found its centre of gravity not under Robespierre but in the Napoleonic years, when careers opened to talents. The Russian Revolution did not find its true expression in the Stalinist years, because suppression exceeded that of the czar.[20] Russia found its way to a new equilibrium after the end of the communist regime, by opening itself to the world.

For the time being at least, the OWS movement has not only lost much of its flame but also remains without a clear direction. The rallies had self-appointed representatives of "the other 99 per cent" of the population (see section 1.5) who condemned social inequality and irresponsible financial practices, but the organizers did not succeed in translating anger into specific demands. Absent of concrete goals, OWS risks splintering.

According to American analysts, there are three main tendencies in the movement. First, there are those who want to build a "new society", but have not yet a blueprint and road map. Critics characterize this group as consisting of people with good intentions but nothing concrete to propose for change – hence it is utopian. However, this is not totally true. Certain notions underpinning this part of OWS reflect a widespread feeling that money has too much a say in the world. What is missing is a pragmatic alternative. Until the details of alternative economic, social and political solutions are spelled out, there will be plenty of discursive arguments which don't permit a firm conclusion on what to do and how. This is a pity because a new way which could shape society's future structure cannot be determined until all issues are put on the table and are analysed and debated – which is a vast task.

Second, there are those who want to make capitalism "more human".[21] This, too, is utopian because capitalism is what it is and the cocktail of capitalism and socialism, the currently prevailing social regime in the West (America included), has made things worse, not better. Capitalistic excesses are the order of the day, as attested by the unprecedented banking crisis of 2007–13 (the fat bonuses for bankers continued unabated), but it is no less true that the "state supermarket" (see Chapter 4) has led to a society which has lost its bearings. There is no better example on the need to choose one way and stick to it than the one provided by Josef Pilsudski, the father of modern Poland. Pilsudski used to be a socialist, but above all he was a nationalist. According to Margaret Macmillan, right after he arrived back in Warsaw after the World War I armistice, his old socialist friends came to see him and called him "comrade". "Gentlemen," he told them, "we both took a ride on the same red train, but while I got off at the stop *Polish Independence*, you wish to travel to the station *Socialism*. Bon voyage – but be so kind as to call me *Sir*!"[22]

Third, there are those who joined OWS to turn it into a wider civil rights movement. To them current Western society is a place of unsatisfied promises in need of change, but any such changes have not gone far enough. The wider spirit in this group of OWS participants is for a merge of a "better" society with "better" (but unspecified) conditions to be implemented after the collapse of the present-day order. In all likelihood, analysts say, in this group are also some anarchists, but there is no evidence that they have control. If the foundations of the West's current social and political structure crumble it will not be because of anarchists, even less because of communists; it will be due to governments' own ineptitude and inability to make choices and take tough decisions.

Governments and the establishment find it difficult to decide in which way they should react to the challenge. This is one of the reasons why critics, who see nothing coherent in government policy against OWS, have commented that both the authorities and the movement are without clear policies. Critics also add that while the participants in the OWS action seems to be motivated, those in charge lack powerful allies to promote it.

It might not be so difficult to find such allies. A comment in the *Financial Times* was that anti-Wall Street protesters, who are giving the banks and other corporate entities a taste of their own medicine, could find allies by turning to the growing community of large institutional investors – including public funds and sovereign wealth funds (as well as labour unions) – that have embraced the idea of socially responsible investing.

By contrast, it will be more difficult to find support among the political elite which is not ready to subscribe to, let alone initiate, major changes. This is precisely where the problem lies. There is no political will for restructuring Western society and the economy, bringing entitlements down to an affordable level and placing more emphasis on relaunching the economy and hence on jobs. Neither is there money (other than inflationary money) to finance such new departures.

In conclusion, the OWS movement might be seen as a way of renewal of American society and of Western society at large, but without a grand plan and some important details public opinion remains divided in its reaction. There was indeed public support as the OWS protests spread coast-to-coast from New York to Los Angeles then to Boston, Chicago and Washington. But public support is volatile and does not last long.

Looking at the umbrella of events connected to the OWS movement, to see how their connections might be improved, one can see that the OWS has missed two important issues. The first is that as long as the West is indebted to the East, job opportunities will be in the East – not in the West. The second is that on the shoulders of each young person weighs not only his or her personal debt but also that of the intergenerational debt – to which scant attention has been paid. Yet this is making "the other 99 per cent" more brittle than it might otherwise have been.

1.5 Intergenerational equity and debt

One of the main issues of our time, which politicians have largely failed to address, is the highly explosive issue of *intergenerational equity and debt*. (Positive) equity refers to assets; debt (or negative equity) refers to accumulating liabilities. Longevity brought this intergenerational challenge up as a sleeping bed-fellow to what OWS has called "the other 99 per cent".

The deep economic and financial crisis which started in 2007 had two effects which weigh heavily today and will continue doing so in the coming years. The first is that it reinforced the defensive position of a two-tier labour market which obliges younger workers to confront job insecurity, while preserving for older workers a high degree of protection. The second is the asymmetric rewards which followed the Western economies descent to the abyss, and which has made young people aware that current entitlements are loaded on the side of the present generation of workers and employees, and who are leaving the succeeding generations with huge liabilities that they will find very difficult to repay (see Chapter 2).

If exception is made of residential real estate where parents still leave some assets to their children – for instance in Germany 23 per cent of households that own their main residence obtained it as either an inheritance or a gift[23] – inheritance has become a poisoned benevolence. The classical notion of "household net worth" has turned on its head and the result has been "household net debt" – a new notion.

The more generally accepted definition of "household net worth" is that it equals total assets net of total liabilities. Total assets consist of financial assets (which include currency, deposits, shares and other securities) and non-financial assets, whose key component is housing real estate.[24] Turning around this formulation, household net debt can be defined as the family's total liabilities, including the per capita public debt, net of total assets.

Household net debt is (or at least should be) a nightmare for everybody, and most particularly for the "other 99 per cent". Seen under the perspective of the indebted common citizen, in the largest possible sense – within the current structure of the economy and of society – this "99 per cent" includes all people who are in a more or less precarious position.

On the other hand, it is an exaggeration to speak of "99 per cent". A more realistic estimate of a Western country's population confronting difficult conditions is between 30 and 50 per cent. Even so, 35 to 50 per cent means that mounting inequality hits almost one out of two citizens or households – and this is unacceptable. It is becoming clear that the Western world is in pretty bad shape – and everybody is responsible for it, whether one is in the "1 per cent" or in the "99 per cent".

"Wealth always means independence and comfort", says Marc Rich, the American oil trader, "but it also means that I can help the less fortunate with my foundations".[25] Not everybody in the 1 per cent is providing this help to the less fortunate, and when it happens it is more likely to take place in America than in Europe. Neither should this "1 per cent" be looked at as a *deus ex machina*. Every man or woman, and most particularly every head of household, should watch the economic situation (including his or her generational equity and debt) and right the balance of income, expenses and prior commitments before it is too late.

This being said, it is no less true that many people in the "99 per cent" have a strong feeling that they and their families are slowly moving from the middle class to the lower class (see Chapter 2), and they have reasons to think so as they are facing hard times. At risk are both their employment opportunities and their ability to continue servicing their debts (including their mortgages).

At its roots, the challenge is political. In an interview he gave to CNN on 26 October 2011, Michael Moore, author and film producer, pointed out that over 45 million people live in poverty right now in the US. Greed started 10 to 15 years ago, Moore said, making life harder and harder for many people. In his opinion, OWS is the result of a frustration felt by many Americans, including:

- Families overspending by buying things they cannot afford;
- Governments spreading themselves thin and getting deeper into debt;
- Banks overleveraging themselves and taking inordinate risks, then distributing their fat profits among their elite.

In Moore's opinion capitalism has become greed but it has powerful friends in government who conveniently look the other way. The Department of Justice did not prosecute those responsible for the deep financial and economic crisis of 2007; nor for the stock market, real estate and other bubbles which preceded it. Instead, taxpayers' money has been used in lavish amounts to pull up short of the abyss the self-wounded banks.[26] Curiously, Moore did not make reference to the generational equity and debt issue which is a most potent factor.

According to other opinions probably the most drastic reason behind the current malaise (discomfort, uneasiness) lies the fact that the American democracy has ceased being sensitive to voters' wishes. Protesters have taken to the street because they are prevented from achieving something with their lives by the two quarrelling sides of the nation's bitterly divided political parties. Protestors perceive a downward trajectory for their future and they are afraid this downside is likely to become even steeper for their children.

Critics say that what has happened during the last couple of decades is the incoherent outcome of a political void. The so-called political left lacks any convincing programme in the neo-socialist world of the state supermarket. The political right promotes the status quo. And both left and right have found their place in an environment in which the dominant motivation is greed.

Left unattended, intergenerational debt is soaring, and the most irrational bailouts are made by governments and central banks with other peoples' money. What the diffused leadership and membership of the OWS movement can claim with evidence is the concern that, in spite of the nanny state or more likely because of it, our society is confronted by a rising inequality with the reasons lying both within and without, including:

- Globalization has put nearly every job in Western countries under pressure;
- Information technology has eliminated plenty of jobs previously deemed secure;
- The global economic and financial crisis, which led to deep recession, has made social pressures much more acute.

Make no mistake about it. We have come to this point because governments have not examined their options in full detail, they have been prone to accept wishful thinking as an answer, and they have not stuck to their guns. They often cave in under pressure from powerful lobbies – and this is only one of their sins. The other is that they let themselves be intimidated by both the "1 per cent" and the "99 per cent".

Mario Monti, Italy's prime minister, provides an example. He took over the reins of a country sinking under €2.1 trillion of public debt, with the aim of putting the balances straight. But in less than two months he found out the hard way that labour liberalization – which could help the moribund Italian economy – was firmly opposed by taxi drivers in Rome who are evidently not part of the "1 per cent"; and the Roman taxi drivers carried the day.

One of Monti's proposed reforms would have opened up territorial operating restrictions (for instance, allowing out of town taxis to operate in Rome). This was brought down in flames by the angry Roman taxi drivers. About a year earlier the same had happened in Athens. Promoted by the EU, the European Central Bank (ECB) and the IMF, George Papandreou's formula for labour liberalization was knocked down by an interminable strike of taxi drivers and pharmacists. Reforms were put on hold, which suggests that it is high time the "99 per cent" takes care of its own reactionary elements. Prime ministers who are brought down in flames by taxi drivers, and the political party they represent, are not viable candidates for any office.

1.6 Globalization's trilemma

"Globalization" is both a process and a state of mind. In terms of labour, raw materials, agricultural produce, manufactured goods and services, global markets open a greater perspective than those that are regional, national or local. Success in global trade, however, requires restructuring of the labour market to make it competitive worldwide and to provide for:

- Flexibility;
- Adaptation;
- Innovation;
- Cost-control;
- Price competitiveness;
- Global marketing skills.

This is the theme of my book on *Globalization's Limits*,[27] which pressed the point that countries and companies that don't meet these prerequisites, or turn a blind eye to their challenges, will be hurt by globalization. It is not at all surprising that, like any other process, globalization has limits; and that when such limits are exceeded it may turn from friend to foe.

Therefore, it came as a shock that in no Western country have politicians dared to explain to the public the real depth of the problems confronting companies and common citizens as some of the developing countries turned globalization to their own advantage. Western monetary policy has been one of the victims. Because of globalization and innovation in financial instruments (read: derivatives), classical monetary policy has lost its punch: central bankers have been reduced to firefighters and the instruments at their disposal are worn out and have become ineffectual.

One of the idiosyncrasies of globalization is that it promotes production in what were called until recently less developed countries. This has hurt labour in the West, and not just those in non-specialized jobs. Globalization has also increased the world's uncertainties in terms of income and wealth. This has destabilized both the common people and decision-makers in a way reminiscent of Goethe's *Faust*, where, frustrated by the constraints on his learning, the hero makes a pact with the devil.

Treaties worked out in the different 'rounds' of the World Trade Organization (WTO) cannot and have not closed the uncertainties gap. People often fail to appreciate that it is much easier to launch a treaty than subsequently to control the execution of its clauses. The devil is in the detail. And detail is unavoidable because running a globalized economy is a lot about judgement and understanding people with diverse objectives and inherent contradictions.

Up to a point, but only up to a point, the growing supply of low-cost goods improved the standard of living of people in Western nations: their money went so much further, hence they profited from globalization. It also served to control inflation. But at the same time it destabilized the jobs landscape of economies to which low-cost goods had been massively exported. Globalization's negatives come step by step in the form of:

- Dislocation of jobs;
- Loss of competitiveness;
- Huge current account deficits.

Only after we first reached then exceeded globalization's limits did we come to realize that globalization includes unsuspected inconvenient facts and unwanted consequences. After the event, a small group of economists, industrialists and politicians came forward with the suggestion that due consideration should always be given to the fact that, just as in science, globalization has no morals (more precisely, science – and by extension globalization – is amoral, not immoral). The party who wins is the one who:

- Is better organized;
- Knows what it wants;
- Has a longer term perspective;
- Possesses financial staying power.

Behind these four bullets lies globalization's *trilemma*. Unlike the typical dilemma which boils down to an either/or answer, a trilemma demands a choice of two out of three options as only two are possible at any time. You cannot simultaneously have everything you want, that is:

- Global dominance;
- A high level of employment;
- Economic and financial independence.

Western countries can have a higher level of employment by making the state the employer of choice. But they will spend their wealth and financial power to feed the state supermarket, and this is hardly a prescription for global dominance in the longer term. Alternatively, they can have a long range plan for global leadership and stick to it, but to do so they have to optimize their finances with a view to the longer term. As a result, employment is sure to suffer.

The trilemma can turn into a *quadrilemma* by adding fiscal policy to the first three factors. This will include taxation, national debt and current account balances. Globalization has complicated the search for effective solutions because of the unknowns it introduced. It also made Western sovereigns undecided in confronting their internal and external challenges, as debt has been piling on debt.

Take America and its accumulated massive current-account deficits as an example. For years globalization was considered tantamount to the US way of living and to the principles of democracy.[28] Then it was realized that foreign liabilities have mushroomed. As people consumed more and more goods "Made in China" both jobs and US dollars moved to the East.[29] This is not just an American phenomenon. It can be found in Britain, in France, in Italy and elsewhere in the West.

This is by no means a call for sealing the borders, but it is as well to appreciate globalization's limits. Nearly two centuries ago, David Ricardo, one of the influential economists of his time, railed against the doctrine of reinforced national borders by advocating free exchange of goods. Since then, his theory of *comparative advantage* has fed the free trade debate. Ricardo's central argument was that even if one country could produce everything more efficiently than another, which is never the case, it would reap gains from specializing in what it is best at and trading its products with the other nations.

What David Ricardo did not say is that there are prerequisites for an effective globalization. These concern first and foremost the restructuring of national economies: from establishing strategic plans to revamping labour laws, to instituting lifelong learning and watching carefully so as to stay ahead of global competition. There are, as well, personal prerequisites, four of which are outstanding:

- Knowledge;
- Adaptation;

- Flexibility;
- Hard work.

Other basic prerequisites are a strategic plan and economic guidance that are able to confront globalization's challenges and which are enriched by the will to make plans succeed. Cultural change is important because, with globalization, all sorts of companies – large, medium and small, as well as individuals – come under stress as competitive conditions get into higher gear.

Global market changes affect products and processes in an environment where competition is king. To survive and prosper companies not only need to restructure but also to *reinvent themselves*. This means taking steps beyond those seen as "most obvious" like:

- Revaluing human capital;
- Betting on innovation;
- Targeting new markets;
- Cutting down the costs of operations.

The winners are those careful to assure a comfortable profit margin necessary for new investments and as a war chest against adversity. Because the exact date is not known it is sure that one day adversity will hit and one must be ready for it well ahead of time.

In conclusion, people, companies and sovereigns are frustrated beyond measure at what they see as the disastrous effects of global capitalism. Up to a point they are right. Globalization should have been done in a better planned way and without loading the dice to the side of *financialization*.

1.7 The advent of "financialization"

"Financialization" is a new term. You would not find it in a five-year-old dictionary. It has been coined to mean the conversion of all sorts of real assets and of debt into tradable financial paper. By knowing that a substantial part of an investor's assets is other peoples' debt (bonds being an example) one can understand that in their large majority financialized instruments are based on liabilities recast in the role of pseudo-assets.

Etymologically, the first use of the term "financialization" was in relation to commodities, in the middle of the last decade, as trading activity in commodity futures intensified. One of the key drivers of "financialization of commodities" was the increasing appetite of investors for holding commodities and financial instruments linked to commodities for reasons of portfolio diversification.

Such a diversification made sense because historically there had been a low correlation between commodities and other types of investments. This, however, is no longer true, given the increasing correlation between commodities and other financial assets – a fact which worries central bankers and supervisory authorities (because it could have adverse consequences for monetary policy and financial stability).

Bank supervisors are also concerned by the financialization of dubious loans, such as subprime mortgages. These have been the trigger which launched the recent economic and banking crisis, after being massively securitized and sold to other banks and to the public with a fake AAA rating regarding their creditworthiness.

The people in the OWS rallies exaggerated when they called all bankers "career terrorists" who fill their pockets with an inordinate amount of money. After all, there are plenty of honest bankers desiring to find a sense of belonging in the community where they live and work. But there is no denying that many bankers as well as politicians supporting them have abused the system in any way they could.

"As thousands have gathered in Lower Manhattan, passionately expressing their deep discontent with the status quo, we have taken note of these protests", wrote Lloyd Blankfein, the boss of Goldman Sachs, in a letter to investors. "And we have asked ourselves this question: How can we make money off them?" Blankfein's answer has been the newly launched "Goldman Sachs Global Rage Fund",[30] which plans to invest in firms likely to benefit from social unrest.

If capitalism and financialization have these kinds of friends, they do not need enemies. Big banks take such an aggressive attitude because they know from experience that their army of lobbyists and lawyers is ready and waiting to pull them out of trouble. They also appreciate that the politicians will be happy to oblige. An example is the shadow that Ron Suskind casts on Tim Geithner, the US Treasury Secretary, as a virtual fifth column inside the Obama Administration for the banks, who are "his longtime constituents".[31]

An urgent job for sovereigns is that of thoroughly re-examining the role of financialization and of screening the behaviour of the financial community to remove conflicts of interest and short-termism. Politicians who respect themselves and their constituents can reach that goal by being immune to favours and by strengthening barriers which should be in place to divide the political process from corporate interests.

But will the lobbyists and other pressure groups permit it? It is a disgrace that after the deep economic and financial crisis, which started in July/August 2007 and saw its major dip in September 2008, no person responsible for it has been brought to justice. Those who profited hugely from the system simply kept their gains and, in many cases, even their jobs. Neither were there any sanctions against regulators who had turned a blind eye.

In early October 2008, under intense questioning by Henry Waxman, then chairman of the Government Oversight Committee of the US House of Representatives, and (in a separate deposition) by members of the US Senate's Banking Committee, Dick Fuld, CEO of the defunct Lehman Brothers, had some interesting things to say. He admitted publicly that his bank had *not* been supervised by the Securities and Exchange Commission. It is the case that:

- *If* the American SEC and the Fed had done their job in terms of supervision, *then* Lehman would not have gone bankrupt, while Citigroup and Bank of America would not have had to nearly deposit their balance sheet which was saved at the twelfth hour by taxpayers money;
- *If* the British FSA had performed its supervisory and financial control duties, *then* Northern Rock, Alliance & Leicester, Bradford & Bingley, Halifax Bank of Scotland (HBOS) and Royal Bank of Scotland would not have gone to the wall.

But not all the ills lie with supervision. Wrong-way financialization also means turning the central banks' printing presses faster through *quantitative easing* as practised by the Federal Reserve and Bank of England. Designed to jump start the economy, and having done so without any success, the central bankers' policy of transforming real assets (a nation's monetary stability) into wall paper has been a failed experiment with severe consequences.[32]

The risks Western economies run with all sorts of financialization and of unorthodox economic measures are those of pursuing wrong goals which, apart from the inflation they bring, also distract them from other more fundamental duties. A case in point is the long overdue regulation of derivative financial instruments. Inter alia, the booming market for credit default swaps (CDSs) provides evidence that in the "casino society" of ours beggars have become choosers. Good sense advises that the CDS market should be immediately, globally and thoroughly regulated, and *if* for any reason this cannot be done, *then* the CDS market should be closed down, as either way the lottery must stop.

Wider and wider communications supported by global networks see to it that politicians cannot fool people the way they used to. The public is not that stupid; it knows what is going on and it is angry. In the week of 16 March 2009 a crowd of shoe-throwing demonstrators gathered outside a conference centre in Canada, as George W. Bush spoke to businessmen. This was his first speech since stepping down as US president. But he was not out of public sight.

* * *

Our society has legitimized a business model which can no longer deliver. But while many people agree that this model is being exploited in an outrageous way by its insiders and has become a house of cards, the Western democracies lack the political will to restructure their society, its economic goals and its means for reaching them – which means the businesses.

This message has been provided in section 1.1, while section 1.2 brought into perspective the growing gap in wealth and income, and section 1.3 focused on the growing population of rent seekers. The OWS movement (section 1.4) has been looked at as the right initiative but one with feet of clay because there is no grand plan or details, while scant attention has been being paid to the intergenerational debt (section 1.5).

Globalization (section 1.6) has been examined in terms of merits and demerits. This is by no means a recent invention: cross-border trade has been going on for millennia. What is new with globalization's reincarnation in the 1980s is the Gordian knot of conflicting interests. Many people profit from it, but at the same time, since 2000, the US has lost more than five million manufacturing jobs which, according to all the evidence, will never come back.[33]

Then there is the concept and practice of financialization which turned the table on old values and on ethics. Its goal is the fast buck and its religion *bigness*. The concentration of deposits in the hands of Wall Street banks has greatly upset the way the American banking system funded itself and led to households and enterprises being deprived of loans. Big banks now control over 60 per cent of deposits, something never before seen in the US landscape. As these references document, a mare's nest of reasons sees to it that "democracies" on both sides of the Atlantic have come to be overwhelmingly dominated by:

- Big egos;
- Big government;
- Big banks;
- Big oil;
- Big supermarkets.

By contrast, there is little by way of *trust* and *confidence* – the factors which make an economy tick. Yet, this is what is needed to get Western economies moving again. Outraged at the excesses that led to the current economics and financial crisis, the public is deeply cynical about politics and politicians – their nepotism, favouritism, wild spending, bailouts, interventions and indulgencies.

"Wisdom cannot be bought, it is the reward of righteousness."[34] The prerequisite for righteousness is that people are directly accountable for whatever they do, not only in front of God but also in front of the court on the high street. "Nothing emboldens sin as much as mercy", Shakespeare wrote in *Timon of Athens*. It was true in the ancient world, and it is true in our epoch.

2
Entitlements

2.1 Galbraith's warning about employment and consumer debt

There are many entitlements the state supermarket and its politicians have granted over the years without the foresight provided by study and confirmation of whether these are affordable and sustainable. As usual, short-termism has had the upper hand. Among these entitlements the most voracious in a financing sense have been:

- Jobs provided by the state;
- Free education (see Chapter 3);
- Pensions (see section 2.4);
- Health care for all (see sections 2.5 and 2.6).

Politicians, and not only politicians, have too often glossed over the economic and financial dimensions of entitlements and the crisis they brought on the sovereign budget. The parties of the left have been particularly keen to spend and spend, finding justification in notions such as democracy (which has little to do with it) and social justice. The parties of the right have struggled even to articulate how a more equitable society can be maintained in times of austerity.

Public spending on entitlements and swelling government employment are benefiting so many voters that it is hard for politicians to win backing to cut them. Yet the survival of Western democracy requires that the reasons why the ballooning universe of entitlements is unsustainable are explained to the electorate.

According to Deanne Julius, "voters must choose whether they prefer high public sector spending and generous entitlements coupled with higher taxes to pay for them, or modest public provision and basic entitlements along with lower taxes".[1] The silver lining of the present deep financial crisis is the opportunity it presents for making such a choice – provided that the options are clearly explained to the public, including the costs the next generations will have to pay. This is practically what Galbraith said 40 years ago.

Neither the right nor the left paid attention to Galbraith's warning. "Inadequate production and employment made all other problems insoluble", he wrote in his book *The Affluent Society*. He also suggested that "without a sense of strategy, liberal economists concentrated on policies designed to ensure an adequate level of demand and therewith of output and employment".[2]

In the first couple of decades which followed the end of World War II, the facts of life in Western societies seemed to confirm the hypothesis about demand, output and employment. This led to a degree of complacency, even if by the mid-1960s it started becoming evident, at least in Western Europe, that with the near completion of reconstruction work of war damages there was a new scarcity of jobs arising – particularly among the young.

One of the first among many economic mistakes made in the course of the following years was the overleveraging of the American economy by the simultaneous demands posed by the Vietnam War and social measures taken by President Johnson: Medicaid, Medicare and more. The belief that the US economy was strong enough to withstand the load was shattered by the Smithsonian agreement of 1972. The end of the dollar's convertibility, established with the Bretton Woods agreement, provided proof that something was unwell with the consumer/producer society which had flourished in the preceding years.

One of the problems economists and sovereigns failed to perceive is that "consumer" and "producer", the two legs of the modern society's model, don't need to march in unison. Consumer demand, once created, can be satisfied with imported cheaper products. When this happens, the consumer is no more a producer. He or she may as well be unemployed and living on debt and government handouts. However, the list of "wants" does not diminish after he or she runs out of cash, and, on the contrary, new wants pop up as people push forward their demands for social peace.

In the decades of the 1970s and 1980s economists who heralded a neo-Keynesian conviction that "almost all social issues could be solved and ills cured by means of more production" saw their dreams shattered. The idea that in an affluent society social equality would flourish and everyone would be well-to-do by getting every year deeper in debt, proved awfully wrong. At family, company or sovereign level, debt can accumulate up to a point, but the day of reckoning will come as leverage through "more debt" must be serviced and contracted loans become due.

What was heralded a new, modern and magnified "social solution" became unstuck. Over the years highly indebted consumers became a dominant feature in the West, while the producers could be found more and more in the East.

It is to Galbraith's credit that back in 1958 in Chapter 13 of his book *The Affluent Society*, under the title "The Bill Collector Cometh", he foresaw that debt was no social solution. In his words, "consumer demand ... comes to depend more and more on the ability and willingness of consumers to incur debt ... There has been an inexplicable but very real retreat from the Puritan canon that required an individual to save first and enjoy later."[3]

In an effort to define the time when that inflection point would come Galbraith noted that from 1952 to 1956 total consumer debt (for reasons other than house loans) increased from $27.4 billion to $41.7 billion – 13 per cent per year. Over the same timeframe, the annual instalment credit increased even more, while that for motor vehicles rose by 25 per cent per year.

Leverage has been a basic reason why the mid-1950s were considered the wonder years of the US economy. The bible became "spend now, pay later" and debt was piled up on a massive scale. No political top gun, no religious leader and no economics luminary alerted the public about the dangers which arise with runaway consumer borrowing. Instead, the cult became one in which sophisticated people leverage themselves and the economy is so strong that bad credits can be accommodated.

It is a pity that Galbraith did not press his point and thus become the apostle of a return to the sound Puritan ethic. He was a visionary because he saw, five decades before the consumer debt bubble burst, the descent to the abyss – but his warning was phrased in too mild terms. The abyss came in 2007 with the deep economic and banking crisis.[4] Half a century of headway to turn the situation around was wasted.

During the decades which followed the 1958 Galbraithian warning, consumer debt acquired its own momentum and became unstoppable. Only slowly, very slowly, sovereigns, central bankers and economists started to understand that an overleveraged society will fall because of its debt weight. By then, it was too late because an interruption in the march of debt meant an actual reduction in demand for goods, therefore of production and employment.

Easy solutions can be no more found by the simple process of "increasing production". To fill the gap politicians got into the habit of reverting to the (bad) practice of offering to those left behind the dubious (and very expensive) benefits of the welfare state. But the state supermarket is no Santa Claus and those who promoted it did not have the brains to establish how its entitlements could be financed without raising the mountains of debt at the personal and state level, and without creating an economy which is bureaucratic and backward looking.

Over the years spending way beyond one's income became a sort of conventional wisdom at the sovereign, corporate and family level. The hardest thing about power is knowing where to stop. As Franklin D. Roosevelt put it in his acceptance speech in 1932, "any governments, like any family, can for a year spend a little more than it earns. But you and I know that a continuation of that habit means the *poorhouse*" (my emphasis).

The *poorhouse* is precisely where the Western economies reside in 2012. We are there because governments did not appreciate, when there was still time to do so, that they had to put the brakes on. Instead, they permitted all sorts of dubious debt to be recycled, packaged and marketed through securitization while new sources of liabilities entered the economy's bloodstream. In this way debt destroyed the capitalist system, as it will do of any economic system accepting tons of financial paper full of unfulfilled promises. Initially, a debt is a poisonous gift; as it continues accumulating, it transforms itself into dynamite.

Nearsightedness has been a key ingredient in this transformation. Since the 2000 stock market earthquake, sovereigns, central bankers and economists who knew that the larger economy was in the doldrums have been carefully watching to see whether American and European consumers will open their purse. Alan Greenspan, the then chairman of the Federal Reserve, was particularly keen that the American consumers come forward by using the credit cards in their wallets which had made them debt addicts.

Back in 1958 Galbraith had suggested the need to kept an alarm signal flying over consumer debt creation and accumulation. Nothing has happened of that sort. Sovereigns and economists were too preoccupied with rearranging the chairs on the deck of the Titanic. Nobody in high places seems to have seen the iceberg; or they were too scared to ring the alarm bell. After the crash of 2007, the meltdowns of 2008 and the continuing deep malaise, different actors have tried to pull up the economy by its bootstraps by throwing at it Greek fire: *more and more debt*, such as Ben Bernanke's policy.

2.2 Jobs, taxes and the middle class

Among the duties the state considers to be its own in a socialist or communist society is *jobs for everybody*. Even under these regimes, however, jobs don't come easily and the best available are typically reserved for higher ranking party members. The others have no choice but to take the low paying unexciting jobs that remain, with no questions asked as to whether they like them or not.

A free economy does not work that way. Finding a job is the *responsibility of each individual*, and not of the state. The government only plays an indirect role by investing in the economy which is a precondition for creating a climate favourable to jobs. This evidently requires capital and, short of using the central bank's printing presses, a fiscal policy that sees to it that there is a surplus for jobs-oriented investments. However, three forces work against this solution. First are large budgetary deficits; second is a subdued or poor economic climate. These first two are universal.

The third force acts against jobs that are specific to Western economies. By acquiring a university or college degree, young people in these economies no longer wish to take manual jobs which are not considered to be appropriate for the middle class. By choosing a career path without a future, a young man or woman's higher education – which in Europe is seen as an entitlement to be paid by public money – is misdirected towards a field easy to study but without employment opportunities. (More on this in Chapter 3.)

This is not yet the case in developing countries, though it might become so in the future. At present, their salient problem is a high birth rate which not only drains their resources but also requires huge investments for job creation while money is scarce.

In 1966 in the course of a research project with the American Management Association I met with the Minister of Education in Brazil. The subject was how the government was planning to enlarge the labour market. He said that it was a tough issue since each medium to lower level job required (at the time) an investment of $3,000 and, given the high birth rate, to create enough jobs, each year the government would have to investment an amount nearly equal to Brazil's gross national product. That, evidently, was not doable.[5]

Nearly half a century down the line the lack of jobs is no longer a Latin American speciality. It has become a sort of status quo in Western countries, and it is one of the reasons behind the OWS movement. Particularly at a disadvantage is the young generation whose unemployment rate ranges from 25 per cent in France to 48 per cent in Spain.

Not only are the social implications dire, but the shortage of jobs is also bad for the economy as a whole. Upheaval in the job market depresses productivity, the tax base shrinks and further employment prospects wane. Already job security has become a memory and many of the jobs lost during the crisis are not coming back.

Young people share the blame for such bad news because as a majority they believe that it is the business of the state to find them a job – and one well paid, please. That's totally untrue. It is people's responsibility to build themselves up, not only to get a job but also, as they mature, to write their ticket (to ask for and obtain the salary they want). Success is what happens when preparation meets opportunity.

And neither is the state's bureaucratic employment as well paid as many young people seem to believe. Indeed, low salaries are another reason why people have got into the habit of spending money before they earn it. "I am a teacher but with my salary I cannot even finish the month without going into debt", said a 30-year-old activist. "My friends and I have been talking about this for years. The system is not working for us. It is not just about housing, but also about taxes, which are very high."[6]

"Our parents and grandparents used to have pensions, they have everything. But they have crushed the welfare state", said another protester. That's an opinion heard quite frequently among the young and in a way they are right – except that rather than being crushed the welfare state has collapsed under the weight of its "free" goodies and of its debts.

In a feature article in the *Financial Times*, Martin Wolf makes reference to Tyler Cowen, of George Mason University, who says: "we thought we were richer than we were". Cowen believes that Americans have made demands, both collectively and individually, that they could not afford,[7] and he is absolutely correct in his analysis. This wrong way of thinking is not only present in America. It is also the order of the day in Britain and in continental Europe and it has led to the triple whammy of:

- The desire to continue borrowing and leveraging oneself;
- The policy of resisting higher taxes to pay for the nanny state;
- The habit of looking at the state supermarket as a substitute for one's mother.

Tyler Cowen further believes that even with an official unemployment rate of 9 per cent the US economy is close to full employment. In his article, Martin Wolf adds another issue of which the reader should take note. The structure of the Western economy has changed in a way that what was once treated as *free* nowadays is *costly*.

Few economists support that view, but Wolf is right. Governments might be able to fudge the issue for a little longer, but not forever. Confronted with painful choices, Wolf suggests, human beings choose denial. The failure to look at problems as they are and to try to solve them has a very negative effect on society.

A lack of jobs and the perspective of a reduced nanny state has put the middle class under siege. Typically, middle-class professions are taken to include medicine, engineering, merchandising, teaching, the law and plenty of government jobs. That's the British definition, where "middle class" has come to refer to people who are actually well off. Now, by all evidence, their condition is deteriorating.

"The big losers are Western middle class and blue collar workers, who have lost out dramatically. The source of this crisis is their decades-long loss of competitiveness and income, which politicians have tried to cover with unserviceable levels of sovereign and household debt. Now the bill is due and nobody will be unscathed," writes Mark Malloch-Brown. "The downward slide continues – the great revolt will come later."[8]

In America the population falling under the term "middle class" is much wider, and not necessarily so well off, but nowadays it is also confronted with fortunes which are not changing for the better. After several decades of improving living standards the American middle class, too, is getting poorer and feeling cross about it. Hence the rise of the Tea Party.

People are fighting to preserve the status and standard of living they acquired through their work. But politicians are divorced from the people's wishes, or at least insensitive to them. Barack Obama has failed to stop the hollowing out of the middle class which started in the 1980s and accelerated under the Clinton and George. W. Bush administrations.

In developing countries similar frustrations spring from a different source, but with the same outcome. A new middle class has emerged in recent years in ever growing numbers. According to some estimates, the BRICS (Brazil, Russia, India and China) added 500 million people to the global middle class during the last decade, and might add a further 800 million in this decade. Will they?

Much of the wealth effect in developing countries has come from working hard as producers for consumers in the West. But with the Western middle class in the doldrums – or, even worse, in decline – it is difficult to see that the producer–consumer global equation (and its imbalances) will continue as in the recent past.

Apart from the debt woes which drain the Western middle classes' income, there is taxation. Taxation eats up about 30 per cent of the average American's total compensation (though most Americans also pay state taxes). Still this compares favourably with taxes at about 50 per cent in Britain, Germany, France and other European countries. Swedes and Danes pay well over 50 per cent. There exist as well considerable differences in attitude towards redistributive taxes for the poorer, which are not favourably looked upon by the middle class.

A high taxation was supposed to pay for the entitlements, but the runaway cost of the state supermarket far exceeds what the sovereign budget can afford. And neither are entitlements being granted by politicians only at times of prosperity. In 1921, at the depth of its economic problems right after World War I, a bankrupt Germany, trying to negotiate relief from the huge economic weight of reparations, was also unable to control its finances. The government took upon itself enormous new social obligations which it simply could not afford:

- Insurance for the unemployed;
- Eight-hour work days;
- Health and welfare payments for the poor;
- Pensions to veterans and widows and other goodies intended to counteract the social communist uprising.

This saw to it that Germany's financial woes were not only the after-effect of unsustainable penalties, wrongly inflicted by the victorious allies in the form of reparations. They were also self-created, making a solution to the difficult fiscal situation practically impossible and leading to the hyperinflation of late 1923. (At least Germany learned a lesson from this and for nine decades has been against profligate budgets.)

Central bankers in the US and Britain don't seem to have learned a lesson from that debacle. *If* they had, *then* they would not have spent lavish amounts of money supposedly to jump-start the economy (through quantitative easing), provide jobs and "help the middle class" – an ill-studied policy which started badly and will finish even worse, for:

- The gains have been ephemeral and comparatively small, providing neither jobs nor relief;
- The cost is the risk of huge inflation waiting in the wings if and when Western economies start moving again.

No-one who made the decision to spend large amounts of public money seems to have read the writings of Joseph A. Schumpeter. After having surveyed the experiences connected to nineteenth-century business cycles Schumpeter had come to the conclusion that recovery is sound and sustainable *only if* it comes by itself. In his opinion, backed by his analysis, any revival merely due to artificial stimuli leaves some residue of the depression and adds a maladjustment of its own to the undigested remnants of other maladjustments.

If Ben Bernanke, Mervyn King, George W. Bush, Gordon Brown and Barack Obama had read Schumpeter and still gone ahead with their ill-advised stimuli and the quantitative easing circus, then they would have exceeded their previous levels of incompetence.

2.3 Rights without responsibilities

The rise of the middle class in developing countries has been interpreted by economists and sociologists as the building of a stability mechanism in a social and economic sense. By contrast, the downsizing of the middle class in Western societies – which became a victim of its own success – is a sign of degeneration of society, and most particularly of a future demise of the all-mighty welfare state.

The state supermarket has promised a social environment in which life will be better year-on-year while less-and-less work will need to be done. Both the left and the right are supposed to promote a miraculous social protection mechanism which constantly improves and whose privileges and benefits are continuously extended. In such an ideal state, risk is eliminated and the next generation is supposed to have the *right* to a comfortable and joyful life.

All this is, of course, baloney. It is sand thrown in the eyes of citizens, but there are people who believe that it is true. Living beyond one's means has been taken for granted as the in thing, with nobody bothering to ask who at the end will pay the bill. The youths participating in the OWS movement are among the first to discover that *they* will be held responsible for all the damages created by their parents and grandparents.

With public conscience awakening to the costs and responsibilities associated with the welfare state, the age of rights without responsibilities, which started after the end of World War II and has lasted for over seven decades, may finally start to decline. Whether this happens or not, history will record this 70-year period as one of *living on debt* rather than living on assets, and of having left to the coming generations the bill of the *deep debt* habit.

The inherent weakness of this no-responsibilities philosophy of the state supermarket, which preaches that everyone should be enjoying life more and more while working less and less, is the hypothesis that there exists a bottomless pit in which to throw all that red ink. As if by magic people will be able to reset the accumulator and start piling up debt all over again.

Politicians of right and left have been uttering this big lie by capitalizing on the fact that the danger of public finances drying up and debt becoming a monster does not show up immediately. (Instead, it hits the hardest at the most inopportune moment.) As mentioned in Chapter 1, it was debt, debt and more debt that unravelled what historians consider to be the golden age of Pericles in ancient Athens.

In times past, as now, with spending on welfare far exceeding the state's income, the advantages of an imperial economic prosperity waned, profits ebbed and Athens started living at the expense of those it professed to protect. Sounds familiar? Almost by necessity the democracy Pericles had inherited turned to imperialism, which led to the 30-years Peloponnesian War that devastated ancient Greece. (By strange coincidence the civil war in Europe ("civil" in the sense that it involved European against European), which started in 1914 and did not effectively end until 1945, also lasted 30 years and has been equally devastating.)

In modern times, the love of debt has grown under the cover of a revolution in technology and applied science: space research, computers, robotics, electronic communications and networks. These technological advances were interpreted as heralding in a better life for all. From families to sovereigns all levels of society had only *rights*, and nobody could take them away.

The furious demonstrations in 2011 in Athens, which followed the government's austerity measures aimed at avoiding an outright bankruptcy, were not done out of a fear of serious hunger or endangerment of health. The protesters thought they had the right to an uninterrupted, continuous prosperity at somebody else's expense. This is pure state supermarket philosophy: that wealth is not a consequence of one's own work, but is an endowment that should be guaranteed for life.

In December 2011, Mario Monti, the Italian prime minister, said the right thing in answer to a parliamentary question, "Why is the European Union not paying Italy's (huge) public debt." Monti's response was that it wasn't the European Union but the Italian governments and citizens who created that debt – and therefore they are the ones responsible for it.

Unfortunately, all prime ministers don't think in this way – but huge debts don't cease to exist because they are ignored. Whether sovereigns or common citizens, those who think they have only rights and no responsibilities for their commitments are dancing their way to the precipice. Zimbabwe provides an example of what is meant by the "precipice":

- It is the most indebted country;
- Its financial stability is long gone;
- Its currency has turned to ashes;
- It has the highest unemployment rate in the world.

In the West, the severe economic and banking crisis which started in 2007 has demonstrated that – unlike the real economy, which we know more or less how to deal with – the virtual economy is an unknown. It is characterized by opaqueness, unprecedented accumulation of risk, and requirements for human expertise well beyond what is generally available. The challenge becomes so much greater as debt allows unlimited leverage all the way to the edge of the abyss, further promoted by fake models of the economy.

Broadly speaking this new and little understood debt-ridden financial environment necessarily involves a responsibility that is ten times higher than that needed for managing real assets. New and complex financial products are difficult to price and untangle, and involve a novel financial alchemy through derivatives that can produce catastrophic fallouts. Globalized markets are regulated by nobody. Moreover, there is great diversity in the economic goals among the 33 nations which meet annually as the Group of 20 (or G20, and known for its meagre results).

Managing the global economy and its entitlements is not a game of chance. It is a difficult enterprise needing the highest calibre of experience and skill which, we should admit, does not exist in an amount commensurate to the requirements. The notion that debt, deregulation, technology and globalization create limitless opportunities, and all we have to do is to collect them like fruits from a tree, is a fiction. Reality is precisely the opposite. It is rather a mixture of unknown factors and probabilities of events and their further consequences that is so explosive that it has the power to blow up democracy. In fact, this is precisely what it is now happening. The loudly heralded age of democracy has turned into an age of cleptocracy, and not only by politicians, speculators and smart bankers.

The whole population participates to it through "entitlements" and by living beyond its means – the writing of IOUs (see Chapter 4).

The citizens' policy of taking more out of the state than they contribute is a prescription for *déclinisme* and decadence. This widespread undemocratic attitude counts on those in charge of public affairs being intimidated and giving way. And that's precisely what they are doing. They have succumbed to the widespread wrong belief in present-day Western society that if the state and its institutions do not make available prosperity for all, then one has to intimidate them and constantly put them under pressure through street demonstrations, strikes and any other means.

The public's anger scares present-day politicians into submission to the will of the masses. Leadership has failed Western countries, but not only leadership. Thomas L. Friedman, the political analyst, put this issue in the right light: "the standard answer is that we need better leaders. The real answer is that we need better citizens. We need citizens who will convey to their leaders that they are ready to sacrifice, even pay, yes, higher taxes, and will not punish politicians who ask them to do the hard things. Otherwise, folks, we're in trouble."[9]

2.4 Who pays the cost of pensions?

As the financial crisis of 2007 turned into a full-blown catastrophe with the economy taking a dive, the weight of health care and pensions on the sovereigns' budgets increased. This worsened an already unsustainable situation. In many Western countries pensions are underfunded. Rick Perry, the governor of Texas and Republican hopeful for the US presidency, denounced social security (that is, pensions only) as a Ponzi game.[10]

An ageing society easily overruns its budget of health care and pensions. According to American experts, however, funds for pensions are easier to fix than Medicaid (for the poor), Medicare (for the old) and Obama care (for practically everyone). Expenses associated with health tend to increase exponentially. Sovereigns find it difficult to cope with the amount of bills and are scared to take drastic measures. By default, their way out of trouble is to get deeper in debt.

In the 1930s, when national pension schemes became an entitlement, their financing posed no problem. The ratio of people working to pensioners was greater than 4 to 1 and the contribution of a working population paid for those retired. This sort of funding is very sensitive to employment, and over the years it has confronted two contrarian forces:

- Longevity risk, with the result that individual pensions may be paid for 20 years or more;
- A sharp reduction in the ratio of working persons to retirees, compound by poor employment statistics in Western countries.

Because of these reasons the pay-as-you-go system established in 1936 in the US and France, subsequently replicated in many other (particularly Western) countries, is now falling apart. The hypotheses on which it is based can no more be sustained by an ageing society's facts and figures.

Due to longevity risk and to employment problems, the ratio of people working and those being supported through social security contributions is well below 3 and shrinking. Pensioners demand "their dues", not for five years or so, but for 20 or more after retirement.

This ratio may worsen, because the decline of job opportunities is so widespread that many households depend on the welfare state much more than ever before and they don't make contributions. Early retirement, too, weighs on the social security budget. Ironically, in the US, the only industry sector adding to jobs has been health care (see section 2.5).

In 2009 researchers at Northwestern University and the University of Chicago estimated that the deficit of American state and local government pension plans was $3.1 trillion. Two years down the line it is reckoned that the deficit is a cool $4.4 trillion[11] – an average increase of 7 per cent per year.

States including New Jersey, Illinois, Rhode Island and Minnesota have taken measures to reform their pensions, like suspending cost-of-living increases to benefit recipients. In 2010, as the funding ratio dropped (the proportion of liabilities covered by assets), Illinois passed legislation to cut benefits for its new employees. In January 2011, it also raised state income tax rates by 67 per cent and business tax rates by 30 per cent.

California provides an example of how far the classical concept of pensions has sunk. Its unfunded pension liabilities are staggering, having been estimated at between $240 and $500 billion. It is not easy plugging that kind of hole, and trying to do so will crowd out other things such as schools and courts.

What Jerry Brown, California's governor, proposed in November 2011 centres on conditions for new employees of state or local governments. They would have to wait until age 67 to retire, as contrasted with many current government workers who can retire at 55. Retirement financing will also be a hybrid of traditional defined-benefit pensions and defined-contribution plans that are now common in private industry.

The governor also wants to make current as well as new employees contribute half of the cost of funding their pensions, as well as banning sneaky ways of upping benefits, known as "spiking". Analysts say that Brown's plan might save at best $1 billion over 30 years, which is peanuts. Critics suggest that a better plan is that current workers start paying much more of the cost of their pensions, which should be part of a welfare reform that is able to fight a dependency culture *and* save money while improving incentives to work longer.

Public pension funds are under stress all over Western countries, but private pension funds, thought to be the better solution, are not doing so well either. In the US, the average corporate pension plan had a funding ratio of just 72 per cent in October 2011, down from 81 per cent a year earlier. (In addition, the funds of those private pensions that are prosperous enough are pirated by the state.)

The federal and state governments are not the only parties having a problem in coping with pensions. The funding gap for American corporate pension plans almost doubled in 2011 as bond yields dropped and the stock market, too, got the blues. Compared to a moderate surplus at the end of 2007, at the end of 2011 US pension plan assets at S&P 500 companies covered less than three-quarters of estimated liabilities: a deficit of about $450 billion.[12]

In Europe where the restructuring of pensions moves much slower than in America, experts are ringing the alarm and warning that benefits have to be redimensioned – or the only remaining alternative will be pension fund bankruptcy. Simply hoping for an investment return to close the pensions' gap is not really credible. Pension fund management needs really good returns to offset that gap, and these are not really in sight (though the welfare reform initiated by the British government could provide a model).

Let's start with the principle that a young working man or woman today has to support not only mum and dad but also grandmother and grandfather. This means that the younger generation is mathematically condemned to lose out unless every entitlement is put on the table and thoroughly reconsidered regarding its affordability. The bad news is that this is not going to happen soon since:

- Embedded interests are ready to fight tooth and nail for what they consider to be their acquired benefits;
- Politicians don't have the guts to go ahead with major changes in pension schemes, particularly so as the elderly are a big voting population.

To take just one example, the American Association of Retired People is not altering its stance on social security, which has been a tough one in opposing any change to the status quo. Eventually, the children and grandchildren of today's retirees will pay the financial bill.

One of the reasons for this resistance to restructuring pension programmes is that people have no nest egg for their old age. Their one and only hope is that the state supermarket will continue to perform. In early 2011 a study done by Wells Fargo, the American bank, found that, on average, 50 to 60 year olds have put aside only $29,000 – which evidently won't go far without support by state or company pensions. People in their twenties and early thirties typically have debts, not savings. Only by their early forties do they start putting some money aside.

In late 2010 a study by Aviva, the British insurance company, calculated the difference between the expectations of European workers for a retirement income and the benefits they will actually receive. The researchers assumed that workers would desire a 70 per cent pension income as a proportion of final salary; but what they would probably get was between 35 and 55 per cent, depending on the country.[13]

Worse yet is the fact that social security outfits and the sovereigns behind them have got into the habit of raping the private pension funds which happen to be well-funded, and unfortunately this practice is spreading in, for example, Argentina, Britain, Estonia, Hungary and Poland.

What the different sovereigns are targeting is the so-called "second pillar" provided by private pensions. In the past, following the World Bank's advice, many governments had promoted this second pillar but, as private pension funds (at least those well managed) prospered, their assets became a tempting target for heads of state and finance ministers.

One of the excuses used by governments engaging in this detestable practice is that they have given tax privileges to pension funds as a means of encouraging savings and of reducing the potential burden on the state of provision for the elderly. But, the governments say, such tax shelters have been exploited by the wealthy, and sovereigns want to be compensated for the privileges they have granted.

In Britain, back in 1977 when he was finance minister, Gordon Brown instituted what became known as a "pensions tax grab", reducing private pension funds' income by allegedly some £5 billion ($8.4 billion) a year by eliminating the tax credit on dividend payments. The government's raid materialized through a change in tax policy on private pensions supposedly aimed at high earners.

Argentina's action was a plain grab aimed at filling the empty coffers of the state. Under pressure to get its public finances in order, Hungary has in effect renationalized its second pillar by transferring more than €10 billion from the private pension system back into the public one so as to reduce the budget deficit. Poland planned a permanent reduction of contributions into the managed funds; while Estonia has (allegedly temporarily) slowed inflows. In December 2010, Poland even struck a deal with the European Commission that will take into account the costs of its reformed pension system when calculating the country's budget deficit and debt. This has allowed the government to dodge sanctions for breaching European public finance rules.

Such a double manipulation was important for Poland, which was running a deficit of 7.9 per cent of GDP in 2010 and where public debt is approaching the legal threshold. The country's nearly 8 per cent budget deficit compares poorly with EU limits of 3 per cent, but the European Commission is in the habit of providing such indulgencies. This should not be done particularly when pensions are at stake.

2.5 Who pays the zooming health care costs?

Bad as the pension situation is, the case of skyrocketing health care costs is even worse. On the one hand, an aged society requires long term treatment and the sick desire that it is immediate and at a high level. On the other hand, costs have escaped control because health care practices have grown like wild cacti. They have not been designed for an aged society.

Both the longer term and the immediate health care services provided by the state supermarket are rocked by inflation and it is hard to curb that inflation because the system has not been redesigned for a mass society. Even in emerging countries, greater prosperity means people are taking greater risks with their health. In America, insurance premiums have surged 9 per cent in the last two years. Western governments confront a trilemma in regard to their health care schemes as to:

- Promoting health;
- Curing illnesses;
- Cutting costs.

The first are widely seen as entitlements. Politicians are scared to inform the public, let alone prove, that the way health care costs are rising is unprecedented. This does not change the fact that costs have become a prescription for sovereign bankruptcies.

Here is an example. The average American puts about $45,000 into the financing of state-supported health care, and he or she gets out of it $400,000.[14] Anecdotal evidence suggests this ratio is not too different from the one prevailing in other Western countries. The system is awfully overleveraged and many economists look at it as a prescription for deep trouble. It could ruin America just as it could ruin Britain or France. But nobody wants to give his or her health care entitlement up.

The US is confronted by the added disadvantage of a patchwork of health care services that – even after Lyndon Johnson's Medicare/ Medicaid (of the 1960s) and Obama Care – leaves millions of citizens with no public health insurance. At the same time, the system lacks discipline over costs with the results that year-on-year spending on health eats up 16 per cent of the country's GDP compared to 5 per cent in the mid-1960s.

This contrasts poorly to the health care bill of other Western countries which currently spend 7 to 11 per cent, though even at this level health spending is the single biggest contributor to sovereign budget deficits. As for the results of such a vast spending of public money, they usually range from mediocre to bad.

In Britain the experience with the National Health Service, a product of the immediate post-World War II years, has been a nightmare of high costs and low deliverables. It's hardly an example to imitate, yet the United States was and is eager to do so. This has been true since Harry Truman failed to push national health insurance through Congress in 1949.

Compared to American expenditure, the health care costs of France stand at 11.5 per cent, Germany's at 10 per cent, Britain's at 9 per cent and Japan's slightly below 8 per cent. In other countries they are around 7 per cent. These, however, are total health care costs including both private and public spending. In the US health care costs covered by private insurance were a little less than 4 per cent of GDP in 1970, are around 7.5 per cent today and are projected to reach beyond 10 per cent by 2020.

While, as these examples bring to the reader's attention, spending on health care rises on a steep curve, nobody seems to have a clear idea on how to bend that curve. The trick is to do so without confronting a wave of public indignation from the beneficiaries who are organized in pressure groups to oppose cuts in health care spending – and can even vote out of office a government which dares to take effective cost control measures.

Yet, the job of downsizing health care costs is doable, because there is plenty of inefficiency and fraud in the nightmare statistic of 16 per cent of US gross domestic product (GDP). Interviewed by Charlie Rose, Senator Tom A. Coburn said that in 2011 medical fraud reached \$452 million.[15]

It takes political courage to cut expenses with a sharp knife. Some authorities are trying. Over the next three years, up to 2015, New York will move its entire Medicaid population into *managed care*. New York City will be paying companies a set rate to tend to the poor, rather than paying a fee for each service. Coast-to-coast, an expanding managed care policy will restructure health care support.

The two biggest challenges are:

- People are living longer today;
- High technology in medicine, novel pharmaceuticals and big-ticket diagnostic tests inflate health care costs.

Theoretically, technological changes in health care have led to big improvements in services. Practically, the word "big" is superfluous because the training of personnel to use the new machines and methods is generally substandard, while their price is not affordable for every clinic or hospital.

It is always advisable to understand technological change and to analyse the impact of advances in medical technology from an economic perspective. The same is true of run-away costs.

It is nearly half a century since Medicaid became a branch of the state supermarket. Its appetite for taxpayer money is ferocious. About 16 per cent of Americans, typically the poorer citizens, are covered by Medicaid for a month or more. Enrolment in Medicaid jumped during the recent economic downturn, from 42.7 million people in December 2007 to 50.3 million in June 2010.

Feeding the Medicaid monster requires lots of federal and local money – more than any other state programme, even more than education for all. In addition, according to current projections, costs will rise even faster when in 2014 Barack Obama's health care reform expands the programme by easing eligibility rules (see section 2.6) – which is the wrong way of looking at the problem.

The low cost-effectiveness of Medicaid should have shielded it from further expansion. It did not. Neither is Medicare (for the elderly) any better. According to Senator Tom Coburn, a Senate study has found that most senior citizens contributed to Medicare by less than $105,000 per person but took out of it more than $300,000.[16] Most evidently this situation cannot continue without the Federal government going bust.

Just as important is the way health care money is being spent. As if to prove Pareto's Law is right, in America 80 per cent of health care spending goes to 20 per cent of individuals. But these people are not the only one's to account for the lion's share of expenses: there are also the people whose medical bills increase most significantly over time. According to critics this is because of *over doctoring* and individuals not really caring for their own health.

Another interesting statistic is that in the US hospitals and doctors account for 63 per cent of the nation's health spending and over the years they have shown little interest in taking a hit to their income. Yet, it does not take a genius to appreciate that if medical costs are to be controlled something has to give. Fundamentally, there are only four ways to pay for universal coverage:

- Raising taxes;
- Rationing health care;
- Cutting payments to medical providers;
- Asking the patients to foot a good part of the bill.

Decisions on which way to go cannot be left to a lottery. There is an unquestionable need for hard choices. Politicians want to solve the uninsured problems, but that's not what responsible people should do without examining all the alternatives and their costs. Being honest about the price is not an option. It is an obligation.

This is true not only of governments but also of companies, the evidence being that those who overspend on health care plans go bust. Prior to its bankruptcy General Motors (GM) was the largest US private purchaser of health services and of drugs – from Viagra to Lipitor. A study the carmaker did in 2004 indicated that the projected cost of providing health care benefits to current and future retirees would be a staggering $63 billion. Medical costs at GM are soaring to fulfil this prophecy, but the intervening bankruptcy interrupted many of the handouts.

GM had to cover health care costs of 1.1 million Americans, while fewer than 200,000 were active workers. The US government, too, has been confronted with this kind of statistic which turn the whole concept of health care's social costs on their head. An economy burdened by this kind of entitlement can never recover.

In conclusion, health care is the Achilles heel of the American economy and that of many other Western countries. According to Tom Coburn, "The goal should be to prevent a debt crisis but we go straight into it." Asked if the debt crisis in America has similarities to that in Greece, he said "Yes" – adding that "we are three to four years away from the dimension the debt crisis has taken in Greece".[17] American experts suggest that the rapidly rising debt curve cannot be bent without major cuts in health care expenses.

2.6 Clinton Care, Obama Care and the looting of the health care system

In the 1990s, in his days at the White House, Bill Clinton wanted universal access to a standard health care plan. To make this affordable he also planned to encourage "managed competition", with groups of hospitals and doctors competing for flat-rate prepaid contracts. The moving gear behind that plan, whose details remained murky until draft legislation reached Congress, was Hilary Clinton whose health care deal had four major flaws.

The first flaw was that it required employers to provide insurance for all their workers, and to pay at least 80 per cent of the bills. Like all extra tax on labour, this threatened to destroy jobs especially in small firms who had been unable to afford health coverage in the past. Clinton's proposed small-business subsidies just brought part of the burden from industry to the (already highly indebted) US sovereign.

The second flaw of Clinton's health plan, which is common to all entitlements underwritten by the state supermarket, was that health care for everybody paid too little attention to the control of costs. As has been explained, high costs put any and every health plan into question. Many people say that money does not grow on trees, but many people think that it does.

In the United States, for example, at the base of health care costs is the employer-paid, tax-exempt private insurance that finances inflationary fee-for-service medicine. The Clintons avoided taxing this issue directly. Employer-paid insurance was scheduled to continue, and so was the tax exemption from it. Yet, in Clinton's White House years this was costing the government some $50 billion a year (it is much more than that today).

As if this was not enough, Clinton's plan had a third big flaw, which it shares with Obama Care. This is the outrageously dishonest claim that its costs to taxpayers are minimal. The Clintons would have had Congress believe that their proposal would provide universal coverage, generous new commitments to cover prescription drugs, long-term nursing and mental-health care, subsidies for small firms, and a big government deficit reduction with virtually no new taxes. Even a blind person with black glasses could see that this is nonsense.

The fourth major flaw of Clinton's health care plan, and potentially the most serious, was a twisted notion which it shares not only with Obama Care but also with all other health care programmes promoted by the state supermarket. Their common link can be described in a few words: nothing is being done to protect the taxpayer-financed "health care for all" from fraud and looting from those it supposedly benefits.

Neither Clinton Care nor Obama Care bothered to learn from previous nanny state failures in health care. Such a universal plan exists in France and Britain, among other countries, and it has been steadily exploited by its beneficiaries beyond belief.

Take France as an example. In practically all years preceding 2010 French social security (health care) has suffered plenty of fraud and has paid large sums of money for useless or unwarranted medical interventions. The government-sponsored health care for all also became a source of frivolous income. Dependable estimates indicate that in 2010 there were:

- Fraudulent activities to the tune of €5 billion ($7 billion);
- €10 billion ($14 billion) spent in unwarranted medical interventions paid by the government's health care programme.[18]

Some of the fraudulent tricks were outrageous. For instance, Dr Said, a general practitioner in Evry, for several years declared to the French public health care authority 147 consultations per day. This was 367 per cent above the maximum of 40 the French social security admits, but nobody had been monitoring his claims. Dr Said also charged €40 per consultation instead of the authorized €22, but his clients did not ask any questions because he specialized in signing justifications for fake illnesses – thereby legalizing absenteeism from work.[19]

Cases that have been detected provide food for thought for an analysis of the fraud suffered by government-sponsored health-care systems:

- Half of the fraud came from clinics and hospitals;
- A quarter came from health professionals;
- Over 10 per cent came from the people for whom the state supermarket health care was established;
- The balance from different other sources including organized crimes.

Such statistics are known, and so are their origins, but neither Clinton Care nor Obama Care provided a system for fraud control. Somebody, of course, pays for all this plunder, and that's the taxpayer.

It looks as if the politicians and bureaucrats designing health care systems want to be taken for a ride, and so they copy one another's designs. No wonder therefore that their plans rest on the same fake premises and are held together by scotch tape and provided with a cosmetic surface.

Lies do the rest of the job. For instance, with Obama Care there will come "major" but unspecified savings in Medicare and Medicaid. Health care "reform" has been nothing else than sugar coating for enacting new entitlements, without any attention paid to the likelihood of fraud, and the false claim that the citizen will not pay for the new licence to spend money through taxes. Nothing is said of the fact that all this tra la is:

- Charging the costs to the next generation;
- Making the quality of health care at large even worse than it is today.

Different estimates on what it is expected to cost come to the conclusion that over the next ten years Obama Care will put the US Federal government another trillion dollars in the red. This is a large sum of money at any time, and most particularly when America's budget deficit stands at a whopping 110 per cent of GDP (as opposed to the 100 per cent stated by Washington), while official unemployment seems stuck at just below 9 per cent.[20]

There is no political will for cost control in health care. Dr Nelson Mohler, a pharmacologist, says the whole system is a nightmare of unjustifiably high costs and of perverse incentives. Because employer-provided health insurance is not considered to be a taxable benefit, people feel insulated from the real cost of their coverage and consequently they over-use it. Since hospitals and medical practitioners face too little competition, they charge too much even for simple intervention and, because of legal risk (the fear of lawsuits), doctors are encouraged to practise "defensive medicine", further driving up costs.

Many people are convinced nothing can be done to bend the cost curve, because health costs are determined by long-term conditions (such as lung disease, diabetes, heart disease and obesity), which are usually linked to lifestyle and diet. Some 15 million Britons suffer from such conditions, which take up 70 per cent of bed-days in hospitals.

As if this was not enough, old illnesses are now reappearing. Tuberculosis is a case in point. Back in December 1945, at his Nobel lecture, Alexander Fleming sounded a warning. There is a danger, he said, that the ignorant man may easily underdose himself and by exposing his microbes to non-lethal quantities of the drug make them resistant.

Penicillin and other antibiotics, whose discovery led to the effective therapy of illnesses due to bacteria, have been both overused and misused both on people and on animals. Louise Slaughter, an American Congresswoman who is also a microbiologist, calculates that four-fifths of the antibiotics used in the US are given to livestock. This, too, creates opportunities for bugs to evolve resistance.[21]

Neither should one believe that technology will act as a white knight in health care. While, properly used, it may correct deficiencies like the lack of proper medical records, the talk of smart clinical decision systems working purely online is hyperbole. Though there are advantages to be gained from innovation, more sophisticated medical devices cost more and they also require a great deal of training in the interpretation of their output. In health care as in so many other domains focused intensive training of practitioners is required, but this has been singularly lacking.

In conclusion, there is plenty of reason for questioning the ability of societies to adequately finance existing entitlement programmes, through allocation of tax revenues by governments. The challenge is to come up with a solution factoring-in pensions and health care but also paying full attention to both the West's geriatric demographics and the economy's inability to carry heavier and heavier social costs.

A general roadmap for coming out of the current mess will not be sufficient. Any plan worth its salt must have lots of detail. Even the best hypotheses have to be stress tested. Population ageing has changed the sort of health problems confronting society and, by extension, the configuration and costing of such services. Increasing dependency ratios because of longevity makes it harder for ageing societies to depend on "kids take care" assumptions. Practically, this unloads everybody into the arms of the vast, highly expensive and mismanaged court of the state supermarket.

3
Jobs and Education

3.1 The price of education

An old Chinese proverb has it that if you plan for ten years, plant rice; if for ten years, plant trees; if for a hundred years, educate men. In a modern society jobs and education go together like horse and carriage. Education is the gateway for jobs if, and only if, the choice of a career is made with great care and what one learns matches the career's needs. Education is also one of the "entitlements": as primary and secondary education in Britain and America, and from maternity to university in continental Europe.

Jobs are *not* an entitlement, though many people like to see it that way. Recurring street demonstrations by students in Paris are essentially made up of those who march against their own future. The dream of three out of four of them is to become government employees – hence, do-nothing bureaucrats. In Britain it is not yet that bad, but neither are employment prospects so brilliant. Among the jobless 16 to 24 year-olds, more than a quarter are students looking for part-time work.[1]

Have these young people learned the skills a modern society needs? Or have they spent their parents' money for nothing? Even if it is an entitlement, education has a price which is paid by their parents. The state supermarket may say that it offers free education for all, but at bottom the notion is fake. The price of education is not just money, which when thrown at the problem produces nothing, it is much more than that. The *real* price of education is steady, unrelenting effort by:

- Parents;
- Pupils and students;
- Teachers and professors;
- The whole of society.

Education starts in the family and continues at school, but even then the role of the parents needs to continue to be present and fundamental. Parents are the first people a child gets to know and, as such, they are also instrumental in shaping their child's mind – even if this involves a layer of prejudice before the age of seven, as Albert Einstein spoke of.

In parallel to the parents' role, primary actors in education are the children themselves. Young people who wish to become somebody later on in life have to learn how to learn.[2] This will help them to search and find ways to complement their education at school – through life-long learning for a successful life.

Take Lawrence Sperry's formative years as an example. In 1898, when he was six, his Sunday school teacher at the Euclid Avenue Baptist Church was a 59-year-old who taught his young listeners moral precepts. These had much to do with investing in one's talents and not hiding one's light under a bushel. The Sunday school teacher was John D. Rockefeller.[3]

A successful teacher is a communicator who has knowledge, experience and the will to help the younger generation. In my book teachers who go on strike are not the right people to teach children. What they offer their pupils is a bad example and a morose attitude which simultaneously depends on and wants to undo the status quo. Motivating teachers is an important subject in the search for the right solution to education. Money is only part of the problem. Governments should make a concerted effort to raise the status of the teaching profession and the teacher's standing in society.

Society itself plays a multiple role from educator to employer, or at least as the agent creating the right environment for jobs. Precisely because of society's offers and demands, jobs and education are closely linked and interact with each other – whether providing hope for tomorrow or creating a depression. From the start, what motivated the OWS movement and gave it a global perspective is that those participating in it could not see a happy future (and most likely they have been right in their assessment).

There was a time when a youngster's future employment was defined through his or her apprenticeship. Apprenticeship was a respected way of learning and, by osmosis, it provided young people with the kind of skills they needed to find a job.[4] Nowadays apprenticeship has been replaced by the theoretically "more prestigious" university course, but there is no evidence that this is a better solution even if it comes at a heightened cost. In most of Europe the much higher cost is paid by taxpayers, and in America by accumulating student debt at levels young people can hardly afford to repay (see section 3.3).

Instead of learning from practice and osmosis, young men and women bet their future on so-called plans for "better education" and for "career development", which come and go but at the end produce nothing. That is the feeling expressed by many cognizant people when in mid-March 2010 Barack Obama unveiled his latest plan for educational reform aimed at encouraging states to evaluate their schools. This they are supposed to do according to a nationally defined set of standards, which were ambiguous at best.

Obama's case of a half-baked educational effort is, of course, just an example. When it really comes to the question of education, the behaviour of all political leaders is just as wanting. In their thoughts and words they don't have the fire necessary to raise among parents, students and teachers the sense of effort required. Neither do they explain the pain associated with education, which is inseparable from changing old concepts and obtaining commendable results.

The primary school is the most basic common denominator of an educational effort. There will never be a knowledge society without a grand primary school system. This effort can succeed only if the primary schools' principals and teachers are given full authority, and protection from legal risk or libel, to improve the performance of pupils by demanding and obtaining first class performance.

Lessons can be learned from the nineteenth century when the institution of free education at primary school had been a major social breakthrough. Superior learning at state schools was accompanied by *strict discipline*, which today is largely absent, and by *parental responsibility*, which is no more the order of the day. There was an incident not long ago when five to seven-year-olds sneaked out at night into their school in Nice, France, and went on the rampage, breaking furniture and dirtying the walls with ink and paint.

This "permissive" society teaches children that they have *rights without responsibilities* and is evidence of decadence. If a teacher dares to punish one of his pupils because he or she misbehaved or failed in an exam, then the bigger brothers show up and beat up the teacher. It can even be worse than this. Not long ago in France, a 13-year-old knifed his teacher, nearly cutting her throat. She had to be rushed to the emergency department of a hospital.

This is definitely the wrong culture. It is not free education but *free recklessness for all.* Any stupidity or aggression has free rein. Dropping out of school is no longer seen as a stigma. The generation of illiterates marches on. It is a hopeless task educating undisciplined wild young children whose rate of dropout stands at 30 per cent or worse – as Nicolas Sarkozy, the former French president, himself said in a televised interview.

Conditions at the level of secondary education are no better. This talks volumes about the breeding of a professional illiteracy of the sort Michael Moore has criticized. Time and again I have seen the after-effect of educational irresponsibility in my classes. Decades ago, student performance was a keyword in education. Now it is not even talked about. The quality of graduate students has dropped like a stone all over the Western world.

One of the unwanted consequences of the lack of educational discipline and absence of corrective action is that, from the earliest phases of learning, pupils fail to make the required effort. The avoidance of learning migrates from primary schools to high schools. Notice that such a lack of educational discipline is found not only in the West but also in developing countries, which depend on a learned young generation to pull themselves up from the poverty level.

In South Africa, for instance, there is a 46 per cent chance a black teenager will drop out of high school. If the teenager manages to overcome that awful statistic he or she may get a professional qualification. But this is a big if. No wonder therefore that for a large number of young South Africans job market prospects are bleak, as the likelihood is high that:

- Their lack of quality education sees to it that they will not find employment;
- Without employment they will remain below the poverty line income for the rest of their lives.

All this is a great pity because, when we talk of human resources, true education has no limits. "I learn as long as I live", Socrates said. In his lectures Richard Feynman, the physicist, has insisted that the power of instruction is seldom of much efficacy except in those happy dispositions where the effectiveness of teaching is documented not by the students passing exams but in the general approach they take towards understanding the subject.

Understand the subject and learn how to correlate ideas. With them comes the power of applying the knowledge the student gains at school, in his or her daily life and in his or her professional work. In conclusion, the true power of instruction is:

- Promoted by an iron-clad discipline at home and school, as well as self-discipline;
- Shown by engaging the learner's mind not only to listen but to pose questions and seek answers based on what he or she has learned.

Both of these conditions nowadays are wanting. It is as if nobody takes notice of statistics showing that better education is associated with higher employment rates, as well as fewer chances of unemployment in later life. But, as it cannot be repeated too often, better education requires self-discipline by pupils and students, who are steadily trained and motivated by teachers and parents who care for their children.

3.2 "Free education for all" is a myth

During the interview he gave to CNN on 26 October 2011 Michael Moore said that right now there are in America 40 million illiterate adults – illiterate, that is, for the work they are presently doing or are supposed to do. This is an astonishing statistic; it is also a very interesting one because:

- It provides evidence of wrong orientation in education;
- It points to one of the major reasons why unemployment is stuck at around 9 per cent in the US and in many European countries.

The wrong orientation starts with the time primary school pupils spend in school, and it includes the fact that their instructors (as well as their parents) are not teaching them discipline. A young child in France works a mere 144 days per year, just four days per week, minus plenty of vacations. This rises to 190 days in Britain and to 210 days in Italy.[5] But in all three countries, which I take as an example, the freedom of the teacher to lead and build up the personality of children, cultivating them into men and women of worth to the society in which they live, is handicapped by laws which say that punishment is not allowed, that the childrens' "rights" provide them with the freedom to do as they please, which results in a loss of discipline which underpins education, taking along with it future job opportunities.

As I noted in section 3.1, the men and women who took part in the OWS movement had a reason: lack of hope for their future. This is so widely felt that OWS immediately gathered support from millions of young people around the globe, thereby proving that there is something wrong with current society – and with those who govern it. Priorities have turned on their head:

- Instead of holding the world's population at a sustainable level, taboos and inertia have given free rein to a wild reproduction of *Homo sapiens*;
- Instead of directing the educational effort towards professions needed for better living, there is a reckless policy of creating bureaucrats and the unemployed;[6]
- Instead of congratulating the teaching profession for its contribution to education of the young, every effort is made to turn it into a class struggle.

In March 2011, at New York City, Michael Bloomberg, the mayor, threatened to cut 4,675 teachers from his payroll unless their unions showed some flexibility in regard to seniority problems. (Another condition was that he got more cash from the state politicians in Albany.) The lay-offs were projected to affect 80 per cent of the city's 1,600 schools – with the last teachers hired to be laid off first, regardless of merit.

This is an antiquated and counter-productive policy. In over a dozen states in America it is illegal to lay off teachers who have seniority – and it is worse in Europe because teachers who are confirmed bureaucrats cannot be fired, period. The so-called "last in, first out" firing policy is demoralizing for young teachers.

As if to increase the inequality between young and old, and good and bad, labour union rules make it extremely hard to fire teachers who turn out to be underperforming at their jobs, even if everyone knows that seniority does not necessarily assure quality. In 2009 Indiana and Florida fired young staff who had been nominated for "teacher of the year". All over Western countries little effort has been devoted to the need to identify good teachers and properly reward them for their effort.

To make matters worse, public-sector unions combine support for higher spending with vigorous opposition to more accountability, by doing everything in their power to demonize competition, transparency and flexible pay based on results. It is indeed curious that labour unions decided to act as the Praetorian Guard of lower educational standards.

Contrary to what different obsolete and counter-productive rules mandate, to improve its schools a country, state, city or other jurisdiction should raise the status of the teaching profession. This requires higher principles, transparency, competition and money in order to:

- Recruit more qualified candidates;
- Train then through a lifelong programme;
- Pay them better, using as reference their performance.

Finland, Singapore and South Korea, for example, recruit only high-performing college graduates for teaching positions, support them with mentoring and other help in the classroom, and take steps to raise respect for the profession. Conversely, educational standards are falling in Western countries where teaching is no longer a high-status occupation. In turn, this means that society is caught between increasing demand and a falling quality of educated people.

That's politics at its worst; and it is backward looking. The place of educators is at the forefront of social renewal, and social renewal can only then become a reality when it is associated with personal responsibility. Part of this responsibility is to see more clearly to the bottom of the shallow waters which are to be found in the educational system and in society at large.

The bottom may be foggy but the message is clear: "Free education for all" is an unfulfilled promise. Money is spent on it but the results are less than stellar. The system simply does not stand on the right foot, and three parties share the blame for this result:

- Pupils and students;
- Their teachers;
- Society at large, including parliaments which vote for laws contradicting the very concept of education.

The impact of the educator was a reflection of the fact that the fundamental notions of education left a large imprint on the public mind. The educator was appreciated as a major cultural agent. This is no more the case, and it is evidence that "free education for all" has missed one of its most basic goals: that of upholding the culture and discipline which underpinned the might of the West.

Nowadays even babies have "rights", though they have no responsibilities – which is a rather pathetic naiveté. Gone is the responsibility of pupils and students to respect their parents and teachers. This twist in the values of society creates a vicious circle, because confronted with a tough bunch of irresponsible youngsters (over which they are not allowed to have any authority) the teachers, too, think primarily of their rights, while their responsibility as educators moves to a second tier.

The disrespect for responsibility and accountability by the main players in the educational system comes as a great contrast to the principles and policies of past centuries which shaped Western civilization. In the eighteenth century, for example, great educators like Jean-Jacques Rousseau had much more influence on public opinion than government officials and well-known politicians.

Critics say that this is the fault of public education, but they are only partly right. While public education is greatly suffering – above all because of widespread public disrespect – the fault falls on society as a whole. Parents who have the means for doing so, send their children to private schools because they think that they get better training than in schools that are free from tuition charges. Costs aside, however, this has two evident constraints: while some private schools are well above average, this is not true of all of them; and, by being paid for tuition, private schools feel a certain (undeclared) obligation to be less rigorous in their exams.

Yet, *rigorous exams* are what make the difference in education and culture. Exams are the common denominator for assessing the various sorts of forces that build up human beings. Let us never forget that culture is the nearest emulation in human society to the laws of the physical universe.

"'We the people' had become marvelously 'we the plunderers'", wrote James Thruslow Adams back in 1931. "The dream of a better and fuller life for every man, had become a good deal like the stampede of hogs to a trough."[7] Hogs are not known to exercise personal responsibilities as they rush along, trying to overtake each other.

In conclusion, "free education for all" is a distortion of reality. No greater calamity has struck our civilization than the collective abdication of personal responsibility. Without personal responsibility for whatever one is doing, (supposedly) noble instincts and lofty aspirations expressed so often (sometimes even eloquently) accomplish nothing. Words, words and words are the state supermarket's motors, promising everything which it neither owns nor can afford to give away.

Without responsibility, without discipline and without a plan for a professional future nothing can be achieved. Eventually, even the future looks bleak. It comes therefore as no surprise that to the protesters in the OWS movement it has become clear that the politicians running the fortunes of Western nations have no idea of how to lead because there are so many things they don't understand and so many other themes they are afraid to talk about.

3.3 Siren song: the saga of student loans

What I stated in the previous section about the lack of discipline in education, and the prospect of an uncertain professional future and a falling quality of human resources, is true all the way from primary and secondary schools to universities. It is particularly pronounced in advanced education because it has to confront the dual challenge of a rapid growth in the number of students in their country of origin, and the fact that excellence in university education is no longer measured within national borders but across the global landscape.

According to the Organisation for Economic Co-operation and Development (OECD), more than 3 million students are enrolled outside their country of citizenship. Three decades earlier, in 1980, this number stood at about 1 million, which was already a large number.

As far as higher education is concerned, over 20 per cent of transborder students go to America. Australia, Britain, France and Germany are also popular destinations. Are there any global measures of excellence? First published in 2003, a league table produced by Shanghai's Jiao Tong University rates high academic institutions primarily according to their performance in research, which is a basic ingredient of advanced education.

It is bad news that from all of Europe's universities only Oxford and Cambridge feature in the top 20 of the Jiao Tong list. The majority in this list are American. In the top 50 entries, Europe has only ten places, and only 32 in the top 100. This documents that over the years the level of knowledge of university students has been visibly dropping. One of the reasons is that secondary schools are no longer teaching the level of mathematics and science they used to. But there are also the reasons for the rapid inflation in the number of university students and the financing of university studies whose costs have skyrocketed in the US and are increasing in Britain.[8]

America pioneered student loans in the mid-1960s, and the results are mixed at best. Students who used to work to finance their education are now instead becoming loan addicts, their debt is rising and default rates are climbing. President Johnson thought it was a great idea that the government should make loans to students so they could continue their schooling at universities. The current amount of outstanding US student loans is beyond $1 trillion,[9] about 85 per cent of it being public money and much of it securitized (see section 3.7).

Americans currently owe for their schooling more money than they owe for their credit cards. Worse yet, young people have acquired the habit of spending money before they earn it.[10] On-credit university education has joined on-credit clothing and cruises. The after-effect has been compounded by the fact that the cost of higher education in the US has soared, median incomes have stagnated and the siren song of money from heaven has become irresistible.

In Britain, too, under the government scheme put forward in 2010, English undergraduates can borrow from the state at low interest rates to cover the costs of their tuition, repaying the debt once they have graduated and are earning more than £21,000 a year. Anecdotal evidence suggests that the government expects 30 per cent of the money being lent will never be repaid.

In France, the solution several students found for financing their higher education is moonlighting. According to an article in *L'Express*: "Elèves le jour, prostitué(e)s la nuit" ("students by day, whores by night").[11] According to estimates by the federation of student unions, SUD-Etudiant, 40,000 students – women mostly – monetize their charms with the internet serving as the communications channel.

The rush to colleges and universities, whether or not one can afford it, has in its background the advice of parents that higher education is the best way to equip oneself and thrive in a globalized world. Theoretically this is right, practically it is not. In Western countries young students rush to the so-called "soft sciences" whose degrees are not in demand. Graduates in home economics and social science, to take two examples, do not have the world at their feet. Yet if the choice of university specialization is wrong, then obtaining post-secondary credentials is a waste of time and money.

Residents in the San Francisco area have organized "UnCollege", a social movement that is trying to change the notion that college is the only way to prosper. The rationale behind this movement is that there is plenty of demand for skills which can be taught in a professional school rather than in a university. Only by keeping close to the professions in demand and learning on the ground will:

- Unemployment numbers be downsized;
- Society not have to pay high university costs "for all";
- The graduates themselves be free from the debt of university loans when they enter the labour market.

The past is not a reliable guide to the future. That educational qualifications are tightly correlated with earnings, today applies only to half of those qualifications. We are at the beginning of a new phase in the relationship between jobs and education. One of the reasons is that the supply of university graduates is increasing rapidly, outpacing the creation of good jobs. Between 1990 and 2010 the number of students going to university increased by an estimated:

- 23 per cent in North America;
- 76 per cent in Europe;

- 150 per cent in Latin America;
- 210 per cent in Asia.

Nearly all countries have been pouring resources into building universities, but the outcome is far from stellar. One reason is that faculties cannot be grown overnight. Professors start to lack personal experience on what they teach, and numbers prove it. In 2010 there were in Britain as many university professors as there were students in 1950.

With all due respect, I would say that such an inflation in faculty numbers does not bode well for quality. Likewise, the multiplication of soft subjects in university education has a detrimental effect on industrial competitiveness. It leads to professional illiteracy of which Michael Moore has spoken. The all-precious skills are missing.

If the West is going to be re-industrialized, then it needs *skills*. This should be a top goal in higher education, the more so as, in the course of the last two decades, important skills for many industrial jobs have disappeared from the Western labour market – a fact which is often attributed to globalization. Some experts say that probably something irreversible has occurred as valuable skills and know-how have been lost as jobs have moved abroad and no focused effort is being made to fill the gap in skilled jobs. We have to create and deliver the skills which they require.

David Cote, the chairman and CEO of Honeywell, when asked for his advice on professional education, answered that we need "many more engineers ... We don't need more lawyers, we need more engineers."[12] This is the right educational policy and, though his suggestion was aimed at the American government, it is valid for all nations.

If we do not do so, the result will be that the West, as well as Japan, will no longer have international competitiveness in the manufacturing industry. Ironically, this comes at a time when foreign direct investment finances the building up of the industrial bases in developing countries. This is good for the developing nations, but not for job opportunities in Western countries.

A fact not always appreciated is that, when jobs migrate to other jurisdictions, the skills which are born and grow around them (over several decades) start to decay until there are no longer available. The lack of skills works against the policy of repatriating jobs, such as has been adopted by France and other Western countries. It also creates other hazards due to the concentration of industrial production in nations that lack a proper infrastructure.[13]

The double whammy of selecting wrong subjects (in the sense of employment opportunities later on in life) in university education, and of the absence of skills, is compounded by the lack of discipline and questionable ethics. Critics say that in some countries the market for academic jobs in public universities is deeply corrupt: "plenty of degree courses have sprung up that seem designed merely to create tenured positions ... a ministry of education cites courses on the well-being of dogs and cats and on packaging, as examples".[14]

Still another problem relates to the policy of free university education for all. Overleveraged sovereign budgets cannot afford high salaries for faculties. The best graduates go to work in industry; they don't stay behind to teach at college. Neither is there a policy of bringing the best professionals after their retirement into university faculties as honorary professors.

All this is not hidden from the public eye, but at the end of the day the quality of learning shows in those who are offered employment. There are moreover economists who argue that, contrary to what was thought to be the case some years ago, post-industrial societies will not be characterized by a relentless rise in demand for the educated. This will be marked by a great hollowing out, as mid-level jobs decline and high-level job growth slows. This will result in:

- The quality of education drifting;
- What is taught not being needed;
- The jobs that used to be in demand no longer being there.

It is indeed a pity that society at large, and governments which should have known better, have left the practice of apprenticeship to die away. Only recently have clear-eyed people started to hail the advantages of apprenticeships practised in Switzerland and Germany, stressing the need to value vocational skills as highly as university book-learning.

It has been a grave error to turn jobs like nursing into graduate-only professions and limiting the "apprenticeship" label to low-level courses and in-house training for adult workers. Correctly, in mid-November 2011, the British government urged the institution of higher quality apprenticeships. This is the right move because, as far as skills are concerned, young people learn them much better in apprenticeships than from books, and, instead of costing money to their families and to society, they earn money while they learn.

In 1980, as a share of median household disposable income, university costs consumed about 15 per cent. In 2010 this has risen to 30 per cent. During the first decade of this century tuition rates at public universities have risen 5.6 per cent a year above inflation. On the other hand, average starting salaries for college graduates have fallen by 10 per cent or more during the last five years of the economic downturn.

In America, this combination of rising graduate debts and falling starting pay has renewed a debate about whether college is worth it. Lawrence Kotlikoff, Professor of Economics at Boston College, argues that if one takes the higher income taxes that college graduates pay, and the years of earnings they forego while studying, a university education is less lucrative than it seems.[15]

This makes students' loans so much more difficult to repay. The simplistic idea that a graduate's future earnings will more than cover the costs of doing a degree has turned on its head, and not only because of unemployment rates. For many decades, the best investment was in people's brains. But this no longer seems to be the case because educational discipline is wanting, learning "soft" subjects does not make sense and the labour market has radically changed.

In addition, the repayment of student loans weighs on family budgets for years. In Britain, critics say that student loans create a sort of discrimination, because students from less well-off families are entitled to state support and after graduation they will not have to face the loans repayment burden.

3.4 The university bubble

Since the end of World War II, Britain and France have seen their universities more than double in number, though not in quality. This happens for several reasons. One of the most important is that experienced faculty members who are well-grounded in important professions – particularly the hard sciences – do not multiply as fast as the "new universities" spring up left, right and centre. When one hears that today British universities have as many faculty members as they had students at the end of World War II, one assumes that these staff cannot possibly be of pre-war standards.

Another reason for the fall in the quality of university education is that, with the rapid advancement of technology, laboratory equipment has become too expensive. New equipment is developed and built at a high pace, while university budgets have fallen behind in providing funds for acquiring such new technology. Nearly everything is being paid by the state, and the state is short of money, as other great consumers of capital, such as public health care, ask for more and more.

No minor role is also played by the fact that the mass of students and prospective students has become so large. In 2012 in America 3.2 million high school seniors graduated from 37,000 high schools, and the majority of them aspire to continue their study in a college or university. The numbers in Europe are not too different with the added disadvantage that socialist governments have either watered down or done away with entry examinations, with the result that many students don't have the knowledge necessary to follow university courses,[16] which leads to the holding back of the better learners and the spoiling of scarce resources which could have been put to better use.

At the same time the courses which new entrants choose are, relatively speaking, the easy ones. They are not those which can offer them good prospects for employment. This is a pity because there exist plenty of vacancies in some professions which cannot be filled because the required skills are in short supply.

A study recently made in Switzerland concluded that 30 per cent of generalist doctors will retire within eight years and that there is a scarcity regarding their replacements. Yet, at an average annual income of Swiss francs 200,000 per year, a generalist doctor has good earnings – but his duties also require a full working day. Hence, it is not the job many young people are seeking.

There is another reason that is bringing university education to an inflection point. A growing number of economists and financial analysts believe that the rapid expansion of university education, and the fact that at the end the treasurer who pays everything is the state, may lead to a *university bubble*. Day-in and day-out this bubble is inflated by the way students are funded to study in colleges and the way universities are being financed: which is taxpayers money here, taxpayers money there.

Back in the 1950s and earlier, young men and women whose family had not enough funds to finance their studies worked part-time. But as already mentioned, in the 1960s President Johnson created a state agency to offer student loans, so those who studied could devote 100 per cent of their time to learning. This was a social act which, as with other entitlements, failed to foresee that the latest tool of the nanny state would end up being overexploited – at the end of which lies a bubble.

According to published statistics every second the compound debt of young Americans who finance their study through loans increases by $2,854,[17] adding to the total debt of student loans (many of them securitized) which now stands at $1 trillion. The nightmare for the US federal government is that it has guaranteed 85 per cent of this stock of debt which means a significant increase to the total debt of the country, due to just one reason and in one go.

Let me put this point in a different light. Lyndon Johnson's initiative was an enlightened social measure, but over the decades it became highly geared and therefore it backfired. In 2012, five years after the disaster created by the subprimes, the US government as well as American bankers and taxpayers are now confronted with a new bubble: that of unpaid (and in many cases unpayable) student loans. This is a credit bubble within a bigger university bubble.

This bigger university bubble will come about as a result of deflation in university enrolment if the student loans bubble blows and the federal government and state governments stop financing students.[18] Universities are caught up in the crumbling logic of many twentieth-century institutions according to Christopher Caldwell.[19] He compares this to what has happened in the housing market, noting that the American university system has been lavishly subsidized by the government (as has every European country in regard to their university systems), and that, at the same time, rising expenses have seen to it that heavy borrowing has been required by its students to pay their fees.

University and college costs are rising, says Caldwell, just as excellent, cheap, learning materials are becoming available on the internet. While I agree with Caldwell's worries, I would challenge this last statement because the best learning is done by osmosis. The student must be near to his or her teacher, in order to observe, ask questions and learn. The internet or any online teaching cannot accomplish this requirement. On the other hand, the cost statistics which he presents are eye opening: Yale costs more than $50,000 a year; for a four-year study (with a Master's degree) this makes a cool $200,000 plus living expenses.

There are of course in the US lower cost colleges, but the Ivy League universities set the pace. Beyond this, for all schools of higher education, sponsored research is the prime ingredient of learning, and R&D income comes from federal or state funds and state-sponsored agencies like the Defense Advanced Research Projects Agency (DARPA), as well as from foundations.

Rising costs mean that practically all universities must increase fees to make ends meet. Nowadays this is particularly true of state universities as government budgets are under stress. Aptly Christopher Caldwell points out that two things are breaking the US higher education model: a collapse in wealth and a collapse in economic equality.

He is right, except that this is not just the American model: it is the post-World War II Western model of rich nations and includes Britain, France, Germany and Italy. Theoretically, by subsidizing education all the way to university, the state has bettered the formation of human capital. Practically, it did not achieve its objective because, as explained earlier on, it has allowed students to choose the course of least effort – and this is not what a knowledge society needs.

As far as human capital is concerned, another piece of bad news is that the quality of education is falling, not only in universities but also in high schools and primary schools. This means that a good deal of taxpayers' money is thrown to the four winds. If one looks at higher education as a product, this product has ceased to appreciate in value. Yet costs continue to rise and the discrepancy between what a product costs and what it is worth leads to the bigger university bubble which, some economists say, is soon about to burst.

A nascent bubble in the school system is the use of derivative financial instruments like collateralized debt obligations (CDOs) and credit default swaps (CDSs) to bypass current budgetary constraints. Classically American school authorities financed themselves primarily through taxes. Over the last few decades, however, they started to issue a swelling volume of bonds to supplement tax money. Bonds are loans to be serviced with annual interest and to be repaid sometime in the future. This is the kind of financing which pushes the problem into the years to come.

Worse yet, following the 2007 burst of the real estate market, the property tax revenues of states, largely used to fund schools, have declined, while in many parts of the US voters have imposed (through referenda) fiscal controls on educational boards. To make ends meet, in California schools have made some "innovative" but highly risky solutions to financing.

Poway Unified, a San Diego educational district, is one of many examples. In 2011 it issued over $100 million worth of "capital appreciation" bonds to finance previously planned projects. These are similar to zero-coupon bonds, hence the school district does not need to start repaying interest or capital until 2033. But the risk is enormous. To compensate for this payment deferral and attract investors, these bonds are paying double-digit interest rates.

When the bond is repaid, the total bill will be some ten times the initial loan. It is highly questionable whether the school district will repay it; most likely it will go bust. At this point in time it is not possible to know how widely this silly bond issuance has spread. As the Securities and Exchange Commission said in early August 2012, the $2.7 trillion municipal bond market is extremely opaque. But the Poway case is not unique as there are other, if somewhat less extreme, cases, and this practice seems to be spreading.

Schools and municipalities are being taken to the cleaners by investment banks, by means of derivative products, and not only in the US. However, some cities are biting back. An example is Milan, Italy's economic capital, which went to court. On 18 April 2012 the city settled with a group of banks, which had sold it risky derivative products, for the sum of $623 million – though details were withheld.

3.5 Reasons for unemployment

One of the often heard critiques of the European educational system is that it penalizes success in the name of equality. This is true both of people and of institutions. In the eyes of the bureaucracy, an institute of higher education that does too well is a candidate for having its funding cut. This raises the risk of *entrenched mediocrity*, which is further promoted by the fact that in some countries (for instance, Germany) academics are all but forbidden by law from getting involved in business (where they can gain precious experience).

In other European countries, for instance in France, where no such laws exist, it is considered unethical for an academic to get involved in business for profits. Yet, for European universities many things have to change for them to regain their past glory. The list includes admission examinations, rigorous curricula, first class research laboratories and the recruitment and motivation of highly experienced faculty staff.

Also of great importance is the need for a policy that reorientates students towards the hard sciences, where there is a demand for graduates, rather than the soft sciences, whose graduates are practically assured of being unemployed. As I have shown in the first three sections of this chapter, there is a cost associated with education, and families are paying that cost even if they are misguided into thinking that education is free for all.

In my book, one of the major reasons for unemployment amongst graduates is that young people are being trained for a world that does not exist. No politician takes the initiative to implement the required changes – the reasons being that there are "other priorities", a public apathy and a resistance by embedded interests.

Yet there is an urgency to institute career planning which serves both individuals and society. Out of 2.6 million unemployed in France, 1 million are young people in their twenties (in November 2011).

It is time for a new departure and the goal should be that of promoting employment, though not necessarily full employment. According to Milton Friedman, the economist, a full employment policy leads to inflation, which results in everybody being paid a poor subsistence wage except the elite which has special privileges. Communist Russia tried that, and failed.

It is a major error to repeat past mistakes, such as displaying inertia when it comes to solving the employment problem through adaptation and reorientation. In 2011 one in five people in the European Union labour force aged 25 years or younger is unemployed, with the figures particularly dire in Mediterranean countries. Better managed countries, such as Switzerland and the Netherlands, have youth unemployment rates below 10 per cent. In America just over 18 per cent of the under-25s are jobless.

Wrong-way shifts in educational policies are as responsible for these statistics as the fact that during the last five decades the European Union has not been able to generate jobs at a decent pace. After nearly full employment in the 1950s and 1960s, largely due to the reconstruction work following the war, the European unemployment rate has marched steadily upwards, due in large measure to *labour law rigidities* which have been responsible for:

- The high cost of labour, which includes a swarm of payroll taxes;
- The lack of wage flexibility, seeing to it that companies think twice before hiring people;
- A relatively high benefit being paid to the unemployed, which creates inertia in looking for a job.

Under conditions persisting throughout Europe today, unemployment benefit is not commensurate with a "back to work" policy. In France, it is as high as 59 per cent of pay for 30 months. In Italy, laid-off workers are eligible for up to one year's severance pay. For its part, the cost of hiring and firing discourages hiring.

Labour taxes, as a per cent of hourly wage rates, are over 40 per cent in both France and Italy, compared with under 20 per cent in the United States. Hiring is hindered when the cost of labour is artificially raised by social taxes, which explains the unemployment statistics. In practically all EU countries, particularly the Mediterranean ones, governments are particularly diffident at taking the initiative to open up labour markets. Current rules lock out younger workers.

In general terms, these issues explain how those who have a job have taken as hostage those who are looking for one. While the fine print of labour laws varies from one jurisdiction to the next, the status quo dominates. Still, as far as labour policies are concerned the term "European Union" is a misnomer. Even with this status quo, member states are characterized by significant cross-country differences in employment protection legislation and in wage-setting, such as:

- The degree of centralization of wage bargaining;
- The extension of agreements to other workers;
- The duration of the contract and other specifics.

While all EU countries have plenty of structural rigidities, there exist as well asymmetries between wages, health services and pensions, which creates negative adjustment dynamics. Spain, for example, is one of the countries with a notoriously dysfunctional labour market. As in France, Italy and Greece, a group of ageing unshakeable insiders keep the outsiders at a disadvantage or oblige them to have to make do with temporary contracts.

Unemployment has been a perennial problem in Spain. However, prior to the financial crisis of 2007–12, Spanish unemployment statistics were more or less kept in check by credit-fuelled growth and a prolonged construction boom. In 2007, Spanish unemployment was just 8 per cent. In 2012 it is officially 22 per cent, and among the young a staggering 48 per cent.

Typically, insiders benefit from their seniority, wage-escalation clauses and the fact that in a downturn the newly hired are the first to be sacked. As we have already seen in connection with teachers, this is irrational; but nobody cares or dares to change it. Time and again the European Commission has pointed out that it is not responsible for employment in member states. Neither is it presumably responsible for leading a movement to renew and restructure obsolete and counter-productive labour laws.

Inertia and accommodation with unemployment benefits are other reasons for long-term unemployment. Not everything should be debited to the economic and financial crisis we are in now. From declining employment opportunities for less-skilled people to rising unemployment rates for the young, Western economies were brewing a jobs problem well before the financial crisis hit and, when it did hit, the day arrived when the young generation have to pay for the overspending and debt of their parents.

The combination of globalization and new technology has reduced the demand for the less skilled. In parallel to this, many workers have failed to respond to the deep changes in the labour market by retraining and re-educating themselves – and students entering universities continue to focus on soft subjects rather than hard sciences. Some people have found a way of living with unemployment benefits.

It takes much more than words to bring about a change, particularly when one sees that jobs figures still disappoint a full five years after the economic crisis began. In June 2012 in the US non-farm payrolls rose by less than 0.1 per cent, the third straight month of meagre growth. Other gloomy employment reports abound:

- The International Labour Organization has warned that euroland may lose another 4.5 million jobs over the next four years;
- The OECD has predicted that Germany would be the only euroland economy to see a fall in its unemployment rate by the end of 2013.

Meanwhile in major European countries a long list of jobs are not filled because the skills and know-how they demand are not available in the market. The same prevails in the US, where there are 3 million unfulfilled positions due to lack of required skills.[20]

When in conferences I bring up the argument that career planning and choice of subjects in university education lack focus as far as market demands and employment offers are concerned, some of the delegates get nervous, saying this is not true. When I press the need for lifelong learning, some people point out that to retrain, retool and re-educate the labour force costs money.

A question frequently asked is "Who will pay for it?". The answer is by reducing waste as well as by eliminating the rigidities introduced into the labour market over decades; also, by revaluing handouts, with a view to eliminating them altogether. Both before and after the recent crisis, governments paid big money to unemployed youths for doing nothing – just to keep them off the streets (this policy was started in the 1960s and became institutionalized two decades later).

An opinion which is gaining ground is that the time has finally come for those who are on unemployment assistance to do something for their community rather than sleep and play. Opportunities abound, from looking after the elderly to planting trees.

In conclusion, the job toll from economic woes and structural shifts is high, but we should not throw money at the problem. Finding a job becomes more difficult as more displaced workers are looking for work, but people should try harder. They should not wait for the state supermarket to pull them up, whether from unemployment or underemployment.

3.6 Filling the talent gap

In his book *The Affluent Society*, John Kenneth Galbraith gave an excellent definition of the state supermarket's underworld, making reference to "feather-bedding unions and gold-bricking workmen and slothful supernumeraries ... [and] the ancient art of evading work [which] has been carried out in our time to its highest level of sophistication, not to say elegance".[21]

Nowadays, Galbraith would have probably added in his examples of evil forces working against society the lobbyists and other non-productive elements that thrive at the expense of common citizens and households. Karl Marx was wrong when he said that much modern industrial work was essentially dehumanizing, reducing people to factors of production. These days lots of people are doing jobs that are even more dehumanizing because there is no human value in being a lobbying careerist or a featherbedding union boss.

Featherbedding union bosses are a nineteenth-century relic. Lobbying has older origins but it flourished in the twentieth-century's second half. Neither makes a contribution to society which is found in creative work. Both are not only an anachronism but also a barrier to developing the successful workers of the future who by all evidence will be open-minded people.

The valuing of human capital starts with the choice of the right career. Revaluing is done through lifelong learning. Valuing and revaluing should be characterized by the right selection of a career – therefore of schooling and education, not vice versa. Here is an excellent example from a study released in October 2012 in Switzerland.

An interparty commission, appointed to study the reason for unemployment among graduates in Suisse Romande, has concluded that the main reason is the current level of the baccalaureate (awarded to students who finish their secondary studies and pass the final exam). Its recommendations are that young people should be guided towards professional studies oriented to branches of the economy which need technicians but cannot find them.[22]

The commission has stated that general studies, like those accepted by the baccalaureate, have been at the root of increased unemployment among young Swiss citizens. Worse, the quality level of the baccalaureate has been dropping over the years. Therefore, the interparty commission has proposed that:

- The baccalaureate's level of quality must be improved;
- The severity of examinations must be raised;
- The students' orientation towards technical professions must be promoted.

The same problems with the baccalaureate prevail in France.

Another challenge confronting young people in search of employment is governments' reversal of the position on working on Sundays, where there are jobs to be taken. Are there problems connected with working on Sunday, other than those who find their origin in ideological differences or in conflicts of interest? What is the percentage of the unemployed, most particularly of the long-term unemployed, who would accept a job that demanded them to work on Sunday?

Open-mindedness, flexibility and adaptation are also necessary to survive in a competitive environment. Experts believe that in the coming years the pace of change will be faster than today – and probably so rapid that people will have to acquire new skills every few years if they want to be part of the lucrative market for scarce talent. If the pace of change is going to be so rapid, then an obsolescence of human capital will follow on its heels and innovative education solutions will be necessary to fill that gap.

Innovation in education should answer the need for lifelong learning. This cannot be done online because education requires close contact with the teacher to learn by osmosis.

But is the pace of change really going to be so fast? Some contrary opinions claim that we have passed the high watermark of breathtaking technological change. According to this school of thought, the coming years will be characterized by consolidation more than by rapid innovation, and expertise in consolidation is today in short supply.

Consolidation may well change the organization and structure of a working environment as we know it today. Peter Drucker once said that the structure under which the master professionals of the future will be working will resemble that of an orchestra with one conductor and a hundred virtuosi, rather than the present-day two-dimensional schema.

The Drucker concept of organization might well be the conceptual structure of creative work in the future, though there are people who doubt it and point out that there are two unavoidable steps for a practical approach to this still theoretical concept. The first concerns a market for the services of virtuosi. The consulting service of information technology organizations like Accenture, IBM and Hewlett Packard (to name but a few) are an early example of such a market. Earlier examples have been the Bell Telephone Laboratories and General Motors Laboratories. But similar examples at that scale are not forthcoming, and as an old proverb has it "one swallow does not make a summer".

The second concerns the closing of the talent gap. Manpower, the American human resources firm, surveyed senior personnel executives. Nearly one out of two (precisely 46 per cent) of them said that their talent gap was making it harder for their firm to implement its business strategy. Only 27 per cent answered that their business had the talent needed.[23]

This talent gap, which those of us working in industry know so well, has been one of the basic reasons for the statement made earlier on in this chapter that university education is largely misdirected. Not only is there today an unquestionable talent gap – in spite of the swarm of university graduates – but this shortage will most probably get worse because of the imminent retirement of a generation of seasoned workers: engineers and scientists with sought-after skills.

Households and the state pay lots of money for the education of the young generation. A large part of this money, however, is wasted because of the number of:

- Student dropouts;
- "Professional students" (who want to spend their whole lives as students);
- Degrees which address none of society's needs.

If this were not true, in early 2012 France would not have had 2.6 million unemployed (of which 1 million are young people) and at the same time 460,000 jobs which could not be filled because the required talent was missing. Similar statistics come out of Germany, Britain and the United States. Germany, for example, has millions of unemployed but 550,000 vacancies whose talent requirements have no takers.

German engineering companies are very much concerned about this talent gap. To try to turn the attention of young pupils towards engineering and the sciences, they have instituted programmes addressed at primary education. These programmes include visits of young children to firms as well as an initiation into career planning.

Such efforts are welcome and they come none too soon. If anything, they should have started 30 years ago: "in 2008, one in four workers in America with a degree in science, technology, engineering or mathematics was 50 or over. Lockheed Martin, an aerospace firm, expects nearly half its science and engineering workforce to retire by 2019 and will have to hire a total of 142,000 engineers. Currently only 60,000 engineers a year graduate from American universities".[24]

This talks volumes of the talent gap in the West. It is indeed very curious that "summits" by chiefs of state come and go, but none has devoted time to the question of overcoming the present talent crisis. Yet, all of them most probably know that even if the economy should pick up, big time unemployment is not going to disappear because the jobs of unskilled workers have migrated to developing countries and talented jobs are not being filled because the sort of know-how that they require is in very short supply.

Don't ever believe that Western companies will hire unskilled workers against their best judgement. On the contrary, in order to confront the after-effects of the ongoing economic crisis they restructure and downsize. Tough cost control keeps up profitability. On the other hand, this limits job growth.

In Germany, for instance, to cut costs Otto Versand (a mail order house) has been skirting notoriously restrictive German labour laws by setting up a 24-hour telephone order service through German-speaking operators in Denmark. French companies, for instance SFR of Vivendi, do exactly the same by using French-speaking Moroccans in Morocco for their help desks and other services which can be accommodated through telephone connections.

In the background of these policies lies the fact that companies can no longer easily pass along cost increases. Businesses today are much more likely to absorb costs and innovate around them for fear of losing market share if they raise prices. Other reasons for such policies are the shorter product cycles and the existence of multiple global sources of supply, which see to it that cost control will remain the major theme of Western business at least as long as they experience severe competitive pressure from globalization.

It is indeed a pity that the European Union's 1994 White Paper on competitiveness and employment, which aimed to set standards for the future, gave trivial answers regarding globalization's effect on Western employment. Public spending, which has been one of the answers, is not a cure for the employment crisis. Pep talks about employment are no solution, yet they have remained a top public issue for years.

During the last two or three decades, every important issue has been pushed for consideration into the future. "You can easily recognize an article by Jean Jaurés",[25] George Clemenceau once said. "All the verbs are written in the future." This fits with the verbs in the different pronouncements of both the EU bureaucracy in Brussels and the member states' governments.

3.7 Revaluing human capital

With regard to the talent gap, I have suggested as a solution the right choice in education: one oriented towards expertise and which is known to be in short supply and expected to remain so. Another suggestion has been steady learning which helps to halt the need for requalification, by providing a continuous and sustainable development of skills.

Like everything else, human capital can decay. Innovation, deregulation, globalization and competition have had a revolutionary effect on the job market. To find a job and to continue being in demand for one's talent, one has to be able to change as jobs are redeployed and new opportunities come up.

Concomitant to life-long learning is the culture of being open to two, three or more different careers in a young person's life. Today most job seekers want a full-time, permanent, career-ladder job, but this is not the way to go because what used to be permanent employment – particularly popular in socialistic states and paternalistic companies – is now in short supply. Today's industry has no trouble filling job slots with part-timers; and the labour market signals a fundamental shift in bargaining power to the favour of those who are and continue being flexible.

Human resources must be steadily revalued. An excellent example of the culture necessary to survive in a highly competitive *one world* is that which characterized the life of Thomas Alva Edison, the most famous inventor of his time. Edison had only three months of formal education in a public school, but as he reached fame he made the profound statement that "genius is one per cent inspiration and ninety-nine per cent perspiration". This was his experience, as well as that of all others who had worked hard to succeed.

Another good example is provided by Charles F. Kettering, who made his fame and fortune by inventing the starter motor and selling it, along with his services, to General Motors, where he became director of corporate R&D. Still another excellent example is that of Lawrence Sperry, the inventor of the gyro and of the parachute, among other things.

Not everybody can be an Edison, a Kettering, a Sperry or, more recently, a Steve Jobs. That is not the reason for presenting these examples. The reason is that behind the success of these people has been a steady effort – the 99 per cent of perspiration to which Edison made reference. Without such a steady and focused effort nothing can be achieved.

Not everybody thinks that way and this is a reason why finding the right people is a challenge. Keeping them motivated once they are on the payroll is an even more demanding task. Surveys have suggested that companies which fail in this dual mission do so because revaluing human capital is not in their philosophy.

The right kind of professional education and lifelong learning, a way of revaluing human capital, is to promote innovation and entrepreneurship. Versatility helps and so does the ability to watch unfolding events like an eagle in order to capture the opportunity – Harold Macmillan, the former British prime minister, was once asked what makes success in politics. He answered: "events, dear boy, events".

One of the best examples to ring up the message that revaluing human resources is the best way to be in charge of the future is risk control in banking. The reason for this is very simple. Even if an institution has an excellent record in risk management, its internal controls are functioning, its procedures are strong and its systems work in a way that could be considered flawless (which is very rarely the case), management control will eventually weaken if not manned by first-class people.

Policies and standards are necessary, but by themselves they are not enough. Speaking from experience, it is nearly always possible to find within an organization a first-class person to fill the shoes of the risk manager, but often he or she is unavailable because his current boss says "I cannot spare this man". There are only a few explanations for the "indispensable man" says Peter Drucker:

- His strength is misused to bolster a weak superior who cannot stand on his own feet;
- His strength is misdirected to delay tackling a serious problem or even conceal its existence;

- He is really impotent, and while he got the name of "doer" he can only survive if carefully shielded from further demands.

Drucker goes on to suggest that in every one of the aforementioned situations, the indispensable person should be moved anyhow, and quickly. Otherwise, whatever he or she may have as a personal competitive advantage would be destroyed. As an example on how to manage subordinates in an effective manner, Drucker takes George Marshall's policy during World War II. Marshall insisted that a general officer must be immediately relieved if found to be less than outstanding. To keep him in command, he reasoned, was incompatible with the responsibility of the US Army.

As Chief of Staff, General Marshall refused to listen to the argument "but we have no replacement". All that matters, he pointed out, is that we know this man is not equal to the task. Where his replacement comes from is the next question. Marshall also pressed the point that to relieve a man from command was less a judgement on that particular person than on the commander who had appointed him.

"The only thing we know is that this spot was the wrong one for that man", George Marshall argued. "This does not mean that he is not the ideal man for some other job. Appointing him was my mistake, now it's up to me to find what he can do."[26] Out of this policy, Drucker suggests, came the future generals of World War II who were still junior officers with few hopes for promotion when Marshall became the US Army's boss.

This is an excellent example of human resources management. No matter how great a firm's market position and its goals may be, if the talent expected to execute what is needed to reach them is missing, or is wanting, the result will range from zero to disaster. Deliverables will remain a pipe dream, unless the person in charge makes things happen.

In conclusion, when the board is presented with high level appointments, its members should always ask themselves: does this person have the personality and clout to execute effectively the CEO's decisions? Does he or she have the expertise and strength the job requires? The board should not suffer from the delusion, which I have found in many cases, that an important and demanding job can be split between different people.

Effective planning and control requires unity of command; and two or three mediocrities never achieve as much as one first-class person. If anything, two mediocrities deliver less than one mediocrity as they get in each other's way. Two things which are wrong don't make one which is right, according to Ben Gurion.

Part II
Households Must Get Their Act Together

4
The IOU Abyss

4.1 Democratization of credit and socialization of risk

There is no unlimited borrowing ability for families, just like there is no unlimited borrowing for companies and sovereigns. There are limits in all cases, a truth which is being revealed to the common citizen the hard way. The deep economic and financial crises which started in 2007 and were followed by the drying up of bank credit were the catalysts of a change in credit policies which is still in process. Five factors characterize a financial bubble:

- Increased leverage;
- High liquidity;
- Much bigger turnover;
- New issuance of money which destabilizes the monetary base;
- The "democratization" of credit along with the "socialization" of risk associated with it.

Since the late 1960s/early 1970s households in the US, Britain, France and the Mediterranean countries have been grossly and increasingly undersaving. Most families have probably assumed that the appreciation in home values is an event which replaces traditional savings. In so doing, they have taken no notice of the bearish view on housing which went on-and-off during the more than four decades since 1970, suggesting, among other things, that assumptions made about a decreasing importance of family savings were likely to be incorrect.

Instead of searching for better ways and means to protect their accumulated worth, which they could use, citizens and sovereigns thought that the economy could only go up. No thought was given to the possible deflation of the housing bubble which would have suggested that they not only needed to save more, but also that this "more" should produce a secure income to keep up their standards of living.

The light-headed solution has been that of living on "I Owe You" (IOU) promissory notes, which has led to an IOU abyss and an "age of irresponsibility", a name that can be applied to:

- Profligate sovereigns;
- Runaway banks;
- Households living beyond their means.

At the citizens' level, a recent theory states that the intervention of the credit card ruined capitalism, limiting peoples' ability to distinguish between real and imaginary money, inciting them to spend more than they have, and breaking the link between effort and reward. This theory has relevance to Western society whose citizens are heavily indebted.

Raising one's debt to a higher level creates many problems. One of the more vicious is the case of a debtor (which may be the sovereign) who intends to make somebody else responsible for his or her debts. Common citizens particularly dislike the way the sovereign is using their money to reward deadbeats. Most families work hard and live within their means. They observe neighbours, who borrowed more than they could afford to buy something fancy, declaring themselves bankrupt. Or they read of a mismanaged bank getting a bail-out to save it from the consequences of its own poor judgement. This is a moral risk which creates unease in society.

Worse yet, a salient problem with the democratization of debt is that, as new liabilities pile up on old ones already on the books, the debt pyramid becomes unstable. A huge level of liabilities created through leverage is not sustainable in good times and it is perilous in bad times as the level of unemployment rises, particularly so when citizens have no savings to see themselves through such times.

The fallacy that personal and family savings were no more necessary, or at least were not needed as much as they used to be, was further promoted by an indiscriminate bank lending to households, by amounts which continued to grow, accompanied by progressively lower credit standards on loans. Good economic conditions were expected to reduce the materiality of risks across nearly all sectors of the economy.

True enough, the financial markets experienced an important development in the post-World War II years, most particularly, since the early 1970s, with the end of the Bretton Woods Agreement. To recycle the petrodollars, banks needed to lend, and this led to the democratization of lending. This has been accompanied by the socialization of risk, as sovereigns tried their best to cover or repair the damages from misfortunes the banking industry had brought upon itself. With the democratization of credit, more and more people were able to borrow and eventually an increasing amount of debt was subsidized by the US federal government.

Selectively and then massively rapidly growing liabilities have been repackaged, securitized and (fake) rated and sold to investors as "assets". The practice has been a cheat, but it provided banks with liquid funds to lend again. At the same time, it expanded the scope of lending and borrowing, and gave birth to the process of financialization.

An easily definable characteristic of the socialization of risk has been the government-undertaken salvage operations of private companies, like US Savings & Loans in the late 1980s, and the massive financial assistance provided to self-wounded banks in 2008 and afterwards. By standing behind good banks and bad banks alike, the US government has in effect cancelled the oldest franchise in banking: that which associated the right to do business with *safekeeping*. (This franchise had started being chipped away in the 1930s with deposit insurance.)[1]

Another interesting development of the last decades of the twentieth century and the first decade of the twenty-first, worth noting, is the reinvention of unsecured paper money. "Junk bonds", which essentially means "securitized junk loans", have played an expansive role in the recent booms and busts, and the same is true of other financial instruments which, whilst worth practically nothing, have been rated AAA. With the socialization of risk, creditors lend more freely than they had in the past and the government intervenes more actively than ever before, mainly to absorb the inevitable losses – by using taxpayers' money.

With the democratization of credit and the socialization of risk, indebtedness became widespread and efforts to assess its impact generally relied on old tools like debt-to-income and debt-service-to-income ratios. The results proved to be inaccurate because, with leveraging and derivatives, debts had transformed into structures difficult to analyse and price.

To evaluate properly the amount of assumed exposure, it is important to analyse the debt to *real assets* ratio. Real assets comprise not only real estate but also other non-financial assets which might themselves have been leveraged or (illegally) used as guarantees to multiple creditors. Particularly important is whether these real assets provide cash flows needed to:

- Satisfy the servicing of debt;
- Serve as collateral for refinancing;
- Be available for sale in case the debtor runs into funding difficulties.

Whether indebtedness analysis is done for households, companies or the sovereign state, an important element of it is the principle that the outcome must inspire confidence. A crisis worsens when business confidence disappears, while all the defects of the system come to the foreground.

This is a different way of saying that the democratization of credit is no free lunch. Not only interest on loans must be paid by the borrower and the capital returned to the lender, but the whole lending system must undergo public scrutiny, because borrowers might have set up a Ponzi game. Moreover, in times of crisis, contagion occurs via the breakdown of confidence.

If an ongoing economic crisis leads to increase in risk aversion among financial market participants, then the market access of other entities may be hampered. This may happen even if the economic fundamentals of the other entities remain sound. In addition, the channels of contagion are likely to be mutually reinforcing. In the 2007–12 timeframe, for example, bank recapitalization had to be borne in large part by the public sector,[2] and this weighed on the sustainability of public finances, while house owners were let unassisted.

The strategy of banks and their lobbyists has been that helping out households sinking in a sea of red ink, through public money, would aggravate moral hazard as far as borrowers were concerned. Precisely the same argument, however, is true of overleveraged banks. If a financial institution knows that it does not have to honour fully its contractual obligations, then it will always be tempted to accumulate excess leverage, particularly so if supervisory authorities do not watch over the preservation of assets.

In conclusion, the democratization of credit allows people and companies to increase significantly their leverage, while the socialization of exposure and losses adds moral risk to financial risk. Exposure increases as households and enterprises (both financial and non-financial) raise additional funds, even when their creditworthiness is in question.

4.2 Consumer spending

In the years Alan Greenspan chaired the Federal Reserve, he looked at the American consumer as the motor of the economy and he was not disturbed when he saw that by spending beyond their means households were sinking deeper into debt. As debt piled up, over-leveraging by households precipitated the mortgage crisis and started the devastating economic and financial downfall of Western economies.

The earthquake of the subprimes, and the huge losses suffered by the average American family in its real estate property, have been followed by a scarcity of jobs. Negative equity affects a relatively large number of households, while stagnating economic conditions make it quite likely that there will be further price falls on family investments (see also Chapter 5).

American households who could afford to do so have tried to restructure their balance sheets, and this was positively commented on by several economists, though a high rate of unemployment worked against deleveraging. This restructuring of balance sheets lasted nearly three years. But in August 2011 American consumers changed gear and started spending more money than they earned. Economists looked at this with mixed feelings.

Consumer confidence did not return to the precrisis level. Both in the US and in Europe the speed of the recovery in private consumption has been relatively modest by historical standards and consumption growth has been weaker than overall economic growth which kept below a low one-digit number.

In Europe, most of the upturn in consumption was driven by households' purchases of non-durable goods and services. The consumption of durables was broadly neutral, as a rather positive contribution from durables such as appliances was offset by a decline in purchases of cars following the end of the government schemes which during the recession had encouraged car purchasing.

The economy found it difficult to take off as households' real disposable income was being eroded by the combination of inflationary pressures and taxes. Higher gas and electricity prices being passed on by utility companies did not improve consumer sentiment, and government austerity programmes weighed on spending – but they were unavoidable as sovereign deficits have been among the largest in recent memory.

The way households and ordinary citizens plan their future and assure their economic independence before and after retirement is of vital importance not only to each one of them individually but also to the economy as a whole. There used to be a time when per capita GDP was a statistic guiding the economist's hand. Now it is household debt as a percentage of disposable income (or, alternatively, of GDP). Debt as a percentage of disposable income has a dismal message for the economy:

- Britain leads with a ratio of about 170 per cent;
- Canada comes next with 150 per cent;
- The United States has 130 per cent, nearly matched by Japan;
- In France it stands at 115 per cent;
- In Germany it is nearly 100 per cent, way too high for a relatively conservative society.

Debt has to be served and the interest paid has to be diminishing by a certain amount of the household's disposable income. Yet, against all logic many citizens and households are again adding to their debt. Governments and regulatory agencies are in a bind. They know that inordinate amounts of consumer borrowing destabilize the consumers themselves, and therefore the economy. But they also want to see the economy kicking again.

Measuring household exposure as the ratio of family debt – to GDP does not make the results any better. In either case the top leverage factor is mortgage debt, which in the US makes up about 80 per cent of total household debt. Comparing mortgage debt to deeply falling house prices reveals that debt relative to assets is very high owing to the steep decline in home prices since their 2007 peak.

In euroland, too, household borrowing is driven by loans for house purchases, while more classical consumer credit has contracted. The consumer credit's weakness probably reflects a lack of willingness to embark on purchases of expensive items in view of high levels of household indebtedness. (By mid-2011, in euroland, the recovery in loans to households levelled off.)

In his seminal 1999 book, *Financing the American Dream: A Cultural History of Consumer Credit*, Lendol Calder castigated the culture of consumption, after having demonstrated how the gradual acceptance of a policy of debt-to-purchase consumer goods represented a change in attitudes of the American public.[3] Calder distinguishes between a period of *growth and stigmatization* from 1880 to 1915 and one of *growth and legitimization* which started in 1916 and continued thereafter.

Instead of 1915, a better cut-off is 1928 because in May that year City Bank's personal loan department in New York opened for business. On the first day 500 applications for personal loans poured in. The next three days brought another 2,500. This was a milestone. Until then a personal loan was viewed as a case of philanthropy, but starting in 1928 it became big business and spread all over the globe.

A large portion of the early increase in personal loans had to do with one consumer product: the automobile.[4] Instalment credit was used to buy many other types of goods. A prominent example of the early years of consumer finance was the founding of credit companies by the main car manufacturing companies to provide the dealers and their clients with the financing necessary for the acquisition of motor vehicles.

The collateral was the car, but as personal loans boomed banks became more and more inclined to disregard the inherent value of the collateral (a wrong move). They also bent their creditworthiness criteria. (Even after the catastrophe of the subprimes in early 2011 a survey by the Federal Reserve found more banks easing standards for consumer loans than at any time since 1994.)

Instead of exercising due diligence when giving loans, many banks depended on penalties which they applied to their clients' accounts.

For instance, they replaced late-payment fees with penalty interest rates, and some charged annual fees on credit cards that previously had none.

The banks themselves have to face restrictions where in the past they had been absent. Rules now in the works, connected to the 2010 Dodd-Frank financial regulation law in the US, require a bank, which would in the past routinely sell off 100 per cent of newly originated mortgages, to keep at least 5 per cent of the securitized instruments unless, among other things, the customer makes a down payment of at least 20 per cent – which few borrowers can meet nowadays.

The case of mortgages under water brings another twist. According to some, households can grow into their debt levels by allocating some of their savings towards asset accumulation rather than solely through paying down debt. Economists suggest that this could be accomplished through an increase in the personal savings rate. For instance, from 3 per cent today in the US to 5–10 per cent, allocating 20 per cent to a savings policy centred on buying assets and using the remaining 80 per cent to pay down debt.

The question, of course, is whether households have a cash flow allowing a tripling of the level of their savings. If they do, then this added percentage will be probably taken out of the household budget. Mervyn King, the governor of the Bank of England, has blamed the fall in household spending in 2011 on a squeeze in real incomes resulting from "world energy prices ... the need to rebalance the UK economy and the cost of the financial crisis in terms of lower productivity".[5]

To help consumers and themselves, sovereigns and central banks do the utmost to keep interest rates at rock bottom. In doing so, however, they forget that nearly zero interest rates have not helped the US, Britain or Japan to recover the health of their economy: it just fuelled the potential for inflation in a period of stagnation and led to speculation.

There always exist unexpected consequences, at least for some of the people, when entering into transactions. While a growing number of delinquent and defaulting loans results in an increasing amount of charge-offs on bank balance sheets, it can be beneficial to households as it is a way of lowering their debt levels. The reader should remember that in the general case the reason why debtors default is because their assets are not enough to cover their liabilities.

4.3 The state supermarket

One of the unexpected consequences of the deep economic, financial and banking crisis which started in 2007 has been the realization that a huge chunk of wealth in Western nations has simply disappeared. For the last four decades sovereigns and ordinary citizens in the West have been living way beyond their means, incited to do so and (up to a point) protected from adversity *by the state supermarket.* Over this period nobody bothered to ask:

- Whether a deeply indebted government is good for society;
- Whether the failure to make ends meet will put limits to, and eventually reverse, the welfare state;
- If the public and household debt keeps on mounting, who will pay the final bill?

The worst possible answer, but also the more frequent one, is "the government". Here is what Golda Meir, the former Israeli prime minister said on that matter:

> The government cannot do everything all at once. It cannot have a magic wand and meet everyone's demands simultaneously: eradicate poverty without imposing taxes, win wars, go on absorbing immigration, develop the economy and still give everyone his dues. No government can do all this at once and at the same time.
>
> In the first place, those among us who are poor mustn't permit themselves to be turned into the passive objects of other people's concern. They must be active on their own behalf.[6]

Meir is right. Few politicians have the integrity, foresight and courage to admit that the government cannot be all things to all people; and at the end of the day too much debt kills the economy. The typical political animal will never accept, let alone admit, his or her mistakes. But there are exceptions. Jim Callaghan, the British Labour prime minister, was perfectly honest when he declared to a party conference in the 1970s that:

> We used to think that you could spend your way out of recession and increase employment, cutting taxes and boosting government

> spending. I tell you in all candour that that option no longer exists and that in so far as it ever did exist, it only worked on each occasion since the war by injecting a bigger dose of inflation into the economy, followed by a higher level of unemployment as the next step.[7]

As the prime ministers of Israel and Britain so aptly stated, the state supermarket is far from being manna from heaven. Citizens, households, companies and governments should be wary of unintended consequences. Entitlements can create perverse incentives which, when reaching a critical mass, hit both families and the economy like a rock. Aside from their dead weight on state finances, they lead to greater complexity and opacity of subsidies, and then allow increases in their misuse, with dramatic impact on the sovereign's debt woes.

Not only is deficit financing by the state supermarket a consequence of unemployment, but there is another Horseman of the Apocalypse: higher taxes. "Too much tax kills the tax," said Jacques Chirac before being elected president of France in the 1990s. After his election, however, he changed his mind. With a mismanaged economy, where the large majority of people expect the state supermarket to take care of all their needs, taxes increased and Chirac simply forgot that taxpayers deserve a break.

One of the ironies of our time is that lots of people don't understand deficit financing is a fraud. The same citizens who are overtaxed and know that their country is deeply in debt, every day continue to look at the state supermarket as the Garden of Eden. The *nanny state* which was born in the 1930s following the First Great Depression has never really stopped growing.

People concerned about the "deeper in debt" aftermath on society's future want to stop this piling up of public liabilities. They are convinced that the missing money has gone to finance the *deficit created by better living* as our society lives well beyond its means. The state supermarket and its adherents have been consuming the wealth created over the centuries when the West had a dominating position worldwide. Spending money you don't have, these people say, is decadence.

The state supermarket has gone well beyond what is usually called "entitlements" (Chapter 2). In the first dozen years of the twenty-first century it has generalized a practice of being everybody's nanny by using taxpayers' money to: pull out of the abyss self-wounded banks; use government largesse to bring back to life moribund car companies; invent any sort of non-productive job; and, at the same time, prevent Western economies from reaching their full potential.

The end result of this policy is that it is killing personal initiative and destroying from within the American, British, French and other Western free enterprise systems. It has done so much more effectively what the so much feared Soviet menace might have done. Working in unison, nineteenth-century socialists and governments' *Homo bureaucraticus* have decreed that:

- Everybody is entitled to health coverage, hence people do not need to care for their health (widespread obesity being an example) since medical and hospital expenses are paid for by the state;
- Mothers and fathers get subsidies for their newborn, allowing citizens to use income from procreation as a substitute for income from work;
- Youths often get more benefits from being unemployed than they would if they worked, hence it is better for them not to look for a job;
- Those who have a job are entitled to all kinds of protection through structural barriers, essentially taking hostage those who don't have a job;
- Every person has the right to three, four or five weeks of vacation, and travel to exotic places, once a rare privilege, has become commonplace;
- Big banks, whose managers have been inept and self-gratifying, are entitled to be rescued by massively throwing good public money after bad.

This vast array of unaffordable and unsustainable giveaways documents that today's state supermarket is not the kind envisaged by classical nineteenth-century socialism, but is something even more wasteful than its priests and believers ascribed to. One can look at it as the sort of beast which came out of two strange bedfellows:

- The feminine one, which was born with the Socialist International and acquired its backbone in the early to mid-1930s with the New

Deal in the US and the Popular Front in France; by contrast the Russian Revolution was its nemesis;
- The masculine one, which saw light in the 1920s and reached adulthood in the 1970s with derivative financial instruments and bank-to-bank trading, earning sufficiently large amounts of money which enabled it to buy any favours it wanted from politicians.

To the adherents of the socialist manifesto, wealth embodies evil; money is the devil. But they find no difficulty reconciling this belief with lavish financial state support – indeed, they milk the state through all sorts of entitlements: health care from the cradle to the grave, free-for-all education and pensioners taking out of the pension scheme much more than they have contributed.

The theory espoused nowadays by the majority of people, that the state should replace their mother and should indefinitely continue paying money to society, has taken root. This turns the principle of equality and fraternity on its head. But because the public has been so poorly informed about the need to reverse the profligate policies of the last decades, they are unprepared for confronting the challenges which lie ahead.

Over the years, the behavioural pattern of the state supermarket has given birth to a generation of largely corrupt and often incompetent public servants and politicians, whose main goal has been the spending of public money for all sorts of useless projects. Parliaments have legislated bastion after bastion of privilege and politicians have assured their re-election by throwing unaffordable entitlements to the masses.

Like military equipment, entitlements are not productive investments. Money spent on them does not multiply like money spent on education, infrastructure, industrial and agricultural equipment, or research and development. In addition, when the money thrown at the problem is just red ink, as is happening today, then its longer term cost is overwhelming. No wonder that the West finds itself in growth recession.

What essentially this means is that there are very difficult choices ahead. To get the economy moving again, the labour market must be restructured and a great amount of attention paid to innovation. This is a "must" so as to get ahead of the curve in the global market.

But money is scarce because these days in the West both sovereigns and households are living in debt.

To save money and channel what is saved to where it counts, all sorts of benefits must be trimmed, from health care to pensions and other entitlements. Society must realign its priorities by putting everything on the table, and a new ethic should be instilled into governments and common citizens: earn the money before you spend it.

In conclusion, with its handouts all the way from big banks to citizens, the state supermarket has been a master in creating *self-made unemployment*. The so-called "social" (but in reality *anti-social*) policies of weak governments have created an unstoppable slide towards more and more debt. Red ink has become king in Western societies.

Even worse, self-unemployment has turned into *rent seeking*, and prospering at the expense of society has become a profession. Its army of adherents, a fast-growing breed, is seeking benefits from the common purse which it does not deserve. But, not unexpectedly, politicians are keen to oblige; it's other people's money after all.

4.4 Household leveraging

The difference between genius and stupidity, Winston Churchill once said, is that genius has limits. This applies to households, banks and sovereigns. There have been no limits to leveraging over the past three decades.

As we have seen, British households are leveraged at 170 per cent of their net disposable income, with Canada, the US and France not too far behind. Already, at the end of the 1990s, when Western consumers acquired the habit of taking on so much debt, some economists began to sound the alarm bells. Opinions were, however, divided, as other economists opted for laissez-faire, suggesting that it would not be long before:

- Caution set in;
- Consumers pulled back;
- The economy found its balance.

The critics of leveraging have also pointed out that consumer-debt obligations have been growing twice as fast as wage and salary gains.

In their opinion, at fault are changes in the availability and use of credit. Laxity by credit institutions has altered the frame of reference of consumer indebtedness and made it more difficult to predict when, and even if, a consumer-induced economic bubble will occur.

This argument has been proven by the July/August 2007 economic crisis which still runs on in high gear. Nothing dramatizes more the peril of leveraging than the unprecedented wealth destruction that went on from the third quarter of 2007 to the third quarter of 2008 and beyond, as household wealth descended towards the abyss.

Financial analysts estimate that at its 2006 peak the value of US real estate was over $12 trillion (some say over $13 trillion) based on home prices and equity valuations. In slightly over four years, from August 2007 to November 2011, the loss has been an estimated 37.5 per cent, representing $7.5 trillion.[8] This provides one more evidence that real estate deflations end in:

- Wealth destruction;
- Economic contraction;
- Destabilization of credit markets.

The aftershocks of a severe real estate crisis can be dramatic because so much more money is invested in housing than in the stock market. While the 2001 tech bubble bursting was no picnic, the peak-to-trough decline in household net worth back then was $4.2 trillion, a 9.6 per cent decline, and real estate losses by US households have been much worse. Even the 1975 deflation in asset values, a period which represented the worst economic backdrop of the past five decades, represented a peak-to-trough decline that was only $160 billion, a drop of 3.6 per cent of household net worth. Compared to these statistics, the deep economic and financial crisis of 2007 brought the destruction of household net worth into a whole new zone, and the frequently used old-fashioned macroeconomic models were seen to have yielded flawed results.

By basing their opinions on obsolete macroeconomics models the laissez-faire economists had predicted that, as long as unemployment stays down, there was no problem when consumers hit a rough spot. "No problem" meant that consumers did not have to stop spending.

Some people even suggested that the economy had a new buffer: the plastic card as payment vehicle. The basis for this argument is at best superficial. It is known as the "rescheduling solution". It now takes on average more than four years to pay off an existing credit-card obligation. By contrast, by the end of last century it took less than three years.

Contrary to many superficial arguments, the credit card has been for consumers a powerful and destructive leveraging instrument. The number of cards in circulation in the US is roughly 25 million, and it continues to grow, while statistics on card receivables jump upwards.

As if to provide an accelerator to household leveraging, banks are making credit cards readily available to a wider range of consumers, including those on lower incomes who cannot afford to be big spenders and those borrowers with spotty credit records. Even illegal immigrants have received applications for credit cards.[9]

Department stores and supermarkets, too, have used increasingly liberal credit terms to spur sales and apparently boost interest charges on balances. By lowering the minimum payment due on their credit cards, companies earned far more income from their credit card operations – even during periods when store sales did not rise very much.

It comes therefore as no surprise that credit cards have been in the front line when adversity hit. At end of November 2007, nearly four months after the deep economic and financial crisis started, analysts at Goldman Sachs reckoned that credit-card losses could reach $99 billion if contagion spread from subprime mortgages to other forms of consumer credit.

Both the charge-off and delinquency rates, which respectively measure the share of balances that are uncollectable or more than 30 days late, have been rising. Among other banks HSBC announced that it had taken a $1.4 billion charge in its American consumer-finance business, partly because of weakness among card borrowers.[10]

This vindicated the experts who, while the good times lasted, warned that the fast growth in consumer debt should not be taken lightly. "It is not appropriate for me to tell people not to use their credit cards as much", said Lawrence Lindsey, a Federal Reserve Board governor who believed consumer debt levels were growing too high, "but it is my responsibility to tell bankers not to put out as many solicitations".

Prudence, however, did not carry the day. Massive solicitations for credit cards continued being sent to people, whether or not they should qualify for them. In one trimester alone statistics indicated that banks had send out 1.2 billion solicitations – five for every man, woman and child in America.

According to some economists over-leveraging by credit cards has seen to it that in America the savings rate is only 2 per cent and that consumer spending is at a record high of 71 per cent of GDP. The average household owns about $40,000 of non-housing durable goods assets; the average household also owned 2.2 motor vehicles and has, allegedly, four TV sets. It is interesting to note that this number has nearly tripled since the debt super-cycle began with the repeal of the Glass Steagall Act by Bill Clinton in 1999.

For households, the decision to purchase a durable good[11] is similar to that of a company making an investment decision, though households typically lack the concept of cost-effectiveness. Companies weigh the cost of purchasing an additional unit of capital equipment against the present value of expected future income that it will generate. The large majority of consumers don't think that way. This makes decisions on durable good purchases much more "light". Consumers adjust their purchasing behaviour in the light of their new expected income rather than as a function of an investment's rationality.

A fairly similar paradigm is a home purchase. Theoretically, when a household buys a home this is akin to the land and factory bought by a company. Consumers however don't think in this way: previously they generally followed the old saying "your home is your castle"; more recently, however, with the housing market in an upswing, they have looked at their homes as piggy-banks.

The policy of trying to sell at a higher price contributed to household leveraging. Real estate could be bought with very little, if any, down payment, and even monthly payments were waived for some time. For a couple of years this policy of buying and selling homes made good profits for its players – but then adversity hit families at the worst possible time, as house prices collapsed and unemployment increased.

Precisely this super-leveraging, elaborated on false premises, led to the record implosion of household net worth. The impact of an unprecedented negative wealth shock on personal savings has been substantial – and expectations that the Fed, Treasury or Congress had some magic wand proved to be wholly unrealistic.

Comparisons with the 1930s have flaws, but analysts who calculated the asset deflation of household balance sheets came to the conclusion that the caving-in of real estate prices, and losses to households because of it, represented more than half of the implosion that occurred during the First Great Depression. Another statistic is more disquieting: it took over three years for the economy to recover from the stock market crash of 1929 and the dot.com bust of 2000. But, from July/August 2007 to today, the time elapsed is nearly five years and we still don't see the light at the end of the tunnel.

It comes as no surprise therefore that, even with a highly reduced cost of capital and rather easy financial conditions, consumers are not spending their precious money. People have (probably) learned the hard way that they should *not* expose themselves to highly leveraged conditions.

But have the sovereigns learnt that lesson? The answer is: "not yet". Looking ahead, one can see serious challenges to fiscal sustainability. Progress with fiscal consolidation has been wanting, therefore risks persist and are marked by significant cross-country heterogeneity. Unsustainable public debt is not only making a mockery of incapable sovereigns, it is also the second main risk confronting households, the first being their vulnerability with respect to high unemployment and a deteriorating economic environment. Through taxation and inflation households are typically paying the public debt.

4.5 It is not easy to restore public confidence

From July/August 2007, when the deep economic and banking crisis started, to the "historic week" of mid-September 2008, when Wall Street descended to Hades, market sentiment became very grim. Apart from other indicators, risk aversion towards questionable assets was exemplified by the fact that more than a year after the crisis the prices of home equity loans implied a default rate consistent with unemployment of around 20 per cent rather than the then prevailing 6.5 per cent in the US. Moreover, the rout of the housing market extended to Britain, Ireland and Spain as well as (to a lesser extent) Italy and France.

In parallel to the financial strain, confidence disappeared among citizens. As unemployment started rising, there was a general feeling that politicians and central bankers, who were expected to be men of experience, had failed in their job. Clear minds saw what was coming. In January 2008, Lyndon LaRouche painted a sombre picture by writing that:

> we are at a point not of an ordinary crisis, not of a financial crisis, not of a mere depression, but of a global breakdown crisis, centered in the trans-Atlantic community, especially the English-speaking trans-Atlantic community, which will radiate, if it's not stopped, to bring every part of the world into a *general breakdown of their respective social systems.*[12]

A torrent of public money thrown to the market by central banks has delayed that day of reckoning, but nobody can guarantee that it will not come. Rather, the apparent partnership between governments and big global banks looks precarious. Some economists suggest that its unravelling will define the high and the low points of the politics of sovereigns and Western economies.

This will be equally true of the highs and the lows of emerging economies because in many of these emerging countries a Western style of credit culture has been rising among the middle classes. Better-off people have found no difficulty in getting into debt, behaving in a way their parents would have found unimaginable. For instance, buying homes and cars by borrowing.

The highest ratio of household borrowing to GDP continues to be in the developed countries, which for several decades have been in the habit of saving less and consuming beyond their means, expecting too much from an economy which has not been in good health. Sovereigns have followed precisely the same policy, with no urgency shown to reducing debt or getting the economy moving again.

The 4 July 2011 financial newsletter by Wegelin & Co., the Swiss personal banking firm, characterized as a "blood-red abyss" the debt spiral of Western countries, which will spin ever faster until it disappears beyond hope into political unrest. And because one misfortune never comes alone, countries whose AAA credit rating was not questioned in the past – like the United States, Britain, France and even Germany – will become the subject of rigorous scrutiny by the rating agencies and of downgrades.

Past glories are now mere pipedreams as confidence has been lost in the West (and in the East about the West). Business confidence, not just money, makes the world go round; and once it is gone it is not easy to bring it back. Households, too, have lost their confidence in the economy and this has dire consequences. Personal consumption expenditure by American households alone represents 15 per cent of the global economy – a share greater than the entire Chinese economy.

To appreciate the impact of these statistics the reader should know that only 25 per cent of personal consumption is discretionary spending. The large majority is not made up of mobile phones, smart phones, handbags and dinners, but is non-discretionary in nature, such as housing, health care, energy, food eaten at home and other household staples.

At the same time, however, while there is certainly room to reduce non-discretionary spending, the area of consumer spending feeling the brunt is that of discretionary spending which includes cars, apparel and travel. In Western countries this 25 per cent of household spending is about equivalent to 17.7 per cent of GDP.

It should also be noticed that the objects of discretionary spending are themselves shifting. In Germany, young people have been telling researchers that their mobile phone is more important than a new car. The same switch is also taking place in Japan where a new car is down to seventh place on the "want" list of young adults.[13]

Another consumption figure highlighting the impact of household confidence on the economy and jobs is retail sales. The contribution to American GDP from retail sales has been declining for over ten years. Excluding supermarkets, retail sales are under 40 per cent of total consumption, or about 28.4 per cent of GDP.

Households finance their purchases of goods and services with what they earn in their jobs, if they have one, through their labour. If they don't have a job, because of high unemployment levels, they will sell some of their assets; but then, at least the better managed households, will be careful in using the money they still have. Non-discretionary items will attract most of the remaining funds.

It follows that swings in "household net wealth", defined as being equal to total assets minus total liabilities, will affect actual consumer spending, both in absolute and relative terms. The silver lining with excessive debt (and up to a point with loss of confidence in the economy) is that people wake up to the fact that they are too deep in the red. Up to a certain level debt has become an economic reality; and for companies it is a necessity. Capital is not so distributed that the required amount is always available precisely where it is needed or immediately at the right amount.

Indeed, the reason for economic allocation mechanisms is that of providing the bridge between the places where capital is available and where it is needed. Banks and the bond markets perform that function. But when debt becomes excessive, it turns into a destabilizer, which is rapidly followed by loss of public confidence. It is an illusion to believe that household and business confidence will return as long as unemployment remains a high single-digit or even a two-digit number and super-leveraging is still the rule at the state, bank and household levels.

Stated in a different way, business confidence will not return until the preconditions are present. These include both debt repayment and employment. Facts, not empty contradictory political pronouncements, bring back confidence; but if one listens to what politicians are saying one would doubt that the economy is on the right track – namely that they will simultaneously reduce the public deficit and create new employment opportunities.

Even a child knows that these are mutually exclusive, but politicians find it hard to make tough choices. If they were not lying to the public they would have admitted that, even with stringent measures, it will take the better part of ten years to clean up both the public deficit and the household debt mess. Over this time, employment will be wanting and the markets will be subdued.

To be believable, business confidence has to pass the test of time. This has not happened yet. The European Commission's survey of business confidence in the services sector, which had been showing a gradual recovery since August 2007, was strongly decreasing in July and August 2011. Other 2011 surveys, however, have shown that business confidence will not return until the deleveraging of sovereigns, companies[14] and households is nearly complete. Excess debt, the respondents said, is scary because it always weighs heavily on the economy.

For their part, governments are at a loss about what to do to restore confidence. This is shown by the frequency with which the headlines announce a "new rescue package". The absence of a solution to debt problems suggests that there are no out-of-the-box ideas. Classical econometric models are outmoded and repetition of the same measures, like quantitative easing, is causing additional uncertainty as both citizens and the markets wait for a *credible plan* on how to get out of the IOU hole.

5 Households and the Value of Money

5.1 Household disposable income

Economists suggest a variety of reasons that motivate household consumption and saving decisions. Theoretically, people base their consumption habits on the income they expect to receive over their entire lifetime. Seen in this perspective, household saving is a way of smoothing consumption in expectation of variations in income over shorter periods and temporary fluctuations, and over longer periods including saving for retirement and other events such as the education of children.

This does happen in practice, but it is by no means the general rule. The culture of spending has a great deal to do with how households look at their expenses, and so does the policy of living beyond one's means. In addition, the spending and saving levels of households are affected by real and imaginary developments in their perceived wealth.

Risk is rarely if ever taken into account. Yet, a family's current purchasing power may well be affected by the uncertainty surrounding future income, such as stresses in the economy, employment prospects and extraordinary events such as a severe illness (let alone divorce). Households who know how to protect themselves from adversity tend to hold higher cash reserves, which they can then use to see themselves through. The spending and saving decisions of households are also likely to be influenced by changes in taxation and a reduction of entitlements which have permitted the unloading of a part of a family's wellbeing onto the "nanny state".

General economic conditions, too, should be taken into account. Stock market blues generally lead to a deterioration in the expectations about wealth holdings. A spike in the risk of unemployment can prompt consumers to reduce levels of debt and increase saving. Or there may be other factors raising concerns about the household's balance sheet.

Entitlements have a negative effect on savings. Chinese households have been saving a much bigger slice of their income than their Western counterparts because of a more limited social security net. They put away money to cover the future cost of health care, education and pensions. In turn, higher deposit rates may boost household income, provided the government (through the central bank) does not cheat the citizen by keeping interest rates near to zero (as has happened since 2008 in the United States and Britain, and followed after a minor delay by euroland).

According to some estimates, during the first decade of this century, the saving rate of urban Chinese households has gone from 20 to 28 per cent of their disposable income. This has happened in spite of the fact that between 2005 and 2008 the government has doubled spending on health care, education and pensions. (By all likelihood the reason is that the total amount of entitlements in China remains relatively low at 6 per cent of GDP, compared with an average of around 25 per cent in Western countries.)

In Germany, where the state supermarket has had a ball (the same is true all over Europe and the United States), prior to the July/August 2007 deep economic and banking crisis, the saving ratio as a percentage of disposable income was nearly zero. It stayed at that level until the beginning of 2008, when it jumped to 4.5 per cent, before falling to 1 per cent for a short while, then rising to 6 per cent, since when it has kept fluctuating between 4 and 6 per cent.

In Italy, where memories of the dramatic World War II wipeout of people's savings still linger, the mood is not one for trusting the government – deposits at Italian banks by households and small businesses stand at €1,100 billion. (At the beginning of World War II the Mussolini government told citizens that it would pay them the going interest, but that they could not withdraw their deposits. When the war ended the value of these deposits was only a small fraction of their original value.)

In Britain, where households are the most indebted relative to disposable income in the Western world, the money saved since the crisis has mainly been directed towards deleveraging. Economists say that the high level of indebtedness hampers the ability of households to spend freely over the years ahead.

In the 1980s the American savings rate was relatively static (it had been so for decades) and total US debt to GDP was about 160 per cent, with household debt standing at around 47 per cent of national income. When the credit bubble burst in July/August 2007, total US debt had risen to 350 per cent with household debt at 100 per cent of GDP. (Since the bubble, household debt in the US is contracting, but it still exceeds the level it was at at the beginning of the crisis.)

As a general rule, households in countries where credit growth has been accompanied by a boom in the real estate market have entered a phase of debt reduction since the burst of the bubble. This represents a restructuring of the balance sheet rather than the savings because liabilities still remain high and therefore the process of adjustment is likely to be protracted. The resulting low propensity to consume, and the muted demand for residential property, has a dampening effect on economic activity, the more so as the correction in the housing markets continues. Some economists now believe that, given the 2007 to 2012 negative experience of American and European households, this decade will see leverage being replaced by thrift – which will hurt consumer spending. While it is certain that the crisis we are in has severe consequences on the Western economy and on spending, I prefer to wait for some evidence before subscribing to this thrift hypothesis.

If the past is any guide, things will not go that way because budgetary chapters with runaway expenses are increasingly difficult to control. For more than five decades by far the main driver of increased consumer spending in Western countries, and most particularly in America, has been health care. Since 1960, in the US, the share of spending on health care related costs more than tripled from less than 7 to 22 per cent in 2011. Whoever says that citizens can control their health care costs is over-optimistic. What they can do, and are doing, is unload their health care expenditure onto the state supermarket, which makes the sovereign much more bankrupt than it already is.

On the contrary, the discretionary share of consumer spending in the US – including travel, clothing, restaurants and cars – has fallen from about 35 per cent in 1960 to 26 per cent today. Moreover, as a share of GDP, total retail sales have been in decline since the early 1970s when they stood at their high-water mark.

Retail sales lie low, but a non-discretionary item instrumental in creating credit bubbles has been home ownership. From 1960 to 2011, in the US, as people bought more homes and made improvements to the ones they had, the rental equivalent of home ownership expense more than doubled. Ironically, until the latest real estate bubble burst in 2007, with the subprimes, these statistics were seen as welcome because housing is a significant contributor to economic growth and is instrumental in boosting investment spending.

The imbalances we are talking about have not been unexpected. If one area of expenditure increases as a percentage of GDP, another one will have to decrease. Health care and housing expenses have both increased. And, as we have just seen, the discretionary share of GDP has dropped.

Another sector of the economy which surprisingly has shrunk by a big margin is food. In 1960, food represented 20 per cent of personal expenditures in the US. By 2000, this share had been reduced to only 8 per cent, and it remained at that level during the first decade of the twenty-first century.

Food is part of non-discretionary spending. If expenditure relating to other items under the same class are added, then the bulk of personal consumption is spent on staples such as housing, health care, energy and food eaten at home. Adding to this figure that of discretionary spending, one is lead to the conclusion that total personal consumption expenditure makes up about 71 per cent of US GDP.

5.2 Household liabilities

Golda Meir once said: "Nothing in life just happens. It isn't enough to believe in something; you have to have stamina to meet obstacles and overcome them, to struggle".[1] This is the best advice one can give to households today, particularly those with large and growing liabilities which, in their race to the stars, have been helped by a "wait and see" attitude.

If household liabilities are to be kept under lock and key, then there should be considerable structural adjustment of factors such as the propensity to debt, which created excesses in the run-up to the crisis and has since been exposed. Particularly in Western countries, both the public sector which swims in red ink and high indebted households and enterprises must consolidate their finances and prune their balance sheets (see section 5.6).

It is by no means easy for deeply indebted households to come up from where they are now. Therefore, families would be well-advised to avoid piling up debts. And they can do so by carefully watching their balance sheets all the time – and most particularly their net debt.

"Net debt" is total debt less cash and equivalents (equivalents are easily liquefied assets sold at more or less market prices – not in a fire sale). The net debt of a household (or of a company) is equal to the overall debt situation in the books after subtracting the value of cash and other nearly liquid assets. If the result is a negative figure, then the family has a net cash position. If short and long-term liabilities exceed cash and equivalents, then the household is confronted by net debt:

$$\text{Net debt} = \text{short-term debt} + \text{long term liabilities} \\ - \text{cash and equivalents}$$

The net debt concept should be taught in secondary schools along with the notions of assets, liabilities and family balance sheets. It is part of every head of household to see to it that he or she understands the difference between assets and liabilities and, most importantly, the problems created by net debt.[2] Secondary education should be responsible for imprinting into the young teenagers' minds the risks associated with debt (as well as with assets) and explaining why, unless appropriate checks and balances are in place, households head towards an impossible situation.

Some people say this responsibility of keeping families out of debt belongs to the state rather than to each individual person. That's wrong thinking. Theoretically, the newly instituted Consumer Financial Protection Agency (CFPA) in the US would police and write rules for the retail products of financial firms. For instance, mortgages, bank accounts and credit cards.

Practically, these rules will soon be ignored, like so many other rules before them. The proof that consumer protection is not welcome is that American financial firms have become over-nervous about the CFPA and allegedly spent some $220 million on Capitol

Hill in 2009 lobbying against it. This has been an over-reaction because they already have lots of experience on how to twist rules and regulations in their favour – as they did with the capital requirements imposed by Basel I and Basel II.[3]

Intensive lobbying has provided benefits to the banks by mellowing down consumer financial protection. For instance, the US House Finance Committee dropped the CFPA bill's simple provision which would have obliged banks to offer simple fixed-rate mortgages alongside more complex products. Moreover, banks with less than $10 billion in assets will be spared regular examinations by the new consumer protection agency (!!) (work out the loophole yourself).

In short, the very creation of the CFPA has been watered down after intense lobbying. What else could one expect from the state supermarket, which talks volumes about one thing and does the opposite? In his years of tenure at the Fed, Alan Greenspan carefully watched whether the American consumer was on a shopping spree. That kept the economy going. By contrast, little attention was paid to the fact that much of what American consumers bought was made abroad with the result that the US current account greatly deteriorated and household debt rapidly increased without benefiting the economy, since producers and consumers were in different jurisdictions.

Another negative which resulted from the rapid rise in personal consumption as a percentage of GDP is that it created a culture of getting deeper into debt. In the background has been the policy of easy credit, pushing people to spend money before they earn it. This was further aggravated by:

- Late twentieth and early twenty-first century lifestyles;
- The pride felt in appearing to live like a high earner;
- Ever increasing health care expenses;
- The steady rise in educational costs.

No serious attention has been paid to the fact that the economy is a balancing act which requires a continuous fine-tuning. Rapidly increasing household liabilities in the 1990s and the first decade of this century skewed the dynamics of Western economies.[4] The crisis which started in 2007 made it a risky time for businesses and households to be contemplating expansion. People sat on their wallets because they felt that the economy was going to get worse and spirits have not been lifted by government announcements that the economy was growing – albeit much more slowly than originally thought.

In a morose economic environment salaries and wages stagnate. When unemployment is high, hovering around 9 per cent, companies have little incentive to pay workers more. A wait-and-see attitude sets in, which anticipates more bad economic data and has the potential to become a self-fulfilling prophecy.

Citizens have also been confronted by headline inflation, even if governments and central banks denied it by lying with the statistics. In the spring of 2011 the sharp increase in energy costs pushed consumer prices in Western countries upwards. Year-on-year headline inflation (which includes energy and food) increased.

Some countries suffered from inflation more than others. In Britain, for example, 2011 inflation was above 5 per cent. In China, consumer price inflation accelerated significantly, from 5.4 per cent in March 2011 to 6.5 per cent in July, and the People's Bank of China raised its policy rate for the fifth time in succession. This was due primarily to a more rapid increase in the price of food, which in China accounts for 33 per cent of the goods basket. Leaving the cost of food and energy out of inflation figures, as core inflation statistics do, is like cooking the books.

5.3 Consumer protection through regulation?

An old adage has it that if you want a job done, do it yourself. If not, you delegate it. The same principle applies in protecting your own and your family's wealth and well-being. Yet many people are happy to delegate that very important mission to parliament and the government. This does not really work to the benefit of the ordinary citizen.

Take as an example the CFPA, which I mentioned above, and its remit. The duties that the CFPA is supposed to perform have been defined in legislation. A positive aspect of it is that it would roll back *pre-emption*, which permits nationally active lenders to answer solely to absentee federal regulators. If local authorities are nearer to the common man, they can tighten the rules when this becomes necessary, such as in the run-up to the recent crisis, when states were more alert than federal supervisors, and, as far as consumer protection is concerned, when state legislators are much closer to the life of communities other than Washington.

This is practically true of all countries. Rolling back pre-emption, however, does not mean that legacy problems resulting from previous excesses will automatically disappear. To protect the consumer truly, governments and central banks have to take extraordinary measures, with rules and regulations putting a limit on how many liabilities households can pile up. For its part, each well-managed individual family must put a limit to its liabilities by using its budget and balance sheet. No legislator and no regulator can be as effective as the households themselves; and it should never be forgotten that sovereigns have conflicts of interest. Democracy is not made of saints.

The twenty-first century's economic expansion began in late 2001 and with it the aggregate household debt-to-disposable income ratio surged from 110 per cent to a record 140 per cent.[5] In six years, up until the bubble burst in mid-2007, households and citizens provided the fuel for the expansion, and by so doing they amassed as much debt as the previous 40 years combined. They did so by dramatically expanding their real estate portfolio and then tapping home equity through loans for consumer spending in areas other than housing.

During that time no politician spoke of consumer protection from excessive debt, and no supervising authority pulled on the brakes. After the bubble burst, mortgage delinquency rates rose to six-year highs and only then did regulators say that lenders should tighten their credit ratings. For its part, the Fed was pushing on a string. It pushed the funds rate down, but did nothing thereafter, even though both supply and demand for credit did not return to their "normal" levels.

During the so-called "good years" early on in this century, American households were not alone in embarking on a debt spree. In Britain household debt rose from 115 per cent of disposable income in 2002 to 170 per cent in 2008; and in Spain that ratio nearly doubled from 70 to 130 per cent over the same period. The curve bent because of the crisis and not for reasons of prudential legislation. In America the volume of consumer credit in 2009 declined by 4 per cent, but then the annual growth rate started creeping up again.

Much of the households' indebtedness was fabricated by credit institutions which specialized in trapping people into buying houses they could not afford. One of the background cases to which Margaret Heffernan makes reference is that of Jack Kaminsky who worked for Countrywide, the go-go mortgage company. His job was to securitize mortgages to sell to other banks. "Everybody turned a blind eye to fraud," he said. "They're still uncovering fraud from four years ago! The frauds were so obvious ... I'd have the same owner buying *seven* properties from seven different banks ... We packaged them up and sold them on."[6]

"Something has gone terribly wrong in the US economy, politics, and society in general," writes Jeffrey Sachs.[7] He thinks that American politicians are the stooges of corporations and that American voters have been tranquillized by saturation advertising – and he is not alone in thinking this way. Besides, this is true not only of the US but also of all Western countries.

Part of the saturation advertising drums up the "merits" of debt. Getting leveraged supposedly means "being modern". People and households fall into that trap. Capital, Sachs informs his readers, has prospered more than labour due to globalization. This could not have been otherwise since debt advanced rapidly to all societies who thought of finding the messiah in globalization.[8]

The high watermark of consumer indebtedness in Western countries has been in 2008, but nobody can guarantee that it will not be exceeded in the coming years. Table 5.1 shows the progression of household debt as a percentage of disposable income.

Over a mere six years Spanish households nearly doubled their debt level. On the other hand, from 2002 to 2008 German households reduced their liabilities by almost 10 per cent. As for French

Table 5.1 Household debt as a percentage of disposable income

	1996	2002	2008
US	100	110	140
Britain	105	115	170
Germany	100	110	100
France	65	75	130
Spain	n.a.	70	130

Source: Bank for International Settlements, *79th Annual Report*, Basel, 2009.

households, at the end of March 2010 Christine Lagarde, then the French Finance minister, criticized their over-leveraging – particularly that of the 750,000 families who between 2008 and 2009 were said to have increased their liabilities by 14.8 per cent.[9] Credit cards played their role in skyrocketing family debt. Lagarde mentioned a French woman who had in her name 69 different credit cards.

We have already spoken of the credit cards' disastrous influence on consumer spending, as well as of the fact they are being pushed by the banks down the throat of consumers. The curious thing is that neither the CFPA in the US nor similar initiatives in Europe are attacking the roots of the problem of household over-indebtedness or the role played by credit cards in getting citizens into a sea of red ink.

Compared to the overexposed American and European households, citizens in developing countries are "debt-light". In 2000 household debt in Russia and India was practically unknown. In China it was minimal, and only in Brazil did it represent about 6 per cent of GDP. But bad habits travel fast and by 2008 household indebtedness had increased in all four BRICS countries (even if not tragically so):

- In Russia and India it reached about 10 per cent of GDP;
- In China it went nearer to 15 per cent;
- In Brazil it rose further, to 20 per cent.

Aside from the fact that Western households are much more indebted, there is the fact that they are exposed to very dubious investment advice by unscrupulous bankers. No legislation or regulation is attending to this. In early 2001, when the Argentinian economy was going to the dogs, Italian bankers advised their clients to put their life savings into Argentine bonds. The bankers were in a hurry to unload them, and their promises were believed. They managed to sell €14 billion of bonds to around 400,000 clients, many of whom were pensioners who had placed their entire savings on this risky investment.

Argentina defaulted in 2011, but until that day small investors being taken for a ride was what had kept the country going. These investors didn't have a clue as to what they were buying; retail clients are typically lured into this sort of Ponzi game because the bankers played on the ethnic and historical ties between Italy and Argentina.

5.4 The budget of a household

The "budget" is a financial plan. Households who are in charge of their finances usually do a one-year budget, which is short term. There is merit, however, in also having a medium-term budget at the three to five years range as well as a long-term budget of up to ten years (more on this after I have spoken of the planning functions of a budget).

Whether we talk of the state, of a company or of a family, budgeting is a crucial part of implementing a chosen strategy. Its mechanics help in translating basic planning assumptions into account representations about financial resources and expenses. "The last Louis wins the war", Louis XIV, the French king, used to say.

Contrasted with the budget's mission, that of the *balance sheet* (see section 5.6) is that of modelling financial conditions by mapping the family's assets and liabilities (A&L). The results which it displays are the household's wealth, its income, its spending and its obligations as reflected in budgetary decisions.

Planning can best be performed when the budget period is of a sufficient duration and budgetary estimates are realistic as well as justified by decisions made or to be made. There is no general rule for determining the period of time for which the estimates should be made.

Some families find it difficult even to make rough estimates for more than a few months in advance, while others are able to make fairly accurate predictions for a few years ahead. As noted already, my advice is to work around the annual budget. An improvement will be to establish and control every three months the *cash budget*.

The cash budget tells the magnitude of the outflow and informs as to whether it is necessary that a source for additional funds needs to be arranged. The *cash flow* for a given period is the difference between receipts and expenditures for that period. The significant figure for the head of the family is the cash available or needed.

The principle behind attention to cash flow is that there is no advantage in carrying on a process of financial planning based upon guesswork. Cash flow projections are critical even if, as the budget period is lengthened, the validity of forecasts diminishes.

In the case of an industrial or commercial firm, the budget's financial underpinning and expected cash flow is that of sales targets which embody the company's strategy about products and markets. The capital allocated to centres responsible for investments and operating expenses reflects these sales targets which, when missed, create havoc and can depress the stock value.

As a financial plan, budgeting establishes benchmarks for management control, whether we talk of sovereigns, corporations or households. In the family budget, the income is what the income-earner(s) bring to the household as salary or business profit. This money should pay for a long list of expenses:

- Housing;
- Education;
- Food;
- Clothing;
- Other goods and services (staples);
- Utilities;
- Discretionary items (cars, etc.);
- Entertainment;
- Travel, hotels, restaurants;
- Medical expenses;
- Taxes;
- Savings.

In the first two sections of this chapter I brought to the reader's attention the way in which these items share the budgeted financial resources. The percentages are not cast in stone; they change over time as households and society at large recast and restructure priorities. This change in personal and family expenditures is reflected in the budget.

As this example documents, it is not difficult to make a family budget, particularly the annual budget, provided there is evidence of expenditure – preferably over the last three years, though five years will be better.[10] Never make a financial plan based solely on memory: it often plays dirty tricks.

As a first attempt, the 12 classes of expenditure in the above list will be enough. But because a financial plan is also used for control purposes, it would be better that the next year's family budget is:

- Elaborated with more detail in each class;
- Includes items of personal expenditure;
- Personalized to the household's own profile of income and expense.

Particular attention should be paid to items which overrun their historical limits over past years. As financial planning and control becomes established at household levels, the family should be keen to flag up out-of-control items, and examine the background reasons and how to bring them under control.

The use of past years' tax returns can provide an added useful insight in structuring the family budget, including the impact of value added tax. For the first time, a spreadsheet will do. As experience is gained and detail comes in there is a wealth of financial software available for computer processing.

5.5 The discipline of a household budget

Two-thirds of the benefit to be derived from a household budget is the discipline which it implies in the way expenses are mapped onto the financial plan. Detail matters all the way from studying projected expenditures to observing how the money is being used. The other third of benefits from the family budget should be credited to the discrepancies which it brings to the household's attention. This identification of discrepancies permits one to know fairly accurately where "the family money goes". Therefore, it serves both the timing and the optimizing of household expenditure.

The best approach to budgeting is to match expenses against income within discrete time intervals. This not only sizes up matters but it also helps to avoid getting into debt.

If the family's income is not enough when measured against projected expenditure, then such expenditure must be reduced – with discretionary items being the first to be trimmed. Otherwise, the difference is made up by indebtedness, and we saw where this leads.

In the sense that the family budget helps in redimensioning projected expenses, the implied budgetary discipline does much more than informing about income and expenses associated with different activities. It serves as the base for comparisons involving estimated figures of a prior income distribution among classes of expenses usually requiring further study.

At year's end the budget observance provides the household with a measure of its ability to stick to the financial plan. Plan versus actual evaluation is an important analysis facilitated by the fact that the family budget is both a qualitative and a quantitative tool – a numerical expression of projected expenses combining income statement, balance sheet and cash flow.

To ensure that both the individual and aggregate figures are reliable, budgeting must consider all the household's activities and account for them. We have already spoken about classes of expenditures. The income side will include salary(ies), investments and other sources of wealth controlled by the family. A crucial subject to watch out for is a possible mismatch between income and expense chapters within each time period, usually for a month or less. Regarding the methodology to be adopted, we can distinguish between top-down and bottom-up budgeting.

In a bottom-up process, the starting figures are written down by all family members (both income earners and non-income earners) and reconciled by the family's top decision-maker(s). The advantage of this method is that it increases participation with the budget process and therefore with the commitment to achieve the budget targets. On the negative side, bottom-up budgeting is a rather lengthy process and needs a significant amount of reconciliation. Also, bottom-up figures may, sometimes, be skewed.

Alternatively, top-down budgets originate with the family's leader who provides guidance as well as yardsticks for performance measurement. A downside, however, is the lack of commitment from the base.

There are also other distinctions in budgeting which are sufficiently important to be brought to the reader's attention. "Line-item budgets" refer to solutions that allow spending only a fixed maximum amount on specified items. By preventing family members from making too bold commitments, the use of the household's financial resources can be controlled more easily.

An interesting practice is the so-called "zero-based budget" which questions the very core of the previous year's financial allocations, which is often taken as a starting point for the next budget. Every activity is built from scratch, and this prompts all family members to think creatively about their expenses. Nobody can serve him or herself by counting as "a minimum for next year" money allocated in previous years (whose reason of existence may no longer be present).

As an alternative, "flexible budgets" rely on cost figures and cost drivers as well as on forecasts of income and expenses to set upper and lower control limits. Flexible budgeting helps to obtain a realistic basis for financial planning, since it offers the possibility of adaptation. The disadvantage is that, because of the risk of downsizing, some people ask for higher maximum limits than those allocated by the head of the household.

As these references demonstrate, the discipline of budgeting is not cast in stone. Alternative methods help households to sort out their finances. The importance of financial discipline has been significantly increased after a decade of over-spending and over-borrowing. An orderly approach to planning and controlling expenses helps to avoid unnecessary expenses.

Reduced household spending is criticized by economists who say that higher savings together with subdued earnings result in relatively weak household spending growth and that this hurts the economy. While such an argument has substance, it is counterproductive to try to correct the ills of the economy by increasingly living in debt.

To put it a different way, there is no denying that Western economies are at an inflection point. For decades they have been led by consumer spending. Thanks to rising asset prices and ever easier access to credit, Americans and Europeans went on a seemingly unstoppable spending spree as they bought bigger houses and filled them with ever more goods. We may note that the lowering of taxation has increased consumer spending, whereas the increasing of taxes and employment uncertainties has acted to decrease consumer spending.

Taxation would be an issue were household budgets and the sovereign budget enter into conflict. In many Western countries, the post-World War II economy has been increasingly propelled by consumer spending – particularly so in countries where the upper bracket of personal taxes is at the 35 to 40 per cent level. When personal taxes pass the 50 per cent mark, the dynamics of consumption change.

People, however, never learn. In the French presidential campaign of early 2012, the Socialist Party said that it would shift the economy away from consumer spending towards *reindustrializing* France and focusing on exports. There is little doubt about the need for reindustrializing the West – which would represent a U-turn from the

Thatcher years – but for three reasons this is more easily said than done:

- Lots of skills have been lost, and it will take much time and money to redevelop them.
- The high cost of production in Western countries, which is precisely the opposite of what is needed for exports.
- The huge dead weight of the Western state supermarket, of which developing countries are still free. This gives them a big competitive advantage over the West in the global market.

The conflict between restructuring households' balance sheets and restructuring Western sovereigns' balance sheets is not going to end tomorrow. While it lasts, families have no alternative than to give priority to restructuring their own balance sheets – because sovereigns always find a way out by debasing the currency or overburdening consumers with all sorts of taxes, while households don't have that freedom and can go bust.

It does not need explaining that household leveraging cannot continue forever and that family budgeting is the way to get control of spending. Savings must be restored to their old prominence. In America the household saving rate fell from 10 per cent of disposable income in 1980 to close to zero in 2007, while household indebtedness raced ahead with the result being a severe recession.

Since the 1970s and early 1980s both Europeans and Americans have got into the habit of spending more than they produce. This has limits. Furthermore, America's consumers were hit by the destruction of trillions of dollars of consumer wealth with the housing bubble and by the implosion of the shadow banking system which once had been a plentiful source of credit. With hindsight it can be stated that if the family budget had been a part of culture in the 1980s, the 1990s and the early years of this century, then the excesses which took place would not have happened because the family finances would have been better controlled.

Indeed, between 2000 and 2007 the average American household increased its personal consumption by 44 per cent. This boom in spending was largely financed by debt and it accounted for 77 per cent of America's economic growth during these seven years – but the results have been too negative to contemplate a repetition of such a practice.

Worse yet is that these have not been "normal" debts. American households extracted $2.3 trillion of equity from their homes. They blew 20 per cent of this on consumption, 19 per cent on home improvements and 44 per cent on dubious assets such as stocks in an uncertain equity market.[11] With the crisis, many investments in equities turned to ashes. No surprise therefore that the hangover from this party has been long and painful to most households. The time has come to exercise more discipline in family expenses.

5.6 Household balance sheets

A decision-maker is generally more interested in summaries of the transactions that have been performed than in a detailed account of each individual transaction. Reasons of operating efficiency require that detail is available on request, but the decision-maker is always anxious to learn about the combined effect of a group of transactions upon the financial condition of the firm – or in a household. There exist two such types of valuable summaries:

- The balance sheet (B/S);
- The income statement, or profit and loss statement.

The B/S can be likened to a still picture of a family's financial condition, at a given instant. At the household level, the income statement is a moving picture reporting the financial activities of the family during a particular period in time – typically one year. The general layout of a B/S are shown in Table 5.2.

Table 5.2 Typical layout of a balance sheet

Assets	Liabilities
Current assets One year or less; plus cash	Current liabilities One year or less
Longer-term assets Fixed assets like the family home, and remaining values in car(s) and appliances	Longer-term liabilities Different charges for assumed obligations which have to be honoured

If a household's assets exceed its liabilities, it has equity; if not, it has debt. This statement, however, has to be qualified in two ways:

1. Timing: current vs longer term.
2. Valuation: liabilities are based on a contractual obligation, hence they can be seen as fairly valued. Assets are often "marked to myth".

As shown in Table 5.2, the word "current" stands for maturities of less than one year. It is short term. This however can vary by jurisdiction. In France and Italy regulators have defined short-term loans given by banks as having a maturity of up to six months.

Cash is a current asset. It is immediately available. Current assets are also securities held by households, such as bonds traded in the market. Conversely, esoteric derivative instruments traded over the counter are bank-to-bank deals – and they are typically subject to a highly uncertain valuation.[12]

It is easier to define current liabilities because the obligations assumed by a household (or, alternatively, by a company or other entity) have a fixed date: the day when they are due. For households, I would suggest that both current assets and current liabilities are written down on a monthly, quarterly[13] and annual basis. This will make a perfect framework for balancing the household's financial resources.

The problem with assets valuation (other than cash) is that it is a perfect ground for cooking the books. It is too subjective to be reliable and quite often assumed values have been subject to manipulation. Several publicly traded entities engage in this, and so the valuation model used by Moody's (adopted by the Federal Reserve and by the European Central Bank) takes as assets, A, the market value of a given firm's equity, its capitalization. The formula $\frac{A}{L}$ speaks volumes about a company's leveraging and solvency. The numerator A is the capitalization, while the denominator, L, is equal to the sum of the liabilities in the B/S. Households should not cheat themselves with fake A values. This would be highly counterproductive. Rather:

- The house should be written on market value (using neighbourhood sales as reference);
- All equipment (car(s), appliances) should be depreciated over the number of years the family plans to keep each of them;

- All securities (bonds, equities) should be taken on market value, while life insurance and other policies are written on a discounted basis in the assets column;
- Salaries and other income should be written on an after-taxes basis.

To keep the B/S simple, in the first couple of years after the household implements it, risk could be left out of the picture. Later on, however, it is wise to account for it, which will reduce the assets value.

A house may burn and what the household will receive in exchange is the insurance taken out on it – and if there is no insurance, there will be no asset left after a major fire. The stock market may crash, as it does from time-to-time, for instance in 2001 and in 2008. Some entities might lose half their value. That's *market risk*. A bond issuer may go bankrupt, hence the household needs to know about *credit risk*.

Credit risk exists with any issuer of financial or other obligations, for instance with sovereigns. Governments persuade savers to buy their bonds. Theoretically, they can service these bonds and repay the principal because they are entitled to tax their citizens on any income they have and/or on their wealth. They also have income because in many cases the infrastructure works on a pay-as-you-go basis.

Practically, however, this logic can turn on its head – not for one but for several reasons. For example, if the debt is contracted in a foreign currency which appreciates significantly against the currency of the government issuing the bonds (see section 9.1); or the country is over indebted but its citizens do not pay taxes or the taxes are insufficient to cover both running expenses and outstanding liabilities. In short, countries go bankrupt.

The same principle applies with households. One or both of their earners may lose their jobs – and so there is no income. Or income derived from existing longer-term assets (such as the owner's claim on a business (proprietorship)) is unable to meet the demands posed by oversized liabilities. Creditworthiness is a universal value, and it should be most carefully preserved. A&L must be watched at all times.

In conclusion, the advantage of a B/S is that it presents a snapshot of A&L. It is a summary of property owned by the family in terms of *assets* and *liabilities* (which are debts owed). We have spoken of current A&L that mature in less than one year, and of longer-term ones.

The point has also been made that it is advisable to group A&L into classifications for purposes of further analysis – and eventually to introduce risk factors associated with each of the assets.

5.7 The management of assets and liabilities

I have above placed emphasis on current assets, defining them as those which can be converted to cash within a short period of time without a fire sale, and as cash. The importance of current assets comes from the fact that a household (like a company) is unavoidably confronted by current liabilities. Debts must be paid when they are due, unless the creditor accepts to roll them over. Creditors typically refuse to do this at the most inopportune moment when the debtor is unable to come up with the money. The result may be losing a house bought on a mortgage.

I have also brought to the reader's attention the fact that a household has longer-term assets as well as longer-term liabilities. Longer-term assets are usually (though not always) fixed assets. The family's house is an example. However, when it is monetized through a second mortgage, as often happens, part of it has been turned into a current asset; the liability has also increased, though it remains longer term.

It is easy to detect between the lines of these two paragraphs that the family's A&L must be managed and the responsibility for doing so rests with the head of the household. An integral part of this responsibility is timing: the *due date*. An example is the repayment of a mortgage: the longer-term liability may run to 15 years, but the interest paid for it, and in cases of partial repayment of the loan's capital, is an annual event.

The management of A&L is assisted by *modelling*, whose strategic aspect is the holistic view it presents of a household's financial status. The balance sheet can be effectively used as a simulator of the family's financial status, its major advantage being that of making mental models explicit. The numbers written on a B/S help to expose inconsistencies in a conceptual model which had not yet been explicitly put on paper, prompting a rethink of income(s) and expenses, and making it feasible to determine future implications.

It is not always appreciated that the B/S provides a rich source of information on the household's financial status. While, in spite of such a holistic view, the leader of the household may not change his or her behaviour in regard to expenses, it is no less true that B/S analysis helps in significantly improving the quality of management of the family's A&L. This is an important activity distinct from the management of investments (which is the subject of Chapter 6).

In fact, even if leveraging persists, the benefit from financial statement analysis will remain. In a way, the deductive process promoted by the B/S is equivalent to a reminder by means of accounting figures. The head of the family can look at assumed obligations and make hypotheses about how he or she can make ends meet. If the A&L pattern represented by the B/S signals no emergencies, then the head of the family will have greater confidence in his or her ability to manage the finances.

Employed for reasons of A&L management, the data in a household B/S are most valuable for visualizing and documenting mismatches. By comparing cash flows to account records and statements, reconciliation can identify chapters that need correction. Controls applied to income(s) and expenditures permit a better balanced dependable presentation of financial data and an optimization of assets, liabilities and their timing.

An income statement geared to household finances will summarize the income earned during a given period as well as the cost of purchases, fees and other commitments (including servicing loans). Expenses must be supported by evidence of the way it is done for an enterprise.

The orderly approach to assets, liabilities, income(s), expenses, budgets and B/Ss has several advantages including, if need be, that of a well-organized reference for obtaining a loan. Truthful, B/Ss are more important than disconnected references in regard to income and cash flows. B/Ss are false when:

- The assets are overvalued;
- The liabilities are underpriced;
- They are based on the so-called "proforma" which evades established accounting rules.

Bloated B/Ss evidently concern poor A&L management – and must be deleveraged. The better managed households have been proactively lowering their leverage through debt repayment. When a crisis hits, households swimming in a sea of red ink pay a heavy penalty – as attested by hundreds of thousands of home owners who have been underwater in the wake of the financial crisis following the mortgage debacle of 2007.

When the worst continues worsening, some common citizens and families seek salvation by declaring bankruptcy. But even in the United States, where there is no stigma associated with filing for personal bankruptcy, this is certainly an unpleasant situation for households. The other side of the argument, however, is that, on the whole, such bankruptcies may be a net positive for household B/Ss but a sure net negative for bank B/Ss.

The reason debtors default is because their assets are not enough to cover their liabilities. There is a failure in A&L management. That shortfall, which is put in evidence by the family B/S, is the cost that lenders are forced to accept. The banks know that this is coming, which is why they are over-reserving and taking the hit to earnings today in anticipation of further increases in future default rates. Alternatively, they refuse to lend. A more rational approach is that they fix the interest rate high enough so that they can take out insurance against default risk, or take reinsurance.

Leveraging of the household B/S eventually leads to the need for greater adjustment than otherwise might have been necessary. Prior to the financial and economic crisis which started in 2007, household debt levels were at historical highs, on both sides of the Atlantic. The increase in debt was especially marked in the United States in the first years of this century. The crisis upset the A&L balance of households: high debt levels, combined with large falls in asset prices for both housing and financial assets, generated large declines in the net worth of households, and, coupled with the increased uncertainty regarding the economic outlook, those declines became an important factor contributing to the need for households to deleverage and repair their B/Ss.

The financial crisis which started with subprimes in 2007 still ripples with effect nearly five years later. The mortgage crisis has had a marked impact on many households' B/Ss which have been severely damaged. A more than 30 per cent fall in house prices and a 45 per cent fall in equity markets has significantly reduced the measured net wealth of households.

In principle, the more the market is nervous, the greater is the need for a well-balanced household B/S and for reserves, because market nervousness hits the family's assets. The top decision-maker must be very careful as to what happens next, to the family's interests, particularly if he or she has taken an inordinate exposure – whether in residential real estate or in the equities market.

As one misfortune never comes alone, the outlook for the labour market (and therefore for household income) may also deteriorate. This is particularly bad for indebted households, as not only interest rates but also unemployment is a source of risk that can affect their ability to service their debt.

In conclusion, when the economy's woes increase, risks related to household income also increase. As an old adage has it, the time to fix the roof of your house is when it is sunny. This is precisely the reason for A&L management, as well as the need to do it with foresight.

It needs no explaining that households facing higher risk are particularly those with a lower level of income. However, a weak and/or overleveraged economy may hold bad news for all families, hence the need for a good B/S and for deleveraging.

6
Managing Family Wealth

6.1 Investments by households

Chapter 5 brought to the reader's attention that a household has assets and liabilities. Its assets may be the house where it lives, other houses bought for rent (or speculation), cars, appliances and financial investments – such as money in the bank (savings and time deposits), equities and bonds. Some households have invested in derivative financial instruments (see section 6.4), the so-called "alternative investments", which is very unwise.[1]

Usually, but by no means always (for instance, there may be a case of social or other commitments), a household's liabilities consist of loans. These may be mortgages, house improvement loans, personal loans or loans connected to bought appliances and motor vehicle(s). During the last decades, to this list has been added the servicing and repayment of novel sorts of liabilities – like student loans, which extend over many years and weigh on the family budget.

When assets exceed liabilities, we often talk of "family wealth", and this wealth has to be managed. An effective administration of household wealth requires: family goals; skills with investments; and a planning and control frame of reference. Goals and planning should take into account the household's obligations and priorities.

Furthermore the word "investment", and the notion behind it as a resource reserved for rainy days sometime in the future, have to be pinned down to something tangible, including possible critical issues which may come up. For instance, loss of job, illness or divorce. It is the job of the head of the family to explain that households distinguish themselves through strong balance sheets (B/Ss) with modest, if any, leverage and properly targeted liquidity reserves.

Investments by households should never be speculative. By diversifying into resilient forms of assets, a family can overcome future troubles and withstand the challenges of an economic environment which may be in recession. Moreover, it is highly advisable that a family assesses its risk tolerance carefully, particularly when seeking exposure to instruments or currencies with an apparently positive outlook but with hidden risk factors, such as due mortgage payments, or the servicing and repayment of other debts.

Managing family wealth calls for a careful look at all aspects of how one earns and spends money. Because each family's situation is to a considerable degree unique, there are no cook book solutions for wealth management. But there are principles which should guide the hand of the head of the household – patience and resolve in confronting financial challenges being one of them.

Some families perform their wealth management duties themselves, while others assign full powers to a bank – which sometimes leads to complications. Provided the household's decision-maker understands the opportunities and risks associated with real and financial assets, self-management is the better solution.

The administration of household wealth becomes more complex if projected to serve multigenerational families, as is increasingly the case. However, whether or not a multigenerational perspective is one of the goals, foremost attention must be paid to the preservation of wealth. The reason is self-evident. Like reputation, a fortune takes decades to build, but can be destroyed overnight.

One of the most basic choices which have to be made by the person responsible for household wealth management is the allocation of income (and possible other assets) between consumption and investment. This is indeed a difficult issue, more so than it used to be because of the stagnation of median family incomes since the mid-1970s and associated shifts in income distribution which favour the better off at the expense of economically weaker families.

Another of the challenges is the moving target of metrics and measurements on which the wealth manager can rely in order to judge his or her performance. Numbers alone tell only part of the story and this is true all the way to gross domestic product (GDP). In the 1950s the best measurement was *real GDP* per head, which in the

US stood at $15,000 in 1955. Six decades later, in 2011, the real GDP per head has been estimated at about $40,000. Theoretically, this is a 266 per cent increase. Practically, it is a significant drop in real GDP per head, because inflation has eaten up the value of the dollar.

For the majority of people, as a share of national GDP, the reward in terms of personal wealth has decreased. Conversely, the risks associated with investments have increased because of the asymmetric nature of the payoff. After the 2007 economic and banking crisis, the upside in investments has been far from spectacular, while the family fortune could suffer a great loss if the risks are severely underestimated.

In addition there is uncertainty over risk definitions and probabilities, and this means that (usually) the worst-case losses are not well-known. As a result, they are taken lightly and investments can be misdirected towards unprofitable, undesirable or outright wrong targets.

The challenge for conservative investors is to find safe-haven assets that offer acceptable real returns. In this connection, particular attention must be paid to wealth preservation. No household should rely on only one channel – be it equities, government bonds or cash – to form the bulk of its investment portfolio. The best policy is diversification with the main goals of:

- Financial security (whose main component is wealth preservation);
- Reasonable liquidity;
- Sound asset returns.

If these are household goals, then investment performance can be measured against them. The head of the family should however appreciate that, contrary to the case of a single investor, the management of household assets is confronted with the need for achieving shared family goals which may present potential conflicts arising from family members who maintain:

- Uneasy relationships with each other;
- Often diverging personal views on risk and return;
- Issues of longevity, health care, college education or other matters.

A frequently encountered case, particularly in the absence of strong leadership by the head of the family, is that the needs of individual members may conflict with the needs of the family as a whole. Resolving this type of conflict requires a properly spelled out governance structure, including not only priorities but also *who* makes the end decision. This facilitates the eventual resolution of conflicts.

To elaborate an effective governance structure, the head of the household must start by understanding the issues confronting family members and the way different requirements are documented. He can help himself in this mission by addressing ahead of time questions on the border between individual earnings and wealth on the one hand, and joint family assets on the other.

I would suggest formalizing the process of this analysis in a document that can serve as a basis for friendly family discussions. Without a written mission statement, the household's goals and aspirations may be open to misinterpretation and argument, even reviving previous disagreements between family members.

6.2 Bond investments

The foremost investment that a young household should do concerns its house. There was a time, before and immediately after World War II, when this was a rather straightforward decision; but that is no longer the case today. Residential real estate has been largely depersonalized, becoming a tradable commodity like any other – with all this means in terms of little known risks. We will be looking carefully into this issue in Chapters 8 and 9.

In addition, while the house is important, it may not be the first investment for a young household which appreciates that being overleveraged with a mortgage is an unwise policy. Don't ever buy a house on 100 per cent credit. A serious family purchasing a house should make a reasonable down payment of at least a third of its price and even better half of it.

In former times a family would have kept the money it saved in a bank until the day came for it to become a house owner. After the 2007 deep economic and banking crisis, however, the interest earned in Western countries on savings accounts is less than 1 per cent, way below inflation. Whoever keeps money in the bank sees it eroded by ultralow interest rates and inflation engineered by sovereigns and central banks to save the self-wounded and misbehaving banking industry.

The alternative to money "in the bank" is investing in financial instruments. Most evidently, this is not without its risks. Neither are all financial instruments in the market suitable for households, derivative financial instruments being an example (see section 6.4). The five major classes of financial instruments are:

- Bonds;
- Equities;
- Currencies;
- Other commodities (oil, precious metals, base metals, agricultural produce);
- Derivatives.

For households, only the first two classes – bonds and equities – are recommended; the latter for no more than a quarter of the portfolio – no matter what the banks say. Because many family heads don't think they have the skills to put together a portfolio of bonds and stocks they choose to buy what mutual funds offer. This, too, is not an investment decision immune to exposure.

A "mutual fund" is a portfolio of financial instruments, put together by an investment firm, which acts as a manager, and sold to investors. As far as the family head is concerned, the value of his or her participation in a mutual fund is equal to the percentage claim of the portfolio's content. A small percentage will represent a relatively small investment. Big or small, that investment may do well or not so well, depending on the mutual fund's quality of governance.

Let's now look into the pluses and minuses of bond investments. *Bondholders* are creditors of the company, government or any other entity issuing bonds. Correspondingly, *stockholders* are owners of the company. Funds invested in the purchase of a debt instrument represent money lent to their issuer. Being merely creditors, bondholders ordinarily have no voting power to elect directors, and hence no direct control over the policies of the company or sovereign.[2] In principle bondholders take less risk than stockholders, since interest on bonds must be met before any income is available for dividends to equity investors, yet they typically receive only the stipulated rate of interest, even though the company may make huge profits and, as a result, its market value appreciates.

Creditwise, the main upside of bondholders is that they have a prior claim on the assets of the company in the case of liquidation. Many debt instruments contain provisions that if the issuer fails to pay interest when due, voting power is automatically given to bondholders. This way they can protect their interests.

Bondholders also assume market risk – with a downside and an upside. One of the causes of a downside is the downgrading of the issuer's creditworthiness. The other downside of a fixed interest rate instrument is a sudden rise in interest rates.

The upside primarily rests on a lower interest rate prevailing in the market (because of a central bank decision, or other reasons) than that prevailing when the bond was purchased; or a creditworthiness upgrade of the issuer and/or the currency in which the bond is denominated. Some currencies like US dollars and Swiss francs become a refuge in the case of a crisis. Contrary to what some books say, with bonds upsides and downsides may be significant, particularly for long maturity bonds.

For an investor the better way to look at a bond is as a loan. With a loan, the issuer assumes the obligation to provide one or more future cash flows to the buyer and return the capital at maturity. The timing and size of these cash flow(s) may be prespecified, or it may be dependent on an economic variable whose value is usually known beforehand. The critical variables of all bonds are the:

- Coupon (the percentage yield);
- Currency;
- Face amount;
- Maturity;
- Credit rating of issuer;
- Credit rating of issue (these last two tend to be confused).

The reader should notice that the term "bond" is generally employed when speaking of medium to longer-term obligations, which share common features, though each may have its own details. The more prominent common features of bonds include: the aforementioned promise to pay an interest and repay the principal amount (at maturity); a statement of the tender or medium of payment; an identification of the currency and place of payment.

There is a coupon attached to the bond certificate, which identifies the interest payment due during the life of the bond. In former times, at interest dates the holder of the bond would clip the coupon and remit it for payment to a bank. Today this is done electronically. The coupon represents the normal interest payments expressed as a percentage of that stated at the time of the bond's issue. Payments are usually annually or semi-annually.

Bonds are of different types. Some examples are:

- Fixed income or flat rate bonds;
- Variable or floating rate bonds;
- Inflation protected bonds;
- Straight bullet bonds;
- Redeemable or callable bonds;
- Zero-coupon bonds;
- Junk bonds;
- Convertible bonds;
- Deeply subordinated bonds;
- Medium-term notes;
- Index-linked bonds;
- Index-linked capital protected notes.

A *fixed-income* bond pays at regular intervals a predetermined percentage of its notional amount (fixed income is usually a flat rate, but it is not always so because there exist covenants). The coupon of a *floating rate* bond is reset periodically, typically tied to a price index. Another form of variable-rate bond is one with covenants associated with issuer creditworthiness. Though flat, or fixed, rate bonds have a nominal coupon which does not change until maturity, their yield may change because of the market's interest rate volatility and issuer creditworthiness. To protect themselves against inflation investors can buy floating rate bonds which are indexed against inflation.

With *straight* (or bullet) bonds, maturity, interest rate and coupon payment are fixed in advance by the issuer. Non-bullet or callable bonds are *redeemable* through a lottery, whereby a whole series is called for repayment.

Zero-coupon bonds make no interest payment during their lifetime. The interest is payable upfront as a discount. *Junk* bonds (frequently called high-yield, a misnomer) are non-investment grade. Their attraction lies in the fact they pay higher interest to compensate for the risk of default.

Convertible bonds, or simply *convertibles*, are hybrids of bonds and stocks used by issuers to raise capital.[3] A convertible offers the investor the right to convert the instrument of which he or she is a holder into a specified number of shares, according to an established conversion price. When this happens the equity generated by the company and given to the investor extinguishes the latter's claim on the debt instrument.

Convertible bonds are subject to rules which are often written in fine print, escaping the typical investor's attention; but rules do exist. For instance, the instruments may be redeemable at the issuer's option, as specified in the applicable pricing supplement; or it may be subject to mandatory redemption.

Moreover, the credit ratings of convertible bonds may not reflect the potential impact of all risks related to structure, while real or anticipated changes in the issuer's credit ratings will generally affect the market value of a bond – whether or not it is convertible. The market marks that through *credit spreads* between *bid* and *ask* prices for the security (usually, though not always, advanced by market makers).

Credit spreads discount a lot of bad news about issues connected to a debt instrument, such as rising defaults, and also include a liquidity premium. In the longer term, risk-tolerant investors capitalize on credit spreads to add credit exposure at attractive levels. This is not recommended for households – for whom a broad diversification without inordinate risk is key to the performance of their investments.

Household investors should appreciate that the creditworthiness of the issuer is a very important reference in choosing a bond. This is a vital factor in determining the *degree of risk* assumed with a bond. Another crucial variable is whether it has first, second, or third claim on the income and property of the issuer.

In connection to each entity there is a definite *rank of priority* of claims on earnings. For instance, first-mortgage bondholders ordinarily have "first lien", that is, first claim to payment.

Independent credit rating agencies, such as Standard & Poor's, Moody's and Fitch, publish the creditworthiness of the issuer (and of the issuer's bonds). There are about 20 graduations in their scale and the most important difference is between investment grade: from AAA to BBB–, and non-investment grade debt instruments below the BB+ level.

Bonds are also classified by maturity: short, intermediate or long term. They can be further segregated by type of issuer: corporate, sovereign, municipal, mortgage-backed or other securitized instruments. All this complicates the selection process. To simplify things, when an investor looks at a bond issue, he or she should primarily look at the:

- Bond issuer;
- Bond rating;
- Coupon;
- Maturity;
- Price;
- Yield (which combines the preceding bullets);
- Taxation.

Bonds may present opportunities for tax optimization. Municipals are not the only bonds which may benefit from tax relief (at least in the US). There are plenty of tax-exempt issues: tax-supported general obligation bonds, revenue-supported bonds, bonds by educational and not-for-profit institutions, bonds from health care issuers, tax-exempt housing bonds, debt issued by public power projects, and bonds issued by state governments, sovereigns and subnationals.

In conclusion, the way to bet with debt instruments is that no two bonds have exactly the same characteristics. Take maturities as an example. There are several reasons why maturities vary from one bond to another and this has to do with the issuer and the market. Issues of high creditworthiness can offer longer maturities – though serious investors don't buy 20 or 30 year maturities because nobody can really tell what the interest rate will be, or whether the issuer will still be in business. Depending on the currency, inflation forecasts and market conditions, three to ten years is a good range.

6.3 Equity investments

Publicly traded companies divide their capital into units of equal denomination known as stocks, equities or shares which are traded on the stock market. Shares allow investors to participate in an enterprise and its future – whether positive or negative. By buying equity in a company, the investor becomes partly the owner of it, though without the power to exercise control over its management. Only major investors have that power (though all shareholders are authorized to vote on important business decisions).

Companies are registered and listed on the exchanges according to rules established by the supervisory authorities – for instance, in the US by the Securities and Exchange Commission. Securities are bought and sold through public auction, characterized by bids and offers coordinated by means of a well-developed trading system served through public stock exchanges.

Usually each company belongs to an industry sector, though conglomerates may cover several. The activities characterizing these sectors differ in their dependency on economic cycles. Examples are cyclical vs non-cyclical business; discretionary vs staple goods; and raw materials vs finished products. Some industry sectors tend to outperform in a nervous market.

A company may also issue *preferred stock* which has both bond and equity characteristics. Preferred stock should not be confused with common stock. It typically pays higher dividends and can be converted into common stock by the decision of the board (provided its covenants permit it). But it is also the first line in the case where the company is hit by major financial problems. In a nutshell, summing up the instruments discussed in this and the previous section:

- Common stock pays a variable dividend;
- Preferred stock pays a fixed (usually higher) dividend;
- Bonds pay a fixed interest (unless they are indexed);
- Convertible bonds can be converted into stock;
- Warrants give rights to buy stocks at a given price.

Depending on the company's financial performance, the equity investor receives dividends declared by the board. Normally dividends should be paid only when the company has a profitable year.

The yield is the ratio of this dividend to share price. The price of a share is determined by the market's expectations about the firm's future performance. If these are optimistic, the share price goes up; if they are pessimistic, the price sinks and investors lose money.

Factors that have an influence on the company's profitability are quality of management, cost control, innovation, marketing skill and the overall economic environment. Broadly speaking, a sound valuation of shares consists in determining whether the equity is cheap or expensive when accounting for:

- Earnings and dividend payments;
- Assets, liabilities and finances;
- The company's future market performance.

When a firm issues new equity, the price tends to fall for different reasons: new equity, as well as options given to managers and employees, is a dilution of old equity; a listed company's share price may also fall because of too much debt, loss of market share, obsolete products or a decrease in dividends.

Dividends are the stock market's barometer because they affect the bottom line for shareholders and, generally, their time series is smoother than that of earnings as management does not like to increase dividends if it might have to decrease them next time around (and vice versa). On the other hand, many growth companies prefer to be self-financing rather than depend on loans; therefore they don't pay dividends. The investor's profit comes from the share's appreciation if the company succeeds.

There are plenty of reasons why companies should not take on an inordinate amount of debt. Some theorists like Franco Modigliani and Merton Miller have favoured debt over equity – to a large extent because of tax laws. Generally, a company that issues debt can deduct interest from profits before paying taxes, while it cannot deduct dividend payments. Debt, however, is by no means void of other risks, particularly so when the company becomes overleveraged or operates in a market which makes it difficult to service its debt out of its current cash flow and profits.

Because indebtedness and quality of management correlate and affect in a significant way a company's financial staying power, when I make investment decisions I always look into its assets and liabilities. This must be done for both the current situation and the long-term one. If, in either case, liabilities exceed 50 per cent of assets I never invest in that firm – unless there exist other overwhelming factors, and even then never beyond a ratio of 75 per cent of debt to equities. (This is one of the key investment criteria.)

Another investment criterion is that of choice between growth and value stocks. Which one to prefer depends on the mood in the market. *Growth stocks* are those that have either historically grown faster than their peers in the industry sector or are expected to do so over the next couple of years. Given this, they will probably be more expensive compared to their peers (they will have a higher price/earnings (P/E) ratio), as investors pay a premium for equity they believe has less risk of experiencing problems with its market standing.

Value stocks are those with superior expected earnings. For this reason they are perceived to be cheaper compared to their peers. What few investors appreciate is that such stocks may be cheap because they have higher risks associated with their balance sheets and earnings, as expected earnings do not always materialize.

As the above pragmatic example documents, like any other asset, an equities portfolio has to be managed. The list below presents in a nutshell 14 basic rules which help in guiding the hand of retail investors. The message carried by most of these rules is self-evident, with the exception of the last two which need further explanation.

- Invest only in stocks quoted on big boards;
- Understand the difference between investing and speculating;
- Decide whether you invest for income or for growth;
- Do not borrow, do not buy on margin, do not leverage yourself and do not sell short;
- Bet on the challenger, but do not buy at peaks;
- Look at your homework as a better guide than listening to "advice";
- Always listen to contrary opinion;
- Learn how to detect and analyse market trends;
- Never chase the return of shares you did not buy;
- Accept responsibility for your own investment decisions;
- Never hesitate to cut losses;

- Apply damage control through limits and profit targets;
- Observe the "5 per cent rule" about investing in any name;
- Appreciate the need for rigorous risk management.

Risk control is the last but not the least of these 14 investment principles. Theoretically the control of risk is an issue for professionals only. Practically, that sort of thinking is fatally wrong. Risk management must be everybody's preoccupation, not only in connection with investments but also in regard to all matter's affecting one's personal and professional life.

The "5 per cent rule" says that because all assets are at risk one should not put more than 5 per cent of one's investment in any one "name". The name is that of the equity or bond issuer. The background to this rule consists of the benefits to be obtained from diversification. Diversification, however, should not be haphazard but well studied. Keeping a close watch on risk and return is the alter ego of investing.

The greater the experience that the head of a household acquires in managing its investments, the broader will be the range of options; but the risk associated with each option should be always kept in mind. Other things being equal, exposure associated with equities will be more peripheral if the investor keeps with shares traded in stock exchanges.

Trading on an exchange involves only *listed* securities (approved by the exchange). There are conditions which lead a stock exchange to *delist* one or more of the securities on which trading has been taking place. For instance, early in 2000 the American Stock Exchange advised Echo Bay Mines that its listing eligibility was under review. The review was undertaken because the company had fallen below two of the exchange's continued listing guidelines: it had sustained net losses in its five most recent fiscal years (1995–9) and, in the exchange's view, its shareholders' equity under US generally accepted accounting principles was inadequate.

All companies listed on an exchange have to look out for reasons which might lead to their delisting. When a reason is found, it has to be addressed through immediate damage control action followed by periodic reviews before disciplinary action can be taken. Being listed on one or more exchanges is not a right: it is a privilege, and for which a listed company may no longer qualify.

A major advantage of a public exchange is that trading prices (bids, asks) are widely known. This is not true with other venues. Households should definitely avoid investment in the off-board, over-the-counter (OTC), bank-to-bank market, in which prices are determined by negotiation by two banks. That is the nearest thing to price fixing and it leaves the investor out in the cold.[4]

Another difference between organized exchanges and the OTC market is that the latter is informal and, to a large extent, unregulated. Traders and brokers effect transactions chiefly over the telephone with other traders and brokers. Household investors have nothing to gain but plenty to lose from such secretive deals.

Instead of individual equities, a household investor may choose to buy *stock market indices*. Typically, a stock market index gives an overview on how a particular industry sector, in the equity market, is doing. It also serves as a benchmark. The performance of a single share can be evaluated against the index of that sector or the index of the equity market as a whole. Important indices are:

- The S&P 500 index, created in 1957. It is composed of the prices of the 500 largest firms by market capitalization actively traded in the US on the New York Stock Exchange and the NASDAQ.
- The MSCI World Index. This includes a collection of 1,600 stocks from 24 countries, which comprise the world's developed markets.
- The Euro Stoxx 50 which comprises the 50 largest listed European companies.
- The British FTSE 100 Index.
- The Swiss Market Index.
- The German Deutsche Aktienindex (DAX).
- The French CAC 40.
- The Japanese Nikkei Index.

Still another investment instrument which over the last decade has became very popular is *exchange traded funds*. They are equipped with the trading characteristics of equities and are prized for their easy terms of trade (they can be bought and sold at any time during the trading day), as well as for the diversification they may offer. But they are very opaque in their management, and therefore not proper for household portfolios whose holdings must be transparent.

Two more words of advice are in order. Household investors should avoid initial public offers (IPOs). Issues of new stocks or bonds are carried out on the *primary market* where the flow of capital takes place directly between the issuer and the investor. There is a fair amount of speculation associated with IPOs.

By contrast, trading of existing instruments (equities and bonds) occurs on the *secondary market* where deals are done through financial intermediaries – normally with no direct contact between seller and buyer. For shares, the intermediary is the stock exchange, while brokers are the executioners of customer orders.

6.4 Households should not invest in derivatives

Etymologically, the term "derivative" indicates that a given asset's value derives from that of another asset. Derivatives can be useful instruments, but when they are used for gambling they become dangerous. First the good news. If, say, the dollar/sterling exchange rate is 1.55 dollars to the pound, nobody can be sure of what it will be tomorrow, in a month or in a year or more. An American expatriate who buys a house for a two-year assignment in Britain takes on two risks: the asset price risk and the currency exchange risk.[5] He can cover himself (hedge) for the first of the two risks by buying from a bank a "forward contract" expiring in two years time and guaranteeing the 1.55 exchange rate. This evidently has a cost, and there exist different pricing mechanisms (but which lie outside the scope of this text).[6]

A *forward* contract is probably the simplest derivative instrument. It is an individual deal made between two parties: the bank and its client. Forwards are not traded on exchanges; they are OTC, essentially bilateral, agreements that have no active market. Their specifications may or may not be standardized; quite often they are customized and agreed between buyer and seller. The forward contract is ad hoc, but it may also have some standard features.

A forward's twin is the *futures* contract, which is standardized and traded in public exchanges. Futures are current commitments that, as their name implies, can be exercised in the future. They take the form of contracts in which the quantity of the underlying and the expiration date are standardized.

Futures and forwards are so-called "generic instruments" which have become institutionalized. Another generic is an "option", which is an agreement between a buyer and a seller that, when exercised, gives the former the right, but not the obligation, to require the option writer (seller) to perform certain specified obligations. For example, an option on an equity gives the buyer the right (but not the obligation) to purchase that equity from the writer during a stated period of time at a stipulated price: if the buyer decides to exercise his or her option to purchase, then the seller is obliged to turn over the equity at the agreed-upon price.

The price a buyer pays to a seller for an option is its premium, which is meant to compensate the seller for his or her willingness to grant the option. The last day on which an option can be exercised, or "off-set", is the "expiration date". After an originally stipulated period of time, an option that is left unexercised expires as worthless.

- A *call option* gives the buyer the right to purchase the underlying asset at the stated strike price, on or before the expiration date;
- A *put option* gives the buyer the right to sell the underlying asset at the strike price, on or before the expiration date.

A *swap* is more complex than these two generic derivatives. As its name implies its objective is to exchange one thing for something else. A swap agreement, for example, may exchange in the future a stream of cash flows – such as by swapping floating-rate interest payments for fixed-rate interest payments, or vice versa. A standard swap involves a period receipt of a predetermined fixed amount and a corresponding period payment of the spot value of a unit of the asset in reference.

Swaps typically engage two parties, which enter into an agreement, who, for a certain period, will exchange regular payments. Traders often look at a swap as a portfolio of forward contracts. For instance, a swap can be used to offset the risk of an uncovered position, seeing to it that there is a future cash flow that would move in the opposite direction to that of a hedged position.

Persons responsible for the management of household wealth are not traders and I would recommend them to abstain from using swaps. Not only might the deal become complex but even the advice one gets on how to use a swap for hedging may be half-baked or imprecise, resulting in financial losses.

There are a couple of other things the reader should know about derivatives. Whether generic or complex, every derivative financial instrument has a "notional principal amount". This is a term borrowed from the swaps market where it signifies the quantity of money on which the transaction is based. This money is a frame of reference, never actually to be paid or received. For instance, in interest rate swaps the notional principal amount is used as the basis for calculating the periodic payments of fixed-rate interest and floating-rate interest.

Also known as the "face amount", the notional principal is specified by the contract. It may be currency units, number of shares, kilos, bushels or other metrics underpinning the derivatives contract. The obligations of counterparties are established on the basis of this notional principal amount – a concept that applies to a wide range of instruments.

As these references suggest, the term "notional" is generic. The same is true with the term "underlying" in a derivatives transaction. This may be a specified commodity price, share price, interest rate, currency exchange rate, index of prices, share price, interest rate, currency exchange rate, index of prices or something else. It may also be a variable applied to the notional principal amount to determine the cash flows or other exchange of assets required by the derivatives contract.

In a general sense, the security involved in a forward, futures, option or other derivatives transaction is the *underlying security*. Notice that while the underlying security may be the price of an asset or liability, in itself it is not an asset or liability. For example:

- Interest rates are the underlying of interest rate swaps;
- Currencies are the underlying of currency swaps;
- Gold is the underlying of gold futures.

Two other subjects to be brought to the reader's attention are *intrinsic value* and *time value*. Take as an example the price buyers and sellers of options are willing to accept at a particular time. This is influenced by two primary factors: intrinsic value and time value of the option. Practically, like any other commodity, options are subject to the law of supply and demand: when demand is low and there is plenty of supply, prices go down; when demand is high and writers (sellers) are risk averse, prices go up.

"Intrinsic" means the value of the option if it were to expire immediately. Intrinsic values are determined by the options market. Essentially, this is the amount the futures price is higher than a call's exercise price or lower than a put's exercise price. For a call option, the intrinsic value is the amount of premium by which the futures price is above the option's strike price.

- An option that has an intrinsic value is said to be *in-the-money*;
- The option is *at-the-money* if the futures prices are the same as the strike price;
- If the futures price is below the strike price, it is *out-of-the-money*.

Some investors buy low, priced, out-of-the-money options in the expectation that the market will turn around. These contracts have a low purchase price because what is acquired is the right to buy or sell at a price removed, or even far removed, from actual market values. The investor gains if the market swings in a favourable direction, in line with his or her guess. If it goes in the opposite way he or she loses the money paid to buy these options.

The *extrinsic value* of an option is its current price less its intrinsic value. Extrinsic value is also called the *time value* because the time remaining for the option to make a move is key to its worth. Time value is a risk premium demanded by the option writer, and it depends on:

- The relationship of the futures price to the exercise price;
- The volatility of the futures price;
- The amount of time remaining until expiration.

A definition easy to remember is that "the extrinsic value of an option is the amount of its value that is not in-the-money". By contrast, "the intrinsic value is the amount an option is in-the-money". Notice that the two are loosely coupled: when one changes, the other may or may not change.

Generic and only mildly complex derivatives are at the lower end of the risk curve associated with modern financial instruments. At the high end are complex, very complex and sophisticated derivatives, as there is practically no limit to innovative designs where exposure is often paid only minor attention. For instance, catastrophe securities are among the instruments in that high end.

An example is *insurance futures*, used by insurance companies as a form of reinsurance whose value is determined by a major natural catastrophe or by an insurance index that tracks the amount of claims paid out during a given year. Another example is *event-linked derivatives* which derive value if a particular event occurs.

Even more risky are catastrophe (or mortality) bonds where the principal or interest payments due might be delayed or forfeited if a qualifying loss is caused by a specified peril, like hurricanes or earthquakes. The same reference applies to industry-loss warranties whose payout is linked to a predetermined trigger of estimated insurance industry losses rather than the loss suffered by the insured (protection buyer).

None of these financial instruments should be in the portfolio of a household, no matter what their salesmen may say about their relatively "low risk" and "high return". In fact the best way to look at derivatives is that generic products like simple forwards might be good for hedging. But as the derivative instrument's sophistication increases risk zooms, a significant exposure may destroy single-handedly a family's net worth.

6.5 The pain of deleveraging

Amadeo Giannini, the man who built Bank of America, advised his colleagues, friends, clients and employees *never to borrow money* to play in the stock market. He also told them that if they owned the shares and their price dropped, they should sit on them and wait for the turnaround which invariably comes.

Derivatives aside, there is nothing more financially risky than leveraged plays in the stock market. This notion can be extended to leveraging at large, because once one gets into debt the tendency is to increase leverage and it becomes counter-intuitive as well as very difficult to get out of it.

What has just been stated also applies to buying a house. If the family buys its house (or anything else) "on credit" then it leverages itself. That's why I have suggested that a household pays at least one-third of the price – even better one-half – as down payment.

Behind this advice lies a practical reason. Many citizens and households contracting mortgages fail to notice that the price of houses may go up or down while developments in the labour market may cost the family the income-earner(s) job(s). The more leveraged is the house deal, the greater will be the trouble later on.

Prudence advises deleveraging. A restructured family B/S is one of the most important predictors of a household's ability to meet its debt-servicing obligations and prune its finances before adversity hits.

Reducing household debt to manageable proportions should be a preoccupation *in good times,* not only when an economic and financial crisis looms. The fact that in the run-up to the crisis and right through it most households find it difficult to reduce their leverage is not at all surprising. Latecomers always confront greater problems.

Deleveraging is important because it allows a family to be independent of a debt's weight, and it should be done in a well-organized way and whose prerequisites are organization and culture. Shredding debt has never been a popular concept because it calls for a change in attitude, but it is necessary and doable.

Economists and politicians who would like to see households as big spenders refer to what Keynes called the "paradox of thrift". This can be expressed in fifteen words: "if people spend less and rebuild their balance sheets, this will destroy companies and jobs". The answer to this argument is that if the household does not deleverage, then its very financial survivability will be in question in the case of severe affliction (the events of 2007 to 2012 are examples).

On 29 January 2009 – a year and a half after the July/August 2007 major economic and financial crisis – the CEO of JP Morgan Chase was quoted as having said that (with unlimited credit) banks had given consumers "weapons of mass destruction". These were actively searched for in Iraq, but were not found there. Instead they were hidden in the courtyard of the consumer society and its credit institutions.

Families must deleverage so as not to be at the mercy of banks and other creditors. Companies should deleverage and rely much more on equity than on debt. Sovereigns should deleverage because their leveraging makes the economy unstable and, at the end of the day, it is taxpayers who are asked to pay for damages which were not their doing. Since the beginning of the most recent crisis, a keyword has been "deleveraging", the natural aftermath of several years that involved a credit boom, then a credit bubble, then a credit bust.

The excess spending and borrowing of the last two decades of the twentieth century, and of the first decade of this century, are naturally followed by a long period of redressing badly wounded B/Ss. The secular impulse to raise savings and reduce debt has resulted in low economic growth and low interest rates – a direct result of the debt bubble.

As shown by Federal Reserve data from July 2007 to June 2009 the net worth of US households continued to fall. Since the peak in household wealth in the third quarter of 2007, the US has seen an unprecedented $13.9 trillion of household net worth evaporate. Wealth destruction of this magnitude is unheard of in the post-World War II era.[7]

A 2011 study by the McKinsey Global Institute brought into perspective the fact that in many Western countries the combined public and private debt burdens had reached historic highs. Extrapolating from previous episodes of debt reduction that study reckoned that once deleveraging began countries would on average spend the next six to seven years whittling those debt ratios back by around 25 per cent.[8]

The least risky deleveraging is one that is *counter* to the business cycle. A common way to measure the expansion–slowdown cycle is through the concept of the "trend" which defines the business cycle as fluctuations in overall economic activity around a longer-term trend. Four phases of the expansion–slowdown cycle can be distinguished:

- *Expansion*: in which economic activity is above trend level and the cycle is upward sloping;
- *Downturn*: in which economic activity is above the trend but deteriorating;
- *Slowdown*: in which economic activity is below the trend and the cycle is downward sloping;
- *Recovery*: in which economic activity starts below the trend, but is improving and leading towards expansion.

Households will be well advised to follow the economic indicators used to predict the direction of and, in particular, turning points in the business cycle. The rise in jobs represents a strengthening of growth. This is the time to start deleveraging as opposed to the widespread policy of increasing leverage. The movement towards an expansion phase is also consistent with higher capacity utilization and positive cyclical developments.

Capitalizing on the opportunities the expansion–slowdown cycle presents in restructuring one's B/S is also important, for another reason. When leveraging is high, deleveraging drags on the economy. To avoid this happening, governments should watch out so as to apply the brakes before the economy overheats; hence before leveraging balloons.

America, Britain and Spain entered a recession in mid-2007 with dangerously stretched household B/Ss. Their mortgage credit system was a mess. Keynesian economists would suggest that the slack should be taken up by government spending. Even if one leaves aside the fact that the government too is highly leveraged, to the tune of over 100 per cent in the US and well over 120 per cent in Italy, higher government spending might (only might) delay the economy going into recession; but it cannot prevent a long hangover.

After the credit boom of 2003 to mid-2007, a credit freeze caused the meltdown of 2007–12. As banks upgraded their criteria for loans, credit simply refused to grow. This resembled the years following the First Great Depression when credit and trading in financial markets were subdued. Short of access to credit, and with unemployment rising, households will not buy real estate. Economists are critical of this retrenchment because (in the US) household spending represents 71 per cent of all spending in the economy – but that's life.

A balanced family budget is a wise policy, as there is little doubt that massive deleveraging is bound to have deep effects. Indeed, it is quite surprising that few economists, and even fewer financial experts, have properly analysed the immediate and longer-term dynamics of "reverse leverage". Yet there is no scarcity of examples.

In the 1970s and 1980s Japan – and in the 1980s and 1990s the East Asian "Tigers" – made great strides with high leverage. Eventually, however, their speedily constructed financial edifice began to unravel – and when that happened the shakedown of their economy was just as fast. In the case of Japan it has also been long lasting.

The meltdown of highly leveraged hedge funds, like Long-Term Capital Management (LTCM) in 1998, and Tiger Management in 1999, provides vivid examples of the results of a debt bubble at company level. LTCM went virtually bankrupt, saved only through a twelfth-hour action brokered by the New York Fed. In the case of Tiger Management (in all likelihood) there has been a similar type of moral hazard. This time the "solution" was orchestrated by the Group of Seven governments and the Bank of Japan (which involved dollar/yen forex deals which had gone sour).

Guessing which way the market may go the next day, week, month or year is a very expensive sport – one reserved for people who can sustain the pain. John Paulson was a successful hedge fund manager, who made a fortune by foretelling the July 2007 economic crisis and betting the winning way. But in 2011 his luck ran out. Paulson's "Advantage Plus" fund, the standard bearer of his operations, lost in that year 51 per cent of its capital.[9]

Wall Street experts now note that something similar might happen at a much larger scale with equity derivatives that are used to gamble in the stock market through, for instance, the Standard & Poor's 500 futures index. Today, the combined value of equity derivatives is a low three-digit number in the trillions of dollars. Unravelling can happen at lightning speed because, when reverse leverage strikes, broker margin loans are called in and speculators have to dump equities to meet margin calls.

Imprudent, leveraged investors are wiped out, and this is where a part of the US households' equity released through a second mortgage on the family home has gone. According to experts, the wounds created by the superleveraging which led to the economic and banking crisis of 2007–12 are so deep that an appreciable and material drop in gearing is unavoidable.

In conclusion, debt increases promote B/S uncertainty and shock waves may hit markets, even those which used to be far apart. In the global economy deleveraging in one market, or even in one major market sector, has caused deleveraging in other sectors and markets, triggering a snowball effect. Because financial markets are interconnected, this can happen at lightning speed, causing what financial analysts now call an "all-out, blow-up" effect – whose origins should be found in excessive leverage.

7
The Market Does Not Crawl; It Jumps

7.1 Qualitative factors and market dynamics

Chapter 6 brought to the reader's attention investment principles and policies which help to manage the household's wealth better. These have largely been tactical issues to be supplemented by knowledge and appreciation of market dynamics – the subject of this chapter. Factors underpinning the way the market behaves divide into two main groups. First, there are those whose after-effect is widely apparent. Examples are the stock market earthquakes of 2000, 2008–9 (in the wake of the Lehman's bankruptcy) and the equity-wise negative investment year of 2011. With only one exception, in 2011 all stock market indices sank worldwide. In continental Europe, Italy's MIB/S&P went down 25 per cent; France's CAC40 17.8 per cent, and Germany's DAX 15 per cent. In Asia the Shanghai index was down 22 per cent, nearly Italy's level, even if China is a creditor nation and Italy is debt-ridden to the tune of €2.1 trillion ($2.73 trillion). Only New York's Dow Jones went up in 2011.

Second, there are those factors which are more subtle and therefore hidden from the public eye, affecting industry sectors and individual companies rather than the whole economy. (We will look at some practical examples later in this chapter.) For a successful governance of household wealth, the dynamics and mechanics of investments have to be blended. The best way for doing so is setting clear objectives and developing guidelines by means of one's own homework. This should always be done, but it is not general practice, which is a pity because objectives guide the decision-maker's hand, while their absence opens the door to short-termism which the family will come to regret.

Setting appropriate investment guidelines requires not only skill but also dedication. Putting into practice these guidelines, and sticking to them – in spite of the siren songs of investment advisors, traders, analysts and other experts – is even more demanding. The head of the household can stick to his guns only if he is convinced that the goals behind the investments he makes are realistic.

Four of the principal goals frequently found behind investments made by Western households are travel/vacations, education for the children, an income added to pensions, and health care beyond what is provided by entitlements. To be both over-extended with commitments and deeply in debt should be anathema to a serious household, though, late in the day, many families are finally appreciating that the state supermarket can no longer ensure its entitlements. With the prevailing uncertainty about the future an ageing population has no alternative than to look after itself.

The return of the notion that savings are important has been the silver lining of the threat of unemployment. As time goes by this notion will run deeper, because, while the reborn spirit to save is related to insecurity about the future, it also reflects the growing belief that the age of multifactor productivity, from which the West greatly benefited in the past, has ended.

For starters, "multifactor productivity" is that part of economic growth that is not explained by the rising inputs of labour and capital – in all likelihood it is due to a variety of factors, such as technology, higher skills and better organization. Some experts are content that in the non-farm sector the growth of multifactor productivity peaked in the first half of the twentieth century, the age of scientific management, and collapsed in the last quarter of that century, briefly surging in the so-called "new economy" before fading again.[1]

Multifactor productivity impacts on jobs because in countries of higher wages it makes the output of the individual worker more competitive. The other factor in Western countries affecting the economy, as well as investment returns, is demographic shifts. We have already spoken of this issue, but we need to return briefly to it from an investment perspective.

Economists warn that, as the so-called "baby boomers" liquidate their investments to finance retirement, there could be a steep decline in the price of stocks and other assets. This effect would be magnified by the fact that markets do not only move upwards – and when they move they do not crawl; they jump. During the 1970s and 1980s in America the need of the baby boomers for housing contributed to home price appreciation, but it also posed challenges to investment policies.

Qualitative factors with an impact on investment risk and return have to do with the company in which investments are made, with its management and its ability to survive in a highly competitive global market. Over the first decade of this century, for example, almost all of the big US airlines have steered straight into Chapter 11 (of American bankruptcy law) as the way to reduce their cost base and shed labour contracts they could ill afford.

AMR, the parent company of American Airlines, argued that its annual labour costs are about $800 million higher than those of its rivals. Bankruptcy gives an American firm leeway to cut pay and benefits by allowing it to reopen union contracts. It also permits it to drop its pension plan into the lap of the Pension Benefit Guaranty Corporation (PBGC) of the federal government which already has to plug billions in deficits.[2]

Theoretically, a company benefits by filing for bankruptcy protection under Chapter 11. Practically its shareholders are not better off because there are no all-round benefits and it takes a long time for the equity to recover. There also exist other unknowns like the after-effect of mergers.

Airline bankruptcies over the last decade were often followed by big mergers, including those of US Airways and America West, Delta and Northwest, and United and Continental. Investors can in no way influence such events, and while they often lose on the bond side, they do not necessarily win through higher equity prices as stocks continue being depressed. There is nothing unusual about this. The pay-off in the market is usually asymmetric.

One of the major challenges for investors is the lack of information about the intrinsic value and scale of risks, coupled with the fact that market insiders are usually better positioned in terms of risks and rewards. The asymmetry of information has important implications for investment decisions. In addition the potential for adverse selection of securities is directly proportional to the moral hazard prevailing in the market.

This problem of business ethics is not well recognized by investors who quite often think lightly about risk events. Another interesting qualitative factor in investments, inasmuch as it impacts on share price, is the rate of innovation attained by a company, as opposed to a lack of new products in the pipeline.

The pharmaceutical industry provides an interesting example with the so-called "patent cliff". This has to do with the fact that most highly capitalized pharmaceutical companies periodically lose patent protection on their best-selling blockbuster drugs. Replication of these drugs by generics companies is a relative easy game as most of the drugs that lose exclusivity are simple chemically synthesized pills. On the day a branded product's patent falls, the market is usually served with at least one generic version of it. In the aftermath there is significant pressure on the firm's line and margins.

In practically no other industry is the effect so devastating. The original drug version suffers an immediate sales decline, often up to 80 per cent or more of what it had been able to generate before. This has been known to investors for years, but, more often than not, investors do not account for this overhang. Pfizer suffered greatly from it in 2009–10, Sanofi Aventis and GlaxoSmithKline in 2010, and AstraZeneca and Novartis in 2011.

The reason why these issues, which are qualitative and managerial in nature (rather than technological or financial), are brought to the reader's attention is not to discourage investing – but to press the point that investing is much more than "advice and numbers". Finding out how an industrial sector and the companies in it are doing is part of the homework every serious investor should be doing, whether we are talking of stocks, bonds, residential and commercial real estate or any other asset. There is no way to avoid doing this homework.

7.2 Never panic

Risk keeps people alert. Sometimes small risks or apparent adversities protect from bigger ones. Events associated with 11 September 2011 provide evidence. The head of a company survived the attack because his son started kindergarten; another person was alive thanks to her alarm clock which didn't go off in time; another person's car wouldn't start and he couldn't get a taxi; a man was late because he was stuck on the New Jersey turnpike due to a car accident; a woman had spilled hot coffee on her clothes and had to take time to change.

The fact that risks involve unknowns should not discourage a serious person from grinding through problems and developing scenarios which help in identifying risks and in avoiding bigger, more destructive, problems. Sometimes smaller adversities hide bigger ones, like one train hides another. These bigger adversities can be real killers and no effort should be spared to learn about them ahead of time. This is the philosophy underpinning "worst case scenarios". When we have identified the worst and prepared for it, all other news is good news.

Markets can go through a low which may last more than a year. This may be a disaster for speculators,[3] but not for the long-term investor, who appreciates that an evaluation of investment performance must take into account not only the upside but also the downside in market volatility, as well as constraints due to the rules characterizing the portfolio. Two golden principles of investments were stated in the early twentieth century by Amadeo P. Giannini, the founder of Bank of America:

1. Never buy equities on credit – invest only your own funds;
2. If you lose money, stay put and wait for the market to turn around – *never panic.*

Never listen to Pan, the ancient Greek God who put fear into the hearts of humans and caused them to flee. What Giannini meant with his advice was never fear. One of a successful investor's great strengths is that he never panics. His self-control overrides the pain which he feels when money is lost in the markets – a wrong move may translate into a calamity for his portfolio.

The market has often been compared to a casino, and up to a point this is true. But there exists a difference. Money lost in a casino never comes back, and by betting more to recover it you can lose your last shirt. After her husband died, my baker in Cap d'Ail gambled in the Casino in Monte Carlo. When her liquid funds were gone she bet the green carpet of her bakery – and this too was gone in no time.[4]

By contrast, if the equity investor is patient and follows Giannini's advice, he stands a good chance of recovering his money. It is not easy to part with the wealth one has accumulated after years of hard work and by overcoming many challenges. But managing money is just as tough as making it, if not more so. One of the market's "secrets" is that after it dives it bounces back. If the investments were properly chosen, and if there has been no panic on the investor's side, then the portfolio will recover and become profitable, though this may take some time.

Pierpont Morgan, the famous American banker of the late nineteenth and early twentieth century, carefully avoided all deals where speculation played a role. In his autobiography, Bernard Baruch says that he presented Morgan with the plan of a major investment in Chile. After going through the figures, and seeing that something was not adding up, Morgan asked where the difference came from. Baruch answered that it was a bit, though the only bit, of speculation. "I don't speculate", said Morgan, and the deal was off.[5]

While there is no one-size-fits-all investment strategy for households, as a general rule risky investments are no good for families. In their attempts to speculate, non-speculators not only fail to create value, they destroy value. The doors of risk and return are indistinguishable, and unaccounted for exposures can turn a whole investment strategy on its head.

Readers might ask that this being the case why not leave equities altogether out of a household's investment portfolio. There are two answers to this query. The first is diversification, since returns on equities are not perfectly correlated with returns of other assets. Holding at least some well-chosen equities reduces the volatility of the family's investment. But never go for a 60 per cent investment in equities as advised by brokers. For a household, up to 20 per cent should be a maximum – and mainly in big companies paying good dividends.

The second reason has to do with the debasing of money. To feed the beast of the state supermarket, sovereigns get deeply into debt. The easiest way out for them is to create inflation which penalizes all citizens, depriving them of what they think they otherwise gain through their entitlements. Equities, at least, represent a partial ownership of companies. At times of stress they can be better than paper money (stocks of well-managed companies with a sound product line tend to return to their past highs).

Diversification has to be managed, without the usual tendency to confuse the familiar with the probable and the unfamiliar with the improbable. Moreover, a serious investment plan must consider asset allocation in the context of the family's liabilities. To the extent that the value of liabilities fluctuates, a fine tuning must be done fairly frequently by the head of the household.

In this and in other walks of life many valuable insights can be gained by studying the biographies of people who made something of their lives. J. P. Morgan, for example, was not only a successful banker, but also an administrator who knew how to run the show. Here is how Ron Chernow describes Morgan's work habits: "[he] was extremely attentive to details and took pride in the knowledge that he could perform any job in the bank: 'I can sit down at any clerk's desk, take up his work where he left it and go on with it ... I don't like being at any man's mercy.'"[6] Moreover, he:

- Examined the cash balance daily;
- Had a sharp eye for fake figures when scanning a ledger;
- Boasted he could pay off all debts in two hours;
- Personally audited the books each New Year's Day.

J.P. Morgan was not a man to panic, but when he found an error the effect could be memorable for the responsible employee. His policy is a good reminder that all financial and accounting books have to be audited and that the person doing it should never be the one keeping the books. Family balance sheets must be audited at least once a year; preferably quarterly.

Two different types of auditing are vital to the well-being of the household's investment portfolio. One is the classical accounting audit by a certified public accountant. The other is the "walkthrough" which seeks to establish how the family's investments have got to where they now are through the:

- Premises;
- Starting point;
- Decisions made;
- Switches;
- Results;
- The full reasoning for the decision being made.

Such walkthroughs can be instrumental in avoiding muddling along. While several dos and don'ts distinguish the investment activities of households from those made by banks, there are also common variables, such as liquidity, time horizon, currencies and taxes, which should attract attention when auditing the management of the household's finances.

Investment cash flows are generally considered to be the main sources of liquidity, but at times they may not suffice. Under certain conditions the family may have to liquidate some assets. Generally publicly traded securities can provide a source of liquidity, but this may come at a financial loss if the market is low. Hence, with the exception of the family house, households are well advised to limit their exposure to illiquid assets. Sometimes a lack of liquidity brings the family to a state of temporary panic.

The time horizon is important in a dual sense. First, in regard to securities whose payouts are timed to match the household's expected obligations. Second, in respect to the broader time horizon of an income source at retirement or for health reasons.

Taxes are another issue demanding a focused study. It needs no explaining that taxes influence the way investment income is planned. Asset allocations should be sensitive to tax optimization offered by certain types of investments, like municipal bonds in the US. It is always good policy to examine beforehand what is written in the letter of the law in terms of possible tax advantages.

In conclusion, swinging between euphoria in good times and panic in bad times is the worst possible policy. Avoiding it requires two factors: self-control and preparation – "luck is what happens when opportunity meets preparation". This section has offered an outline of the issue for which you should always be ready, and to be ready you have to do a good deal of homework.

7.3 Investments can turn on their head

The task of setting investment guidelines goes way beyond analysing trends, buying equities of solid companies which pay good dividends, and examining the creditworthiness of bond issuers. Investment guidelines must include targets and ratios – particularly regarding real estate (the family house), bonds, equities and other investments – and what the expected returns are.

A great amount of attention must be paid to the consistency of the investment, as well as the way in which the assumed amount of exposure may change. Risk control is an integral part of investment guidelines because it is the cornerstone to effective wealth management, whether the market is euphoric or there is an economic downturn and market turbulence.

Take house prices as an example. They can go to dizzy heights and even stay there much longer than seems possible. Eventually, however, homes become painfully expensive in relation to incomes and they are vulnerable not only to an increase in interest rates but also to a turning point in market psychology – as the first decade of this century has shown.

Between 2003 and 2006 in many economies around the globe zooming house prices were a powerful motor of economic growth. From 2000 to 2006, the total value of residential property in Western countries skyrocketed. Such an increase was nearly equal to 100 per cent of the combined national incomes of those countries which experienced the real estate boom.

Countries, in which house prices have gone up most, enjoyed the strongest growth in consumer spending. Homeowners who found themselves wealthier spent plenty of money, without accounting for the fact that paper profits could be wiped out as fast as they were generated. Little attention was paid to the nasty question: How much fuel is left in the housing engine? The answer came in mid-2007 with the subprimes crisis and the unravelling of residential real estate investments.

Households who cared to study historical records had no difficulty in finding out that the residential real estate market is volatile (the commercial real estate is too) and that when it unravels it can go down a long way. Moreover, the more leveraged the housing market is, the lower it is going to go – and the longer it will stay in the trough.

As the careful reader will remember from prior discussion, the families most hurt from the housing market's collapse have been those with the greater leverage and those who used their home as a piggy bank by taking out second mortgages. Did they have in mind speculation when they bought their home? I doubt it. In the majority of cases this was not part of the household's investment goals and guidelines. It arose later on as an "easy profit" opportunity – but that was a Fata Morgana.

In the US alone, in less than two years after the 2007 subprimes crisis started, the aggregate loss in household wealth was in the trillions of dollars. By the end of 2011, as the real estate engine refused to restart, there has been an estimated 20 per cent decline in household wealth since the peak in mid-2007. Wealth destruction of this magnitude is unprecedented in the post-World War II years:

- The 1975 equity asset deflation yielded close to a 4 per cent decline in household wealth;
- The 2001 equity crisis of the dotcoms saw a 9.6 per cent decline in the net worth of US households.

The differences between then and now are not at all surprising. The housing market is so much more important to an economy than the equity market, and it also suffers much more in a downturn as demonstrated by what has happened with US, British and Spanish real estate.

This brings us back to the advice of Amadeo Giannini. As long as the house is used for living and is not a speculative investment, even a major correction is not catastrophic – provided that the house value is above the value of the remaining mortgage. What made the crisis which started in 2007 most dramatic is that so many houses turned out to be under water (i.e. the market price of the equity is below the price paid by the investor when it was acquired).

People with an open mind have also learned that leverage is a very costly business and can turn the household's wealth on its head. Whether we talk of money in the bank, real estate or financial investments, the typical household is not totally aware of the risks it confronts with its hard-won savings; and most evidently it should not increase these risks by getting deeper into debt.

Some economists say that the risk of losing everything in a downturn is a basic reason why so many households choose to spend and live on credit rather than to save. This may be true, but it should not be the case because uncontrollable risk is worse than illness. Risk should be managed. The financial crisis of 2007–12 has highlighted two queries everyone should ask themselves: Am I able to confront a long recession and honour assumed obligations if I lose my job? Do I have anything in my portfolio that would help me to survive under the worst circumstances?

Crucial issues behind these queries are whether households have acted with prudence or through too optimistic judgements about the commitments they have assumed. Are they able to stay ahead of the moment? Lack of care about tomorrow is not acceptable because it can bring frightening times as households suddenly find themselves coping with the fourfold problems of:

- A stagnant level of employment;
- Falling house prices;
- Tighter credit;
- Runaway expenses for food, oil (petrol) and education fees.

Other things being equal, households who avoided leverage and had a diversified portfolio have been able to weather the storm by positioning themselves against market forces. As I never tire of repeating, the diversification of household assets is important because every investment class has an inherent exposure. Corporate bonds can have lots of credit risk, and government bonds are not immune to it, as the cases of Greece, Portugal, Spain and Italy document.

Another risk which may upset the household's goals and guidelines is that governments print money as a way to pull themselves up by their bootstraps. Therefore, one of the worst investments may turn out to be a 10 to 30-year government bond which was expensive to buy but lost its value because of rising inflation.

As a rule, inflation is higher than that shown in official numbers, as governments always underplay its effect. Shortly after he became president, Ronald Reagan, who was a good communicator, gave a televised interview to explain inflation's effect on the ordinary citizen. He asked his audience: Do you want to know what a dollar in your pocket at the end of World War II is worth today? And he put on the table 33 cents.[7]

Households will be well-advised to stress test their portfolio of investments not only for inflation but also for other events which might upset their goals – always keeping in mind that the market does not crawl, it jumps. The target should be to study beforehand the impact of multiple stress scenarios such as that associated with:

- *Equities*, such as a 30 per cent decline in equity prices for shares in the family's portfolio;
- *Creditworthiness of bonds*: such as a three notches downgrade of both issuer and bond, for instance from A+ to BBB;

- *Interest rates*: such as the effect of an interest rate increase by the central bank by 300 basis points, for example from 3 to 6 per cent.
- *Educational expenses*, such as the aftermath on the family budget from a near-doubling of the cost of college education of both children;
- *A catastrophe loss-event*, such as the aftermath of losing one's house because of fire, hurricane or tornado;
- *Unemployment risk*, such as the family's ability to withstand unemployment by one or both income earners, given its commitments, liabilities and investments;
- *War or terrorism*, such as different levels of loss of property or bodily damage because of hostilities;
- *Worst-case scenario*, such as the combination of several of the above scenarios, their human and economic after-effects considered by the head of the family to be the worst cases.

In conclusion, factual and well-documented investment decisions, including assumed risk as well as the impact of events beyond the household's reach, are so important because there exists no magic formula to avoid the negative after-effects of happenings which are possible – no matter how unlikely they may be. What if one loses one's job or one's house, the market crashes and inflation takes off in a big way?

Risk should always underpin investment analytics, and a peculiarity of our society is that the list of risks is growing. For instance in 2008–9 the taxpayer was asked to pay the bill of huge losses by highly mismanaged banks. There is always a hidden handholding between government and big business – and this, too, is a risk.

7.4 Can we depend on prognostication?

Prognostication, sometimes described as the ability to read tomorrow's newspaper today, is by no means an exact science, and in the general case it is more subjective than should be the case. In a bull market the guiding spirit is *euphoria*; in a bear market, it is *doubt*. Though there should always be thoroughness of study and analysis in the background, this is frequently lacking – and yet prognostication is not altogether useless. Far from that.

Analysis and the critical questioning of different assumptions should underpin our effort to prognosticate future events. Quite often, we also use models. When I was young I often designed models and looked at them as one of the gifts of science. Experience teaches otherwise. All models are wrong, but some are useful, and their usefulness comes from:

- The questioning attitude they require;
- The need to challenge the obvious;
- The careful identification and analysis of key variables;
- The pattern of their behaviour which more often than not is stochastic (probabilistic).

Whether we talk of credit risk or market risk, this pattern acts as an eye-opener, particularly so if it is characterized by thoroughness in analysis, which should never slacken. As advice, this runs contrary to the usual practice with business cycles where prosperity is marked by an increasing inefficiency in financial research – both on the side of companies and on that of investors. Yet investment action in the West's virtual economy requires more than ever:

- A significant amount of study and analysis in an attempt to prognosticate the effect of current decisions on the future course of economic events;
- The ability to turn on a dime and resolve to implement the needed changes right after we are able to detect what may be coming;
- The patience to go through the turbulence which accompanies major changes, particularly so at inflection point(s) when tough decisions are a must.

Let me repeat the message conveyed by the first bullet. The best possible contribution of prognostication is not that of coming up with a clear picture of future events (which is rarely if ever the case) but of providing us with the ability to test the future impact of current decisions so that we are forewarned of after-effects due to turbulence and can better exploit business opportunities which always exist when our environment changes.

As secretary of defence, Donald Rumsfeld distinguished between "known unknowns" and "unknown unknowns".[8] In the first, we know that we do not know the behaviour and/or we do not have definitive information about particular issues, relations and events.

The stress tests outlined above aim to provide this sort of intelligence. Prognostication is the goal, and reasonable approximation is what we are after.

The case of unknown unknowns is different because what they bring is totally unexpected. We don't even know that we do not know about them, about their existence; therefore, even a series of warnings becomes meaningless because nobody believes in them and therefore no-one pays them any attention. Experience and brainstorming, however, can go a long way in turning unknown unknowns into (albeit imperfectly) known ones.

In my practice I have found two ways for doing just that. One is reading history and taking good notice of what has happened quite unexpectedly in the course of two epochs: during the last five centuries during which what we now call "the Western economy" has developed[9] and during the time of Ancient Greece and Rome (the first major banking bankruptcy, for example, took place under the Roman Emperor Tiberius; until then this was an unknown unknown event).

The second way is by stress-testing for a way out of the long leg of the risk distribution: at 25 or 30 standard deviations from the mean. When this is done a strange-looking hypothesis starts to show up – and a feeling of inevitability begins engulfing what until then might have been considered absurd events. The first method helps the second because one can always ask: Did Tiberius have an advance warning of the deep banking crisis which hit the Roman Empire? If yes, what might the signals have been? If no, how did he come up with a solution which at the time of the deep crisis made good sense?

In terms of gaining insight and foresight, it is rewarding to study, for example, how real estate crises built up over the last 200 years. Easy credit and leveraging aside, which other common characteristics exist between the post-Napoleonic years and today? Or between the late 1980s housing bubble and the descent towards the abyss in 2007–12?

Much can be revealed by analysing what, in both cases, the behaviour has been regarding a longer-term relationship between house prices and rents. Can the changes observed in this relationship be used as a prognosticator of a coming real estate bubble? Is the existence of a temporary price misalignment telling us something really important? How should we account for the effect of limitations to the income derived from real estate property, such as in the following?

- Rent regulation;
- Structural economic changes;
- Fiscal policy measures related to housing;
- Conditions characterizing the evolution of credit and other issues.

The more we try to dig deeper into the rent–house price correlation, the greater becomes the impact of various forms of rent regulation like caps for rent increases, rent indexation and changes in the laws relating to taxation of rental income. Which other conditions have, in the past, combined with these events to burst the real estate bubble?

Several factors see to it that the relationship between house prices and rents is never linear. Moreover, supply constraints and the substituting of buying and renting for one another affect the prevailing relationships and drive a wedge between rents and residential property prices. Other factors are mortgage interest rates, various types of property taxes, subsidies for the "first" family residence and expectations for future house-price developments.

Much can be gained by way of prognostication by establishing whether or not (and by how much) an economic downturn has a negative impact on: the level of income from housing; real estate prices falling below outstanding mortgages; an increase in the number of people unemployed among those who have bought apartments or individual houses and find it difficult to liquidate the investment.

Other things being equal, an increase in the proportion of households in the lower income levels, and in those with a head of household who is unemployed, translates not only into a higher debt-servicing ratio for families with a mortgage outstanding, but also into an increase in the number of debtors with arrears. One of the goals of prognostication in a deeper economic crisis will be to foretell, as a percentage, the number of households with a perceived level of income below that needed to make ends meet, and to outline basic steps to overcome this adversity (including immediately applicable tighter credit) before adversity hits.

In conclusion, prognostication is by no means meant to tell today what will happen tomorrow. Rather, its remit is to help in clearing up to a point a given situation, to warn on likely after-effects, and to focus on crucial issues. Forgetting about something which is really important can turn an otherwise prudent asset allocation on its head.

7.5 The government is not a white knight

While, as we will see in Chapter 8, investments in family homes are by no means free of risk and challenges, investments made in the financial markets top them. "Like the ocean, global financial markets are never at rest. Like women, they are never entirely predictable", said Sir George Bolton. For his part, Amadeo Giannini aptly suggested: "No man actually owns a fortune. It owns him."

The real cost of any investment is steady vigilance. When adversity hits, even portfolio positions which have been well-studied and look secure stand on a razor's edge. Market conditions change in the most unexpected ways. Right after World War II, British gilts (government bonds) offered attractive interest rates. By the mid-1970s, three decades down the line, those who bought them lost three-quarters of their money in real terms. Conversely, in 2011 investors in British gilts were rewarded with a 17 per cent profit.

Investors who bought Japanese equities at the stock market's peak in 1989 had plenty of reasons to regret it. Twenty-two years later, as 2011 came to a close, they were still sitting on a nominal 70 per cent loss.

Watching the changing fortunes and trying to project one's investments is necessary but not enough. One must act. It serves nothing by sitting on the fence. In 2011 people held cash – plenty of it – as they waited for the other shoe to drop, but they were also worried about missing a surge in the stock market.

Investors who went through the dip of September 2008 and held steady saw the upside which started in April 2009, tapered off in 2010 and in August 2011 went downside again. Those who suffered the most with the market's blues were leveraged, as leveraging dramatically reduces flexibility and turns the investor into a sitting duck.

Anecdotal evidence speaks of a New York hedge fund which early enough in 2011, foreseeing a major market correction, sold its equity holdings. Then, as the market held, it bought them back, just prior to the August 2011 dip. The investment was by all evidence leveraged and with the equity market in a new trough by November 2011 the hedge fund lost half the money it had invested in the equities. Not to be outdone, Advantage, the flagship hedge fund of John Paulson, closed 2011 with a strategic 51 per cent loss of its capital.

The fact that experts make such mistakes with the choice and timing of investments is troubling. Just think for a moment of being in the shoes of households confronted with the challenge of entering and exiting a nervous market. In former times their goal would have been to invest their money to make a profit. In late 2011 and early 2012, however, wealth preservation, not earnings, was supreme.

Diversification, avoidance of leverage, patience and self-discipline is the way to wealth preservation. Investors who wait for governments to rescue the economy prepare themselves for deception. Particularly in connection to the challenges of the twenty-first century, governments and central banks don't have the right policies, the tools or the money. They spent all their dry powder in 2008 and the subsequent years.

Prior to the latest crisis, fiscal and monetary tools used to be powerful weapons. Today, after years of unsuccessful efforts to kick start Western economies by getting deeper into public debt, these tools are inefficient, crude and often counterproductive.

Paul Volcker, who as chairman of the Federal Reserve launched the successful fight against the ruinous inflation of the 1970s, once said that "the truly unique power of a central bank is the power to create money, and ultimately the power to create is the power to destroy".[10] It is most likely that we are finding ourselves in the middle of that destruction cycle.

Side-effects from government intervention are sometimes worse than the problems they are meant to solve. Examples are the extraordinary liquidity being created by the Federal Reserve and the unstoppable deficit spending by the US government – policy measures which, while increasingly aggressive, are still no match for the contraction of credit and the record deflation in asset values suffered by American households.

The Japanese government, too, is heavily indebted (to the tune of over 200 per cent of GDP), but somehow it manages its financial issues a little better. Household cash savings are no more the

$3 trillion that they used to be in the 1970s, but together with household assets they represent an appreciable $146 trillion (yen 1,127 trillion).[11] Compared to this the Japanese social security funds stand at $2.6 trillion (yen 201 trillion).

These Japanese figures leave other Western countries in shame. Savings rates in America and in Europe differ between jurisdictions and over time, but as a general rule they are low. This has an adverse effect on investments. In the past, mismatches between desired levels of savings and investments were brought into line by Western central banks through the interest-rate mechanism, but even this is now out of action because interest rates are purposely kept below inflation level and, in some countries like France, that minimal interest paid on savings is taxed by the state.[12]

Bill Gross, Chief Investment Officer of Pimco and manager of the world's largest bond fund, the $245 billion Total Return Fund, has argued that investors in US Treasuries are not being compensated for the risk of inflation. Yet, this risk is a real and present danger which erodes the value of savings, time deposits and a bond's fixed-interest payments.

In Gross's opinion, complacent holders of Treasury bonds are akin to the frog in boiling water. Ajay Rajadhyaksha, head of US fixed income strategy at Barclays Capital, says: "if you own Treasuries you should sell them at this point. You are getting compensated nothing for the next ten years".[13]

Who would then buy the Treasuries? For obvious reasons China has been a big buyer, but it needs no explaining that the West cannot continue borrowing from the East with impunity over long stretches of time. Neither can the US government continue with a deficit of over $1 trillion per year, nearly 8 per cent of GDP, without very serious economic consequences. The overhang of public debt is to a large measure the result and the source of slower growth and higher unemployment.

Entitlements are behind these extremely large public expenditures, but not only entitlements. Another big negative contributor is unnecessary foreign wars, like the eight and a half years of war in Iraq and a decade in Afghanistan – both characterized by negative deliverables. Who will pay the bill for all these extravaganzas? Predictably, the answer is US households.

No matter what the reason for which they have been created, a large debt overhang and continuing budget deficits eventually lead to stagflation (the joint effects of economic stagnation and inflation). There is not much to look forward to, and trying to escape forwards by listening to the (unfulfilled) promises of politicians is no solution either. Ultimately, there is only so much debt a household, company or nation can absorb. The securitization of debt and its resale does not solve the problem either – it becomes a Ponzi game.[14]

7.6 Wrong solutions and their consequences

By pooling loans and securitizing them, banks distort the market and make investments more unsecure than they would be otherwise. Tossing securitized instruments together, leveraging the lot and resecuritizing them builds up a pyramid scheme which makes little sense but creates great opportunities for profits and bonuses – until it crashes. And when it crashes investors and taxpayers pay the bill.

The scams are legendary. Sovereigns, municipalities, companies and households have been taken repeatedly to the cleaners. Over time banks make a killing and bankers make fat bonuses until the edifice crumbles and governments are called to the rescue. Just as an example, in the third quarter of 2010 alone American bank-holding companies made $12.2 billion from derivatives trading.[15]

Freewheeling derivatives markets have not been the only cause of the crisis, but they were major contributors to it by playing the unwelcome role of both multiplying and hiding leverage. From private citizens to companies and governments, *end-users* took positions with derivative instruments which they did not understand and were not even remotely in a position to value their risks.

Quite evidently there have been unintended consequences. Back in the early 1990s municipalities became early victims of the peddlers of derivative instruments. The bankruptcy of Orange County was the first warning sign. Plenty of others followed. A more recent example is that of derivative products bought by the City of Menton, in Southern France.

On Thursday 27 October 2011, during the presentation of the budget for 2012, the city authorities admitted that they had bought derivative instruments and lost money with them. Menton took a loan from Dexia (the Franco-Belgian bank which went bankrupt twice in three years), supposedly to free itself from what the bankers/salesmen called its "toxic loans" contracted in the past. They were replaced with one "neat derivatives package", reportedly more toxic than its predecessors.

The icing on the cake made it look like a Christmas present, but it was a gamble, and the cost of this gambling with derivatives by the city administrator (who knew nothing about what he was buying) has been €1,000 ($1,300) for every family, living in the city and its suburbs.[16] Write this down as *the cost of ignorance*, with the citizen paying for someone else's mistakes.

If municipalities bend over to the siren song of structured instruments sold by derivatives peddlers, private households stand no chance of resisting them. Particularly less-well-off families have been hooked and advanced the practice of "negative amortization". This means a build-up of debt during the term of a mortgage, rather than proceeding with debt reduction. Widely used in fixed-rate graduated-payment mortgages, as well as in adjustable rate loans, negative amortization takes control of a borrower by allowing him or her to pay an artificially low rate and add the deferred payments onto the principal owed to the lender.

Normally, final pay-off of the full debt is not required until the house is sold or the mortgage refinanced. But when home real-estate values are soft or sagging, the hooked-up home-owner feels the heat. Therefore, mortgage industry experts should warn buyers to stay away from one of the most popular leftovers from the go-go 1980s: the aforementioned "I win, you lose" form of financing.

In theory, by permitting negative amortization lenders create more affordable financing packages. In their words, they make it feasible to refinance a current mortgage and pull money out of the equity. In practice, as critics of twisted mortgage lending practices suggest, this approach is risky and loaded with liabilities. The owner may end up by losing his or her house.

Widespread use of negative amortization was a fad in the 1980s, when homes in most parts of the United States were appreciating in value. But the housing economy – first in the 1990s (with values flat and a recession looming) and then in 2007 (with subprimes and Alt-As (alternative A ratings)),[17] as well as thereafter when housing descended towards the abyss – led to negative amortization becoming a trap for many house owners. (Negative amortization became popular principally due to the fact that in many cases the borrowers did not understand what they were signing up for, even when the feature was fully disclosed. They looked at the low payment, or initial no payment of even a relatively low rate, and they were taken in by the salesman's clever words. With this, they assumed they were getting the best deal in town, which was a long way from reality.)

Other examples on what *not to do* with your family's wealth, and most particularly with your house, come from Britain. The race to derivatives in the real estate property market started in 2004. While there were several attempts during the 1990s to create such products, in September 2004 a socially unfortunate change in the law occurred which provided real estate derivatives with favourable tax treatment and made them attractive to the wider public.

Until this change in British law, capital gains tax was payable on profits from property derivatives, while losses did not qualify for relief. Another "favourable" impulse in promoting speculation through real estate derivatives came from the Financial Services Authority, a watch dog. Most surprisingly, it allowed insurance companies to use property derivatives for portfolio management. With a smile from supervisors and a tax advantage assured by law, Britain became the first country in the world with a fully formed property derivatives market.

Still another contributor has been the fact that, contrary to other jurisdictions whose cadaster (land register) is in a mess, Britain has a wealth of property data collated by Investment Property Databank, which is an independent research company whose index tracks the return on over £100 billion of property.[18] Barclays had already offered bonds and Abbey National had savings products where the payout depended on movements in real estate property prices. But in late 2004, a blockbuster real estate swap was the first snow-white derivative in the sense that no money changed hands when the deal was contracted.[19] Notice how, with the politicians' help, the market fulfilled its own prophecies: early financial products did not allow investors to bet against the property market; swaps made it possible to take positions without committing funds, yet while expecting future payments.

That's a gamblers' paradise. Promoters of the new instrument capitalized on the fact that real estate is a very illiquid market in which deals can take months with charges on a physical property changing hands reaching 6 to 8 per cent. The real estate derivatives swap is done without such costs and delays of a physical deal, but the risk is always there – and it is not immediately transparent.

In addition, even if the deal is opaque, the future looks brilliant. In Britain alone billions in real estate property are expected to be unlocked over the years, as elderly homeowners look for ways to boost their retirement income. The more classical means of doing so is by remortgaging or selling part of their homes but, theoretically at least, derivative financial instruments offer to home owners a way to leverage their residential real estate asset.

According to experts, leveraged real estate deals have no problem finding eager players in the so-called "equity release market" which is rated for huge growth. With endowments ebbing, people are forced to take more responsibility for funding pensions, paying for long-term care and confronting education costs of offspring. This however can go wrong if the necessary regulatory and supervisory framework is not in place. Control of any market, particularly one of derivatives, is a battle between arithmetic, which is predictable, and the momentum of wheeling and dealing, which is not.

Not all properties, of course, will qualify as prime sites but alchemists will easily give, even to dubious instruments, an AAA rating and sell them on. Clear-eyed people can see the precipice at the end of the line. "We have reached the point of diminishing returns with easy money," said a trader in an interview with CNBC on 18 August 2011, "but the Fed has not yet understood that. The lowering of the interest rate to practically zero has made the market uneasy."

Tectonic economic and financial shifts will occupy much of the market's attention over the coming years. In his book on Warren Buffett, Roger Lowenstein provided a good example of what comes when unknown unknowns can lead to a precipice. "Buffett said: 'What do you think the odds of this thing making it are?' I said 'Pretty good. One out of two.' He said, 'Do you think that's good? Why don't you go on an airplane with a parachute that opens one out of every two times and jump?'"[20]

8
Home Ownership: Shelter or Burden?

8.1 Your home is your castle

"Your home is your castle," says an old proverb. Your home is also your house, and your house is a real estate investment which – like it or not – is subject to market cycles and whims which eventually confront the home owner. House prices are volatile, mortgage interest rates rise and fall, and the heavy hand of the government as well as the law of the land (evidently, including the tax code) shape the house owner's behaviour (see the contrast between Canada and the United States at the time of the Clinton Administration's push for home ownership in sections 8.2 and 8.3).

A real estate cycle can be seen as an interval of time which has ups and downs. Throughout history, for any commodity, ups and downs repeat themselves. Housing is characterized by demand and supply imbalances which create conditions for swings from boom to bust. Banks add to these ups and down by adopting, respectively, a loose or stringent credit policy.

For a real estate speculator, the challenge is to know when to get in and out of an investment. Predicting a cycle is not easy. If a householder looks at his or her house as a castle, he or she should not have a prediction problem because the term "castle" automatically suggests a longer perspective. There exists, however, an exception to this statement: if a family is on the move, changing place of work and moving every couple of years or so, and if the house has been bought on credit with a minor down payment, then a real estate market slump sees to it that the house may be worth less than the outstanding mortgage when the family needs to sell it.[1]

Particularly vulnerable in this second group are those households who bought property at the peak of the market because they did not do their homework (see section 8.6) and so are confronted with negative equity. This also includes those who, particularly in the US, took out subprime mortgages "with no question" being asked by their bankers who only wanted raw stuff for securitization.

With the collapse of the housing market, and the severe banking crisis which followed it, by the first quarter of 2009 an estimated 10 million Americans found themselves in negative equity. When the cost of a mortgage exceeds the value of the home to which it applies, it demolishes the hopes of the family who can no longer see the end of the tunnel. Those unable to meet their payments lose their house.

In the second term of the George W. Bush Administration subprime mortgages increased by leaps and bounds regarding their share of the total mortgage market. The after-effect of this should serve as an alarm signal, though it has not received the attention it deserves. In the US, subprimes zoomed from 7 per cent in 2001 to over 20 per cent in 2006. As a result, the delinquency rate reached 22 per cent by the end of 2008, compared with only 5 per cent for prime loans – while by early 2011 an estimated 5.5 million households were tied to mortgages that were higher than 20 per cent or more of the market value of their homes.[2]

Leveraging is a greater evil in home ownership and it destroys families in a downturn. Typically, albeit not always, the ordinary citizen buys shares outright, but homes are bought on a margin. If share prices fall by 15 per cent, they lose 15 per cent. But if house prices fall by 15 per cent, they may lose their geared-up (leveraged) house.[3]

On the one hand, home ownership benefits society because it encourages more stable communities and has a favourable impact on future generations. There is evidence that the children of homeowners do better at school. On the other hand, however, leveraging destabilizes households – particularly when due payments are further handicapped by the loss of job by one of the parents (even worse, by both). This creates behavioural problems for children and sometimes for adults.

Gearing (leveraging) may help to make a quick buck (if one is "lucky"), but the preservation of wealth is not promoted through leverage. This destructive behaviour by the citizen is promoted by the banking industry through easy credit and by central banks by keeping interest rates near zero. *Cheap money* is inflating the value of assets. At the end of the day this is a great disservice to households and to the economy. Leverage, and therefore debt, sees to it that real wealth takes a hit.

As the careful reader will recall from Chapters 6 and 7, what has just been said about leveraging in real estate holds true also for financial investments. In the end, citizens who try to beat the professionals through gearing lose their hard-won wealth. People who buy overvalued assets with borrowed money do not make themselves richer but poorer. Economists who forget the facts of life and promote leverage should be asked: will a policy of leveraging assets boost the amount of goods the economy produces in the long run? Or will it have negative consequences in the longer run, destabilizing households and eventually restricting economic activity?

Different economists tend to answer such queries in diametrically opposite ways; yet financial history teaches that the second alternative is much more likely than the first. Just remember how much taxpayers' money has been spent by governments intervening to rescue self-wounded big financial institutions. The printing presses were kept busy for the superleveraged companies with political clout, while nothing was done to save households from losing their leveraged home property.

Political clout aside, one of the reasons for wrong-way action is that in the minds of people, including those who govern, there is plenty of confusion about the nature of wealth. Theoretically, wealth consists of goods that people wish to consume and assets – land, houses, factories and machinery – with the latter providing the ability to produce goods. But in the case of superleveraged entities, where liabilities exceed assets, what is left is red ink – not wealth.

It used to be a rule of thumb that a household should spend no more than 25 to 30 per cent of its annual income on housing, including mortgage or rent, utilities, taxes and house repair. Taking a household's annual income figure as a reference and applying this rule would mean that a family should spend a measurable amount of its income on its home – and this amount should be recorded in its balance sheet. Everything above that limit is supported through leveraging and it is sad to know that more than three-quarters of residential real estate properties in the US are encumbered by mortgages of greater than 80 per cent of their value. (In Europe the corresponding statistics are somewhat better, but still irrational.)

Critics say that the US government's obsession with home ownership has contributed to this superleveraging of residential home property, and therefore to the meltdown of the housing market in 2007. The irony is that both the Bush and Obama Administrations depended on Fannie Mae and Freddie Mac, the government-sponsored institutions to hold the residential real estate dam from breaking when they knew that Fannie and Freddie were bankrupt (they were taken over by the sovereign in early September 2008).[4]

Neither were home purchases the only case of household leveraging. Practically all Western households have run up a large credit card debt. In America credit card debt also zoomed in an attempt to maintain the repayments on a mortgage that now exceeds the value of the family's home. A 2008 study found that the typical family who filed for bankruptcy in 2007 was carrying 21 per cent more exposure in secured debts, like mortgages and car loans, and 44 per cent more in unsecured debts, like credit cards, medical and utility bills, than at the time of the stock market crash in 2000. As should be remembered, 2000 was also a year of a bubble burst and stress. In essence, within seven years the economy went from one speculation to another – from a stock market bubble to an even more severe housing bubble which rapidly spread through the Western world.

The bubble mentality has been instrumental in transforming home ownership from shelter to burden as houses got under water. Evidence from price trends, market swings and interest rates used as a monetary policy tool shows that many real estate cycles have acquired idiosyncratic elements. Generally, real estate cycles have a length of roughly ten years, but:

- They are now showing up more frequently;
- They do not begin concurrently in different markets;
- They do not have the same intensity worldwide, because the reasons behind them are different.

In the early years of this century the main reason behind real estate booms and busts which occurred in the US, Britain and Spain was speculation. Other cycles in countries like Australia, Canada and

Brazil were fuelled by the commodities boom. The rise of residential markets in Asia (apart from Japan) was driven by cheap money, which was artificially prolonged by credit expansion after the financial crisis of 1997–98. But no matter which has been the primary reason, leveraging made a bad situation even worse.

8.2 Home mortgages and the law of the land in Canada: a case study

A real estate bust is a risk not only to speculators but also to indebted households, particularly to those with a stretched financial position – and by extension to the national economy. In March 2011, a study by Bank of America Merrill Lynch looked at the proportion of indebted households with debt service ratios greater than 40 per cent.[5] The researchers estimated that in Canada about 6.5 per cent of households have this high debt service ratio, representing some 12.4 per cent of the total debt outstanding (this level is the threshold limit for mortgage insurance) – and they found that this was way below comparable US statistics.

What might be the reason for such a discrepancy within North America? The Merrill Lynch study brought to attention some important differences between Canada and the US, ranging from the law of the land in regard to mortgages, government guarantees and leverage ratios. Based on these findings, the study concluded that the differences which exist shape the behaviour of households in regard to the way they treat their mortgages and condition their response when times turn against the indebted house owner.

In the case of Canada, legal recourse laws reduce the likelihood that households are able to walk away from their mortgage. This implicitly improves lending quality. About 90 per cent of mortgages have full recourse in Canada, creating a more lender-friendly environment. Conversely, in the US the house owner can leave the estate and mail the keys of his or her home to the bank. No wonder, therefore, that reports of abandoned vacant homes came in en masse as the overall economic situation reached a low.

Credit institutions are well aware of the impact of the law of the land on mortgages by households. In Canada, roughly 30 per cent of the mortgage funding market has a federal government guarantee which reduces the risk of a US style funding freeze. Moreover, during the height of the recent credit crisis, the Canadian government initiated an effective Insured Mortgage Purchase Program which kept the mortgage market functioning. Nothing similar was done in the US.

Greater stability in the housing market has also been promoted by the historically lower leverage ratios in Canada as contrasted with the US. While with the recent crisis the balance sheets of Canadian households have deteriorated and families have entered into more risky contracts, like variable rate mortgages, subprime lending has been practically non-existent. Families have preferred conventional mortgage options to the casino society.

The evidence provided by the Bank of America Merrill Lynch study suggests the need for rethinking and revamping the current residential real estate laws and rules, not only in the US but also in other Western countries, Britain included. This is in line with the call by several experts for strict limits on mortgage terms and regulations, including clauses that force banks to set aside money for possible losses.

In the opinion of real estate experts, there should be measures which can be effectively used to deflate asset bubbles and avoid a repetition of the same mistakes which characterized the first half dozen years of this century. The reader should however appreciate that these are prescriptions with future impact rather than reliefs to current distress. In an article in the *Financial Times* Mort Zuckerman, a real estate investor and publisher, asked "What is to be done?" in terms of immediate relief – and he concluded that the options are all bad. In his opinion:[6]

- A moratorium on foreclosure would be opposed by people struggling to keep paying their mortgages;
- A repeat of the tax credit given to first-time borrowers is unlikely to be supported in Congress, given the government's indebtedness;
- The expansion of the role in Fannie Mae and Freddie Mac in mediating housing markets must overcome the perception that they distorted mortgage markets;[7]
- Reducing the principal of mortgages to the value of the underlying properties would see the cost to the lenders (banks and the taxpayer through Fannie and Freddie) run to the level of $1 trillion.

Longer-term measures – such as rules on credit targeted at specific risks, caps on the loan to value ratio, or mortgages and limits on bank lending in overseas currencies – are being debated, but Zuckerman is right when he says that short-term relief must be given a priority, even at this late date.

Last but not least, a law should be passed by Congress which ends once and for all the frivolous arms-twisting in favour of "social home ownership", like the one by the Clinton Administration, supposedly to benefit those who could not afford buying a house. Nothing like this ever existed in Canada, or in any other Western country that I know of, and for good reason.

8.3 The Clinton Administration's scenario on home mortgages: a case study

The Clinton Administration's scenario on home mortgages was totally different from the Canadian model. Its origins were populist and pro-banking, beyond the perennial lust and greed. To the untrained eye in the background, the subprime mortgages[8] and their twins the Alt-As (alternative A ratings, which was a myth) were overstated assets and falsified documents. But that was only the one-eighth of the iceberg which could be seen.

At the start, the seven-eighths were made up of political pressure to the banking industry to give mortgages to people who could neither afford them nor sustain them. Initially the banks resisted the Clinton Administration's pressure because they violated orderly credit practices. Before too long, however, bankers and banks understood that subprimes were manna from heaven for their bottom line, because steady fat profits could be made with them. Hence, they aggressively went out for "clients" – while bank supervisors turned a blind eye.[9]

Roberta Achtenberg is the name of the Clinton Administration official who put the US home loans world on fire; and Angelo Mozilo, the CEO of Countrywide,[10] is widely considered to be the prime agent of the US real estate debacle. Mozilo, of course, had his friends. According to Lawrence McDonald, he provided Senator Chris Dodd with a mortgage that saved the Connecticut Democrat some $75,000 in interest payments.[11]

McDonald traced the history of Countrywide and found in the first year of this century that the mortgage lender had had revenues of

$2 billion, with net income of about $320 million. Six years later, at the subprime market's peak, its revenues were well over $10 billion, with an income of $2.5 billion. Then came the crash.

The first half dozen years of this century make interesting reading because there was something extremely ambitious in the subprimes craze, with ordinary people being hooked up and each big player facing tough competition from its peers. Not just Countrywide, but also Washington Mutual, the best of savings and loans (building societies), MGIC Insurance, Radian and even the US government-sponsored Fannie Mae are some of the names which left their mark on this bubble.

Clinton appointee Achtenberg, whom US Senator Jesse Helms allegedly referred to as that "damn lesbian",[12] is credited with the feat of having harnessed the power of the government, supposedly to help the economically weak – while in reality pushing banks into the business of selling houses to people too economically fragile to afford their own house. According to McDonald she did that sometimes, threatening and in other cases berating or bullying.

Citing innate racism on behalf of banks for their reluctance to give mortgages to people of doubtful or non-existent creditworthiness, Achtenberg pressed on with what became the raw stuff of subprimes. Working for the US government as Assistant Secretary of Housing and Urban Development gave her leverage. She was hyperactive for about two years: enough time to build up a national grid of offices staffed with investigators and lawyers who acted against the banks for discrimination if they refused to sign up subprimes.

Compare this to the policy followed by the Canadian government in terms of housing. The contrast is one between a smooth progression and a spike which turned into an ugly bubble. In the six years following 1993, over 2 million non-qualifying home owners came on record – themselves and their houses becoming cannon feed for subprimes.

Prodded by the Clinton Administration, "the competitors" in this deceiving business line aimed to create a gigantic portfolio of subprimes and Alt-As whose rating might have been "C" at best. These were immediately recycled into collateralized debt obligations (CDOs), christened AAA (with the complacency of credit rating agencies, the highest credit rating) and sold on with tremendous profits. In parallel to this, there was a bidding war to acquire banking companies rich in subprimes – at prices having little to do with their worth.

Critics of these exercises in absolute credit irresponsibility say that practically all of the players in this perpetual money machine thought it would go on forever. Having been out of their senses, they could not see that sooner rather than later it would explode. What was supposed to be the national watchdog, the Center for Responsible Lending, estimated that loans for 2.2 million people would end in foreclosure. In effect, this was an underestimate.

The market psychology radically changed from euphoria to near panic when rumours had it that the biggest beasts among subprime lenders and structured instrument producers were finding it nearly impossible to sell the CDOs. Their selling price had to be drastically cut, if it were to move them at all.[13] Banks and investors who thought they had made the deal of the century with their pseudo-AAA mortgage-backed securities – stamped, signed and certified as *riskless* by Moody's, S&P and Fitch – found out the hard way that they were valueless.

The perpetual money machine had broken down and, as usual, the worst hit were the financially weaker homeowners who defaulted on their loans, lost their houses and with the ensuing economic crisis also lost their jobs. Subprime and Alt-A loans became delinquent by the score. Institutions and investors who eagerly bought instruments which they could not understand had only themselves to blame for their plight.[14] But millions of people found themselves in a sea of red ink as their assets were swept by the economic and financial crisis.

Not everything was, however, in vain. Some banks and their executives became filthy rich. From early 2000 to July/August 2007, the day of reckoning, Wall Street had created an estimated $1.8 to 2.0 trillion of securities, backed by the homes their owners could not afford. The fallout was worldwide, even if the bulk of it was concentrated in the US, where the producers-consumers of pseudo-AAA securitized mortgages were located, and in Europe, where many of the financial victims to the con game could be found.

8.4 Benefits and risks from real estate investing

This century's great real estate boom started in 2003, had a high-water mark in 2006 and hit the public eye in 2007 at the time of the housing market's bust. Those who benefited the most were those who rode the wave as early as 2003 or 2004 and had the foresight to limit their speculative presence in the real estate market to a couple of years. As always, the latecomers and the "greedier" were left holding the bad stuff.

I have brought to the reader's attention the great difference in wealth management viewpoints between people who look at their house as their home and those who speculate on real estate prices. This being said, even the serious long-term investors in residential real estate who have the financial staying power to survive the bursting of a bubble, must be aware that there are also other risks which may hit them in the longer run. Two of these exposures will concern us in this section: that of liquidity risk and government-takes-all risk.

Investments in real estate have merits; but there also demerits, one of the most evident being their lack of liquidity, which is partly associated with the time that elapses before the property is sold. Even if the waiting for a deal is not expected to take ages (which is still not a certainty), market liquidity may not be on call at the time one wants to sell the house. Generally, real estate is not appropriate for investors who:

- Have a short-term time horizon;
- Make frequent changes in asset allocation;
- Are regularly concerned with liquidity on a short-term basis;
- Have difficulty in properly pricing a real estate property when they buy and sell.

The lack of liquidity in real estate investing is heightened by unrealistic estimates of current values in volatile markets. Misrepresentation of values can make it difficult to get in and out of a real estate property, even when the market is hot; in a down market, this may become a nightmare. The difficulty of liquidating holdings where there are few buyers should always be kept in mind, particularly when the market has gone through a period of overinvestment.

It is generally difficult to determine an acceptable level of assurance of the fair value of a real estate property. The most frequent benchmark is deals recently done with nearby properties; but no two real estate deals are the same. This is true all the way from a single house to the national housing stock. Let me repeat the reference just being made. What is frequently used as a benchmark is the relationship amongst:

- One's own house and neighbouring houses;
- House price indices;
- Disposable household income or rents.

Like any indicator, the latter two provide a longer-term average. Deviations from a given trend serve as a measure for overvaluation or undervaluation. The problem is that the consistency of historical averages with fundamentally justified relationships is largely based on assumptions. Some of them are backed up by regression models, but others are poorly documented.

One of the rather questionable assumptions is that house prices have an "equilibrium value". This is challenged by several economists who think that if properties were systematically undervalued in the past and current market prices exceed model forecasts, then the conclusion that there is an overvaluation is wrong.

Assumptions about an equilibrium value in real estate have also been invalidated by the sharp rise and fall in prices in the housing market which does not depend only (let alone mainly) on whether asked prices have moved significantly from an appropriate level as defined by theoretical determinants. Practical determinants are most critical and they should be given full weight, such as:

- Location;
- Supply and demand;
- Market liquidity (this and the previous bullet being influenced by such factors as bankers' bonuses in London residential real estate);
- Market psychology;
- Regional differences.

Bubble effects are another critical factor. After a bubble has arisen, there will be by all likelihood an abrupt correction to the prevailing mispricing. Other practical factors are construction indicators, like private housing expenditures, building permits, housing starts or new house sales, and existing house sales reflecting quantity adjustments on the supply side.

The rise and fall of economic indicators prevailing in the area where real estate property is located evidently affects pricing. Worse hit in a downturn are the less diversified economies. In the United States, for example, after the District of Columbia (which relies on government) and Alaska (whose lifeline is oil and gas), Nevada has the least diversified economy. In the aftermath of the economic and financial crisis, between 2007 and 2011, Nevada lost more than 10 per cent of its jobs and home prices fell by more than half.

Overwhelming taxation is a different but just as serious threat. When governments need money they shake down the citizenry, house owners included. Both commercial and residential real estate are at the frontline of the government's lust for money through taxation, all the way to their citizens' impoverishment. Several relatively wealthy Germans mastered the risks of their country's hyperinflation of the early 1920s because they owned prime real estate. But after the hyperinflation was over, a needy German government put prohibitive taxes on real estate and threw into despair many people who had saved their wealth through real estate.

Some German citizens lost half of their fortunes, and this is by no means an outlier. When in late 2011 Italy's Berlusconi government fell and Mario Monti took over, the new government's foremost worry was to find the money to avoid bankruptcy as public debt was due both in 2011 and early on in 2012. Between February and May 2012 Italy needed to roll over some €300 billion ($400 billion) (i.e. money handed over by German taxpayers).

While investors reacted positively to six-month credit, the market test done in the last days of 2011 by the new government, by way of floating ten-year bonds, failed. It looked like default was the next stop. Some Italian economists said that short of a deus ex machina the only solution was taxing the Italian citizens' wealth which consisted of €4.0 trillion in real estate[15] and €4.8 trillion in all other assets.

Taken together these two figures amount to an impressive €8.8 trillion ($11.5 trillion). Those who looked to a policy of wealth taxation as being the country's salvation said that if the sovereign taxed 15 to 20 per cent of this wealth, the catchment would make the Italian government one of the richest in Europe.

Sounds impossible? Not so, because nothing will stop a government that is super-hungry for fresh money. In neighbouring Greece, confronted with a public debt of €350 billion ($465 billion), the government did just that. While it reduced salaries and pensions for public employees, it imposed a new residential real estate tax roughly equal to a monthly rent. The monthly rent of a house or apartment is the benefit its owner derives from his or her investment, but when things get tough it may be taxed away.

Real assets have intrinsic value. Governments tax the real estate based both on a cadaster value and on derived income. Cadaster value is, quite often, not updated; sometimes it is a number out of a hat. However, while the value may be wrong, the asset is tangible and – unlike financial assets – it cannot be hidden away.

This has been one of the main reasons, albeit not the only one, why *financialization* (see section 1.7) took hold of real estate. While there are real estate instruments that are similar to strictly real assets, the large majority of financialization has been *paper* land and stones, involving an income stream with a tangible asset underlying the revenue stream. This makes real estate more like equities than strictly real assets. (Investments in real estate derivatives possess an income stream with exposure to an underlying real asset. Real estate derivatives are discussed in Chapter 9 but the reader should remember that they are *not* instruments for households or for retail investors at large.)

For many investors, albeit not for everyone, the rationale for investment in real estate has been classically based on its theoretic appeal as a hedge against high inflation, its rather competitive returns over time, and its aforementioned low correlation to financial assets – hence acting as an effective diversifier. Nowadays the weight of these attributes is being transformed, and by all likelihood the extent and length of this transformation is not yet fully appreciated.

The financialization of real estate assets has altered the dynamics of wealth management. In an investment sense, until quite recently real asset returns had low correlations with the returns of financial instruments in a portfolio. This has changed in the course of the last couple of decades – derivatives played an important role in this transformation.

In conclusion people who think that, compared with equity, investing in real estate is a relatively simple, not-so-demanding enterprise live to repeat their hypothesis. As we have seen in this section, this is far from being true. Moreover, while classical real estate deals are not exchange-traded, paper real estate is also a two-party deal with added risks to those already featured by real estate properties like land and houses.

On the other hand, real estate still provides a basis for diversification in an investment portfolio, since different assets react differently to a universe of factors. The theoretical assumption is that the returns of different asset classes will not be perfectly correlated over time and, hence, will act to diversify against one another. But as we have seen in this section, while real estate investments feature benefits, they are also subject to a number of risks, well beyond price volatility, which can cause dramatic reversals in real estate returns.

8.5 Family homes and foreclosure risk

"Buy land", an old saying has it, "they are not making it anymore." This is true, but it is not a reason for buying land and houses at any price and, over and above that, getting geared-up or leveraged by doing so. The recent crisis has provided plenty of evidence that not only households but also the national economy suffers from a residential housing bust.

The evidence, if any is needed, is that residential real estate can find itself in a perfect storm. In the opinion of the European Central Bank (ECB) favourable financing conditions and expected capital gains in the 2004 to 2005 timeframe have supported strong demand for housing. At the same time, however, the rapid pace of increase in real estate prices created its own momentum, which became unstuck from the classical notions of affordability and creditworthiness.

This rang alarm bells. Since the mid-1990s in some countries – particularly Ireland, France and Spain – there have been calls for close monitoring, given the potential implications for these economies and the region as a whole.[16] One of the key reasons why central banks became interested in housing prices has been that developments in residential property prices are an important factor in assessing monetary policy decisions, particularly those aimed at maintaining price stability over the medium term. In addition changes in residential real estate prices affect households' consumption behaviour and the housing market has a two-way relationship with credit, as well as indirectly impacting upon inflation through an increase in rents.

Badly informed in respect of the aftermath of a housing bubble – and as long as the euphoria of the real estate market lasted in the first decade of this century – sovereigns looked favourably on rising prices, interpreting them as vigour. Conversely, many central bankers were concerned by the nightmare of the Great Depression of 1929–33, including its sheriff's sales (forced sales made by the sheriff following a court's order) and home foreclosures. The risk has been that both can return with a vengeance while governments drum up the merits of an "ownership society" and brag that the number of new homeowners is "the highest in history".

Almost forgotten in the government's prodding and in the consumers' rush to property ownership has been the principle of *affordability* and, in its absence, that of *foreclosure*. In early 2009, after the real estate bubble had burst, Lehman Brothers was relegated to oblivion, while the US government found itself obliged to salvage in a hurry Fannie Mae and Freddie Mac. Conversely, little, and way too lightly, has been done to relieve the pain of households under stress confronted with defaults on their mortgages and foreclosures.

It was as if a huge hole had been opened in the residential real estate market in America (also in Ireland, Spain and, to a somewhat lesser extent, Britain) through which family wealth drained. Between early 2006 and early 2009 about 5 million homes had entered foreclosure in the US alone and experts suggested that over 9 million more would enter the process over the following four years. By contrast, in normal times, new foreclosures run at fewer than 1 million a year.

The real estate cataclysm found the Barack Obama Administration totally unprepared and unable to decide on its priorities. It focused its attention on salvaging the self-wounded big banks rather than the millions of households. Yet, the domain of family houses was precisely where the greater attention needed to be paid to stabilize the market by avoiding the falling of millions of families over the financial precipice.

In all likelihood, the bureaucrats, who were expected to decide which way to look and where to turn a blind eye, were further confronted with the fact that previous efforts had flopped. An example is George W. Bush's first plan which aimed at assisting a quarter of a million delinquent subprime borrowers to refinance their debts into government-backed fixed-rate mortgages. Only 4,000 did so.

In another case, a Democrat-inspired $300 billion plan to guarantee up to 400,000 mortgages attracted a little over 500 applications. Lenders balked at the requirement that they first write down the principal. Critics say that there is no surprise that these different initiatives failed because their original conditions were wrong. Politicians and bureaucrats did not succeed in correctly diagnosing what was driving the wave of foreclosures. Was it that:

- Homeowners could not afford to pay?
- Or, after years of loose credit, banks closed their purse to home owners?
- Or they did not put good money in after bad since their homes were under water?
- Or, households had lost faith in the government's willingness to help them avoid foreclosures?

Mortgage payments were not affordable because of unemployment; and the White House had in mind a stimulus to create 3.5 million jobs over the following two years and lift more than 2 million people out of poverty. This was a vast plan with a certified high probability of failure. Neither goal was attained at the end of the day.

If negative equity was the real problem, what sort of measures could the government take so that principal could be reduced to stem the foreclosures? Left to their own devices, lenders were reluctant to do so. They worried that: many homeowners who could afford their mortgage payments would ask for principal reduction; write-downs, whether voluntary or court-ordered, would destroy their capital; investors in securitized mortgages would sue them.

The February 2009 housing plan by the Obama Administration included some $50 billion in subsidies for loan modifications for overstretched borrowers. That plan, too, had questionable deliverables. Critics said that it had several flaws. For instance, it failed to create a standardized framework for dealing with "at-risk" mortgages.

Confidence in the government's willingness to help the citizen avoid foreclosures was in short supply – and as already discussed, confidence is the oil which lubricates the business machine. Within the prevailing negative climate, where no one trusts the other party, the concept of a Homeowner Affordability and Stability Plan (HASP), promoted by the Obama Administration as a way to deal with the crisis, was judged to be too little, too late.

HASP was supposed to contain at its core a programme for the mass modification of "at-risk" mortgages, coupled with a refinancing programme. The latter was intended to broaden the benefits of declining mortgage rates limited by collapsed loan to value ratios. Theoretically that plan aimed to expand refinancing opportunities for up to 5 million borrowers whose loans were owned or guaranteed by Fannie Mae or Freddie Mac.

Critics said that it would have been more valuable to stabilize the real estate market than to try to solve the problem of "toxic" real estate assets by supporting borrowers to pay through temporary interest rate reductions. This was a mode of foreclosure mitigation but, as critics pointed out, it is too optimistic to think that servicers and lenders will automatically qualify mortgages meeting eligibility. Eligibility is a rather complex and subjective notion, and the better way to proceed is to study and decide case-by-case.

In addition, past efforts at foreclosure mitigation demonstrated that there are limits to the ability to keep a borrower in the home because of, among other reasons, a repeated default risk. Too optimistic scenarios for employment and house prices do not mitigate the downward spiral of home price declines and foreclosures.

Rather than the aforementioned plans whose applicability was at best questionable, some economists asked for federal money to relieve the pain of homeowners under stress in a practical way. In their opinion, the Administration's housing plan was too theoretical and unlikely to prevent further declines in house prices.

The trouble was that while in mid-February 2009 the Obama Administration had pledged $75 billion to reduce the mortgage payments of homeowners at risk of default that money was not enough to satisfy its announced aims; nor was the government's effort to leverage it successful. The background policy, that lenders who help people to refinance their mortgages were to receive matching subsidies from the government, did not have any traction.

What the Obama Administration had in mind was to reduce a borrower's monthly payments to as little as 31 per cent of his or her income (supposed to last for up to five years). That was the carrot. As a stick, Obama reiterated his intention to alter the bankruptcy code so that courts could reduce mortgage principal. Lenders did not think that Obama could pass such a law through Congress.

Nothing really seemed to work, and in the following year, 2010, the US was braced for 4 million or more foreclosures, while the government was still searching for an effective way to stop the rot in housing. And as a piece of bad news never really comes alone, under the Home Affordable Mortgage Program (HAMP) a mere 170,000 borrowers received permanent loan modifications. This was well below the target of 3 to 4 million. For their part, American taxpayers were stuck holding the bill of the Administration's different unsuccessful programmes.

8.6 Do your homework prior to choosing a property

In his book *Fragments of My Diary* Maxim Gorky makes reference to a Russian priest who once placed one of his boots in front of him and said to it impressively: "Now then – go!", followed by: "Ah, you can't?" With dignity and conviction the priest reprimanded his boot: "You see! You can't go anywhere without me!"[17]

No investor, not even the largest financial organization in the world, can say to the market: "Now then – go!" The market's community intelligence outweighs and outstrips that of every other entity taken alone. The only way one has to understand and (maybe) appreciate what the market might be thinking about tomorrow is to do one's homework with dedication and diligence. If this is true of big organizations with huge financial resources, it is even more so of households – whether their interest centres on real estate, equities or the bonds market.

For wealth preservation and management, first and foremost, family heads will be well advised to learn the lessons of repeated financial folly. As I have already mentioned, salvage by the heavy hand of government is practically synonymous with losing your estate.

Financial research must be productive, always questioning "the obvious". Even big names in business cannot be trusted to perform well. In business, and therefore in investments, it is relatively easy to conceive a plan. The difficulty is in executing it through the right choices and proper timing of moves. In 2011, a year the Dow Jones ended slightly above zero:

- The biggest Dow Jones loser was Bank of America at –60 per cent;
- The best Dow Jones performer was McDonald's at +40 per cent;
- The biggest Standard & Poor's 500 loser was First Solar at –75 per cent.[18]

As for experts knowing what they are talking about, Advantage Plus, the flagship hedge fund of John Paulson, who in 2007 had made a killing of $2.5 billion as the housing market descended towards the abyss, lost a cool 51 per cent of its capital. This did not happen because Paulson did not know how to do maths, but for the reason that past glory makes people blind. Pride comes to the foreground and homework takes second place.

We can significantly improve our market insight and foresight if we draw the lessons that historical context provides us with. Worst case analysis can be the mother of great lessons. Analysing the worst possible outcome raises qualitative and quantitative questions – questioning the linkages between the housing sector and other sectors of the economy beyond the dynamics of:

- Consumption and wealth;
- Volatility in house prices;
- Consumer expenditure;
- The effect of demographics.

The proper homework should include both national and local supply and demand in housing, credit availability, collateral constraints, size and role of down-payments, new financial instruments and how financial innovation changes the transmission of housing price shocks (see section 9.3). An integral part of the house owner's, and future house owner's, homework is the lessons to be learned about the range and depth of housing crises: what is the reason that three years after a crisis house prices continued falling in 8 of 16 Western countries in North America, Europe and the South Pacific?

To assess the risks of a further slump, the family head studying this pattern will be well advised to track two measures of valuation: the price-to-income ratio which focuses on affordability; and the price-to-rent ratio, which helps to value the intrinsic value of residential real estate. If both of these metrics are well above their long-term average, this is a signal that the property is overvalued. In turn, overvaluation raises the question: if residential real estate is overvalued, are prices near the cliff? If yes, how far can they fall? If, on the contrary, prevailing house prices look cheap, are they set to rebound? If yes, by how much?

These "if" questions must be answered with great care because they define whether residential real estate prices may have reached a peak or a floor. Even if there is no guarantee of an imminent price drop or bounce, knowing about cliffs and floors helps the decision-maker to be clear in his or her mind and to improve his or her judgement.

In the mid-1990s, in Britain and Sweden, prices undershot fair value by nearly 35 per cent. After the British prices bottomed they did not really start to rise for almost four years. (The careful reader will remember the reference to linkages between housing and the other sectors of the economy made above.)

In addition, global market dynamics challenge the often-heard argument that the real estate market's problems are solely the concern of overstretched developers and their banks. This is near-sighted at best, because a real estate boom is promoted by a number of factors, and conversely a property crash has implications for the economy as a whole.

Within this broader perspective must be examined all factors entering into housing prices at a given location and time. After being identified, these factors should be stress tested in regard to the importance of real property to banks and business. The security that underpins banking loans fades as property prices crash.

Political events outside the realm of the real estate industry may significantly affect market psychology and precipitate a rise or fall in prices. In the autumn of 1998, just after the near-blowout of the world monetary system because of the collapse of the Long Term Capital Management hedge fund, a decision was allegedly made by the Clinton Administration to create a national real estate bubble by dramatically lowering long-term interest rates and changing the tax code to encourage high turnover in real estate transactions.

According to an article in the *Executive Intelligence Review* (*EIR*), this decision was made at the top by Alan Greenspan, then Federal Reserve chairman, who forced his roadmap on a weakened Clinton Administration. For its part, the US Treasury Department put through two key tax code changes: the limit on profits exempted from taxation in the sale of a primary or secondary residence was raised to $500,000; a home could be sold as frequently as every two years (less, under some loopholes), without a tax impact.[19]

These changes fit well with the developing culture of homeowners, who are less and less interested in the longer term, accompanied by a large increase in adjustable rate mortgages as well as in the interest-only loans where no equity is secured. Estate agents, bankers and mortgage brokers saw this trend as "good for business" but at the same time dangerous in the cases of an interest rate spike or a sharp break in the economy.

In *EIR*'s opinion the Fed's roadmap kept both these issues under control, while the emerging business opportunities with residential real estate carried the day. Spurred on by banks eager to contract loans and earn the fees from making the deals, builders in many cases obtained relatively short-term mortgages. The idea was to complete the building, fill it with tenants and use the cash mortgages on favourable terms. But it did not work out that way.

As loans became due, and banks knew their quality was not the best, they became reluctant to refinance them. As more of those loans became due, almost none of them got an easy rollover. As nothing was learned from the experience of the late 1990s, in 2006 the Federal Reserve worried about a slowdown in housing but did not take measures commensurate with the possibility that the loss of market confidence could cause a financial crisis.[20]

As a case study about what the authorities should not do and prospective home owners should not rush to embrace, the Greenspan housing bubble provides valuable lessons on plenty of things which can go wrong – and therefore on what to avoid. "To err is human; to persist in the error is diabolical", wrote Seneca.

"Housing is the crucial issue. To get a soft landing, we need some cooling in housing," Ben Bernanke, the Fed Chairman, is quoted as having said when summing-up the economic situation in March 2006. "We are unlikely to see growth being derailed by the housing market."[21] This statement highlights the failure of the Fed's top brass to spot the great danger to the financial system from subprime mortgages – a complacency which set the stage for the crisis that began in July/August 2007.

Apart from the fact that home owners have been devastated and foreclosures have reached a new peak, the collapse in property prices affected the banks' ability to make new loans, because it cut both into their capital base and into their willingness to take more risks. As asset prices fell, the collateral provided by these assets diminished in quality, and this meant even more trouble for lending institutions.

Seen in unison, the case of Alan Greenspan and Ben Bernanke emulate the way in which a century and a half earlier, in 1862, Alfonso La Marmora, Piedmonte's former prime minister and most incompetent general, lost the battle of Custoza against the Austrians because he positioned his troops the wrong way round and so could not protect his assets. La Marmora's failed strategic plan and his battle's shortcoming have been extensively studied by general staffs as an example of what *not to do* in order to win.[22] Precisely for the same reasons, the Greenspan–Bernanke strategic plan for lifting up the residential real estate hecatomb is a precious case study on what not to do.

9

A Chapter on the Blind for the Benefit of Those Who Can See

9.1 Mortgages with currency risk: a case study on Hungary

Within euroland and its 17 economies, some countries have made a serious effort to rein in their finances: Germany, Holland, Finland and Austria are examples (though, like Ireland, Austria has fallen victim to the aggressive expansionism of its banks, which try to recreate single-handedly the Austrian empire). By contrast, other member countries and their citizens have been living well beyond their means. Greece, Italy, Portugal and Spain took a collective leave of their senses. (A special case has been the Irish sovereign which got into trouble because of the blank coverage it (unwisely) provided to its self-wounded banks.)

Euroland, however, is not the only area with unprecedented debt problems, and the next crisis may well come from a source which has not attracted too much attention: Hungary's thirst for the Swiss currency. Between 2004 and 2008, some 4 trillion forints' worth of mortgages and consumer loans were made in Swiss francs as citizens wanted to profit from the much lower Swiss franc interest rates. As 2011 came to an end, the accumulated mortgage debt in this strong currency represented 60 per cent of all Hungarian mortgages and a cool 16 per cent of Hungary's gross domestic product.

True enough, Hungary is not alone in the predicament of having heavily borrowed in a foreign currency and left its own in the dust. Somewhat comparable situations exist in Poland and Croatia, though they are not as extreme and, therefore, they are much less risky. Moreover, because of its own overleveraging, the Hungarian government finds it difficult to auction state bonds, while at the same time Hungarian subsidiaries of euroland banks deleverage, reducing their lending.[1]

The problem with the Hungarian consumer loans and household mortgages is that the citizens who took them out were unaware of the currency risk, or simply paid no attention to it. Back in 2008 the Swiss franc–forint exchange rate was at 160, while by late 2011 it stood at 240. As a consequence the value of franc-denominated mortgages and consumer loans increased by 50 per cent. No wonder that indebted Hungarian households are under stress, and so is the Hungarian economy.

The problem resulting from this 50 per cent appreciation of the Swiss franc against the Hungarian forint, and the impact it had on mortgages, can be seen in the fact that the non-performing loans ratio in Hungary stands above 10 per cent, while it is only 1.5 per cent in Poland. Temporarily, to ease households' debt burden, the Hungarian government introduced a foreign exchange (forex) pseudo-fixing scheme aimed to help troubled borrowers: interest payments were to be made at a fixed franc–forint exchange rate of 180, 25 per cent lower than the ongoing market forex rate; and, for the resulting gap between this fixed rate and the spot exchange rate, a bridging loan had to be issued by the bank to be repaid after 2014. This simply pushes the stress on homeowners a few years down the line.[2]

A country has a currency and a currency needs a country to depend on. Well-managed economies and countries rich in resources have a strong currency. If the currency slackens, then the households, economy and banks which provided the loans are in trouble. Let's now look into currency risk.

From the start of 2010 to the end of 2011, the Swiss franc and the Australian dollar have risen 22 and 19 per cent, respectively, against the US dollar. Critics say they are among the most overvalued currencies, measured by how much can be bought with them (their "purchasing power parity"). But the Swiss and the Australians know that currencies which do well are based on a strong economy – and therefore they are safe currencies (though this poses a problem with exports).

Precisely because an overvalued currency can put the economy under stress, on 6 September 2011 the Swiss National Bank (SNB) announced a "minimum" exchange rate of 1.20 francs per euro and said that it would buy unlimited quantities of foreign currency in exchange for Swiss francs (which had become a haven for investors fleeing the eurozone's debt crisis). Right after this, the franc fell from 1.11 to 1.22 francs to the euro (for a very short time prior to the announcement, the Swiss franc reached parity with the euro).

What essentially happened is that the central bank drove its currency down by putting the printing presses in action, in a way not too different than that adopted by the Federal Reserve and the Bank of England with "quantitative easing" (QE). Like all other central banks, the SNB can create francs without limit if it wants to (the price for doing so will be inflation sometime down the line).

No tool in a central bank's armoury is risk-free. QE is a show of weakness, not of strength. Officially the Federal Reserve has denied that dollar weakness is the explicit aim of QE, but the dollar's inherent weakness was part of the game, given the weak economic outlook both in the US and in the global economy.

Moreover, a policy of keeping the currency weak is rarely reached by default,[3] though most governments would like to see their currencies fall to give their exporters a chance of seizing a bigger share of global trade. As in the late 1920s and 1930s, the risk is of *beggar-thy-neighbour* devaluations which can escape the central bankers watch and lead to a round of currency wars, and from there to a depression.

The US dollar used to be a safe currency. A loose monetary policy – both in the early 1970s and more recently after 2007 – have seen to it that this is no longer the case. Still the US dollar has some strength. Its share of average daily foreign exchange turnover is the highest in the world (about 81 per cent) – way ahead of the euro's share which is the next high daily turnover currency – and practically all major commodities are priced in US dollars.

Political reasons, too, work in favour of the US dollar. It appreciates when investors are worried about the state of the global economy or there is fear of a new major war. While such instances do not challenge the long-term downtrend of the greenback, the American currency has psychological and commercial assets to hold it up. With dollar interest rates at rock bottom, Hungarians would have done better taking their mortgages out in dollars rather than in Swiss francs.

What has been said about the US dollar, the Australian dollar and the Swiss franc is evidently not the case for the forint and other weak currencies which face the risk of currency collapse, whether through an "orderly" or "disorderly" scenario. The latter would be the worst case, but even an orderly bankruptcy of Hungary and a highly devalued forint will worsen the plight of Hungarian households. At the time of writing, Hungary is near bankruptcy, though this may be averted.

Neither was the Hungarian economy helped by the currency risk assumed by its citizens. To appreciate better what this means the reader should know that, according to economists, one in three Hungarians lives on or below the poverty line. The fact that about 70 per cent of all household and business debt is denominated in foreign currencies is a problem over and above the one referred to that makes the country hostage to currencies over which it has no control.

To make matters worse, successive Hungarian governments did not do much to improve their country's gloomy economic outlook. In 2010 the (then) new government's plans looked ambitious, but their rationale was questionable, as proven by the fact that they did not work.

Just as questionable has been the government's policy towards foreign-currency-denominated mortgages. As we have seen, the banks have been forced to swallow a big part of the difference in the exchange rate. For the most past these were Austrian, Italian and German banks that were active in Hungary's home-loan market. The banks said that the government undermined the rule of law. The government answered that the banks should not have lent so recklessly in the first place.

With a large portion of the currency exposure not hedged – the mistake of the credit institutions – foreign banks found themselves at risk of a surge in non-performing loans. Part of the blame should go to the credit institution's own strategic plan of expanding heavily into Eastern Europe without the appropriate checks and controls.

According to the Bank for International Settlements some 80 per cent of Hungary's banking sector is foreign-owned, with Austria accounting for 27 per cent and Germany for 21 per cent. Eventually loans which might go bad due to the collapse of the forint could migrate westwards. Should Austria lose its AAA rating by Standard & Poor's because of its banks' exposure, or should it come under more pressure, this would most likely send shock waves through euroland. Austria has so far been perceived as a safer member of the common currency's core and, according to analysts, a big negative event could induce a reassessment of the euro's stability.

The irony is that since the late 1980s Austrian households too have fallen into the trap of Swiss-franc-denominated mortgages. Many Austrian residents who worked in neighbouring Switzerland and earned Swiss francs thought it sensible enough to borrow in the same currency since Swiss interest rates were lower. By the end of 2007 almost one out of three Austrian household borrowing was denominated in foreign currencies. Other countries which took the same road have been Bulgaria, Estonia, Latvia, Lithuania, Poland and Romania. It is silly to gamble, without considering currency risk.

9.2 Alternative investments and paper oil

The financial stress which confronted Hungarian homeowners found its origin in a mass effect amplified by ignorance of the markets. Households went long[4] on the Swiss franc without any measure of the risk they were assuming and without hedging. In many cases, they had just heard from a neighbour that this was an opportunity not to be missed for owning a home – and we have now seen the results.

Buying something in a sack without prudent examination of the horrors that may be hiding in it is by no means a practice exclusively associated with residential real estate. Quite the contrary, it is the philosophy underpinning nearly all alternative investments.[5] The term "alternative investments" is derived from the way in which capital is employed, which is typically significantly different from that followed by traditional investment methods.

For instance, one of the strategies a hedge fund manager uses is to "go short" when the price of an equity or commodity is high, and cover his position when the price drops. Essentially, he is shorting the company whose equity he sells (and sometimes the economy). Shorting has major risks because equity prices can recover unexpectedly and covering leveraged short positions becomes very expensive, if not outright ruinous.

No two financial institutions define alternative investment in the same way. In fact, few have come forward with a precise definition other than to say that the old investment strategy of buying and holding stocks or other assets is no longer valid because the market has changed. With this argument, they promote among investors a (questionable) policy of diversification by placing something like 20 per cent of investors' capital into alternative investments – which, to put it mildly, is silly.

Such an allocation of one's financial resources to *highly risky, illiquid, leveraged several times over* and *non-transparent* instruments is poor advice and bad practice which can have disastrous results. It is therefore both curious and disturbing that retail banks try to sell financial toxic waste to their clients and that the use of derivatives has reached the housing market. Your home is no longer your castle.

The better way to appreciate the effect of multiple leveraging which characterizes alternative investments deals is to think of the different layers composing the structure of intermediaries between the instrument and the end-investor. This structure consists of at least four layers, each with its own risks.

First, at the bottom of the chain are the derivative instruments, many of them novel and complex. These are designed and inventoried by movers and shakers working for banks and hedge funds. They would use practically anything as underlying raw material, doing literally as they pleased because the contents of alternative investment portfolios are not audited even by an unreliable, Arthur Andersen type, certified, public accountant.[6]

Second, next to the bottom of the chain are the hedge funds, which take on the crude risk. Among them, a relatively small number of funds (typically 10 to 20) that work with a given commercial or retail bank on alternative investments constitute what is known as the "multimanager concept". The existence of multimanagers gives the reason for being of the following, higher-up layer.

Third, above the hedge funds stands the "aggregator of risk", with its aforementioned stable of 10 or 20 hedge funds, each weighting a variable share of its alternative investments portfolio. Many of the claims the end-investor hears about liquidity, security and "high returns" (without mentioning assumed risk which is even higher) come from the aggregator of risk. As for the control of exposure, commercial banks that are in this business say "we monitor it daily" – a claim based on very shaky grounds because it is not explicit what they monitor or against which standards.

Fourth, at the top of the layered structure is the broker, who sells the alternative investment instrument to the client, the end-investor who is assuming the *full risk*. The broker and the commercial bank may be the same entity. Whether the commodity underlying the alternative investment is equities, sub primes, an ill-fated foreign exchange deal, equities, oil, cargo ships, commercial or residential real estate, the aggregator of risk and the broker try to offload the exposure which they have assumed on their customers.

At the core of this offloading business is *distribution* and its swarm of salesmen. Not all of the claims being made are untrue, because however many players in the hedge funds industry target the same instruments, markets and end-investors returns are questionable and it is difficult to distinguish the "right" from the "wrong". Moreover, distribution has become less effective than it used to be and this is undesirable because the less effective is the moving of assumed risk around the market, the greater is the likelihood that the end-investor will be left holding the can.

Housing used to be a product sold according to rules established centuries ago, and real estate has been a staple for a long time. More recently, however, staple commodities have started to be traded in *futures markets*. Energy futures was the first case and as might have been expected real estate followed in that vein.

To appreciate this transformation and its impact, we should start by briefly looking into the conversion of a commodity from a tangible to an intangible (paper) asset. The evolution in oil trading provides a practical example. Since the end of World War II, the lion's share was changing hands between big international oil companies and oil producing states through long-term contracts and fixed prices. Up to the beginning of the 1970s, roughly 5 per cent of crude oil was traded according to the free market rule of supply and demand.

For every practical purpose, the spot market for oil was created in 1969 by Philipp Brothers, then the world's largest metals trader. Marc Rich, one of Philipp Brothers' young and upcoming dealers, started selling small quantities of Iranian crude oil to independent refiners. This relatively minor operation got the wind in its sails with the oil shocks of 1973 and 1979. The aftermath has been a 180-degree shift in oil pricing, away from long-term contracts and towards the Rotterdam-based spot market.

Spot trading inserted into the oil business a swarm of financial middlemen and their income streams. It also changed the trading practice. In the spot market one buys the oil only 24 to 48 hours before taking physical (spot) delivery, as contrasted with buying it 12 or more months in advance while the barrel (159 litres) of oil is still in the earth. In parallel to this, supply and demand became the great embodiment of the oil trade.

As far as the oil producing nations have been concerned, the spot market came at the right time. In August 1971, after President Nixon abandoned the gold standard, the dollar lost nearly a third of its value. With oil, like all other commodities, being priced in dollars, oil producing nations decided to take control over their black gold, and this led to:

- A wave of oil well nationalizations;
- A substantial increase in the price of a barrel of oil;
- New rules in oil market dynamics which, as with all other commodities, went beyond spot deals.

If oil can be sold spot for delivery it can also be traded while it is still underground and waiting to be pumped. The next step in the evolution of commodities trading has been the use of derivative financial instruments – specifically the *futures* market. Two principal exchanges dominating oil futures trading are the London-based International Petroleum Exchange (IPE), established in 1980, and the New York Mercantile Exchange (NYMEX), which is more than a century old, and which in 1983 was the first to start trading oil futures.

Also known as "paper oil", oil futures contracts are in essence a claim against oil. Since the futures markets are leveraged, paper oil is far in excess of the volume of oil produced and delivered at oil terminals. Additionally, oil traders say that a futures contract may change hands 15 times or more before the underlying barrel is pumped out of the earth.

In the course of four decades, traders, investors and speculators have bought and sold on the NYMEX and IPE a horde of oil futures contracts, each one of them representing 1,000 barrels of oil. Millions of oil derivatives deals are made each month in the exchanges, while the leveraging associated with a futures contract pulls and pushes the price around. For instance, if traders bet long, the price of a barrel will rise because bets pull up the price of the underlying (of the derivatives contract).[7]

This happens with all underlying commodities, and as such it magnifies price movements (though it also helps in price discovery). At the IPE, for example, one can buy a futures contract on a margin of less than 4 per cent, which represents a 2,500 per cent leverage. If the trader buys a single futures contract, representing 1,000 barrels of oil at, say, a price of $110 per barrel, then the contract has a given price tag of $110,000, while paying only a $4,400 margin. Conversely, a margin of $110,000 will give the trader control over contracts worth almost $2.75 million.

If this sort of gearing is effectively done with oil, then it can be done with any commodity – and in the last analysis everything is a commodity, including the homes of people. An integral part of knowing how the change from classical trading to futures trading works is the skill of appreciating the most likely way in which a given commodity's market will transform itself (the market transformation of real estate will be discussed in the next section).

Of course, profit is by no means the only option, as end-users of alternative investments and other leveraged instruments know from experience. The user should take good notice of the fact that the aforementioned deals have plenty of risk and that they may regret the day when they made them. If the price of oil falls, then the broker will ask the investor to come up with collateral. If the investor is unable to do so, then the broker will sell the investor's holding (under his control), in order to protect himself from someone else's exposure.

One of the foremost criticisms of paper commodities is that by using leveraging and their market connections a small group of players can control the world's oil price. The daily turnover of Brent crude (North Sea oil quality) futures contracts on the IPE alone has been roughly equal to twice the global daily production of oil.

Other criticism concentrates on the amount of assumed risk, though this is a speculator's issue. The risk being taken by investors is commensurate to their lust and greed. A by-now-classical example dates back to the early 1980s with the Hunt brothers who tried to corner the silver market. They started with a wealth of $8 billion (inherited from their father) and ended by being some $15 billion in debt. In their descent into the abyss they also took along Bache, their broker.

Precisely because the price of futures contracts is dynamic, speculators (let alone investors) must keep enough reserves to respond to adversity. They must also have in place a system of *cash deposits* and *margin requirements* whose dependability requires:

- Steady monitoring of every inventoried position;
- Uninterrupted information on paper profits and paper losses;
- Real-time adjustment of positions to be ahead of the curve.

Sound management of geared investments requires that all positions are revalued at their current *settlement price* by *marking-to-market*, keeping well in perspective the fact that margin requirements can exceed by leaps and bounds relatively small cash deposits made when buying a contract. Practically all futures contracts represent a much larger notional amount of money, and the day may come when the speculator has to put it on the table. Short of that, he or she is one of the blind whose misfortunes are written for the benefit of those who can see.

9.3 Paper houses through real estate derivatives[8]

One of the "novel" instruments banks and securities firms have been offering since the mid-1990s is the "index certificate", also known as the "participation certificate". This is sold as a structured product with a variety of characteristics theoretically tailored to meet a range of investment objectives. Banks establish bid–ask prices for index certificates practically each trading day:[9] if the certificate is based on a performance index, then, on expiry of the period, interim earnings on the underlying asset can generally be collected as capital gains.

People with a positive reaction to the paper commodities indexes say that using this and similar instruments comes down to magnifying (read: gearing) one's assets. But what's the real cost? In all branches of finance, the major question to ask in terms of leveraging is: on whose balance sheet do the risk and return take place. For instance, in the case of paper ships, is it the ship owner's (or real estate owner's)? Or the bank's? Or is it a special investment vehicle that lies between the bank and the owner of the asset?

A key challenge is that of pre-calculating life-cycle risk, which is tough, but it is also prerequisite to the realistic pricing of, say, the paper ship index. As with any instrument, the pricing affects the issuer, the buyer and the market as a whole. Still another challenge is that of arriving at a factual and documented answer to the question of how far the paper commodity index is effective in laying off risk. This question is valid for any underlying real asset; for example with real estate.

The promoters of index certificates cite as their advantage that: they have relatively low transaction costs and comparatively good liquidity; they require a low minimum capital outlay (which means plenty of leveraging); and they provide a basis for risk diversification – a claim difficult to prove when banks are designers, vendors and price fixers of structured instruments.

These considerations are quite important in regard to real estate derivatives. Investors must keep in perspective the relative position of such a certificate in relation to their other assets and liabilities, which is not so easy because index certificates have become complex – and they are neither transparent nor liquid (and that lack of transparency also prevails in connection to their pricing).

True enough, right pricing is a challenge with nearly all financial instruments, but the more complex they are, the more opaque they become even to their issuers. Basically, the value of participation certificates is derived from their underlying; which, for instance, may be the underlying of key domestic and foreign share indexes.

Structured assets have also been used for speculative purposes and the "paper ship index" is no exception. Ship owners who know how to play with the system can use it to hedge the future value of their assets, while speculators employ the paper ship index for gambling, as this index provides the ability to page the value of assets. In addition some of the counterparties providing protection are also speculating.

Structured instruments like those discussed in this section are not traditional forward contracts. Their handling requires a lot of sophistication that does not yet exist in many commodities, or among companies which are small to medium-sized, family-run organizations. There is also the opinion that, as has happened with other complex instruments, while the new generation of commodities dealers seems open to the derivatives market, these are players with a limited understanding of what hedging is and how it can be done using futures and forwards.

When hedges are improperly designed or poorly executed, and the market moves the opposite way to what the hedger or speculator had guessed, the result is a double whammy. In such cases, it is irrelevant whether we talk of paper oil, paper ships or paper real estate. The disaster is evidently greater if the bids are leveraged.

* * *

The constraints and likely perils described in the preceding paragraphs had not been accounted for when the race to create derivatives in the real estate property market started. This happened in late 2004, some ten years after the invention of paper ships. While there were several attempts during the 1990s to design and market real-estate-based derivative products, only in September 2004 was the tax treatment under British law changed in a way to make them attractive. Until then, capital gains tax was payable on profits from property derivatives; and conversely losses did not qualify for tax relief, which evidently was an asymmetric treatment.

At least in Britain, another push in the direction of virtualizing real estate came from the Financial Services Authority which allowed insurance companies to use property derivatives for portfolio management. With a smile by supervisors and tax advantages assured by law, Britain became the first country in the world with a fully formed property derivatives market.

Still another contributor has been the fact that, contrary to the majority of countries, Britain is considered to have reliable property data collated by the Investment Property Databank, which is an independent research organization whose index tracks the return on more than £100 billion of property.

Starting with the British experience, real estate property derivatives have been largely swap-based. Swaps, however, have not been the first novel financial instrument in the property market. Barclays offered bonds and Abbey National saving products whose payout depended on movements in property prices – a different way of turning a tangible asset into an intangible one.

An interesting retrospective in the history of the development of derivative financial instruments is that prior to the use of real estate swaps financial products did not allow market players to bet against the property market. Swaps made it possible to take dual positions, such as reducing exposure to office building and increasing exposure to, say, residential real estate.

Within this dual betting, 13 January 2005 saw the completion of the first property swaps deal[10] consisting of a £40 million contract for difference that involved the exchange of exposure to the property market without the transfer of physical assets. The underlying logic has been that if returns from the British property market outperformed the Libor interest rate, then the insurer would simply pay the difference. If the returns trailed Libor, then the property company would pay the difference.

In these cases, the investor's/trader's estimate on how the market will move made the difference between winning and losing. Today this betting of £40 million may be looked on as almost pocket money, as experts estimate that, in Britain alone, this market's potential size ranges from several billion to 3 trillion pounds. Some people think that real estate swaps have come at the right time, as an estimated £4 billion ($6.4 billion) is expected to be unlocked from people's property over the next five years in Britain alone.

The reason underlying this estimate is that in Western countries elderly homeowners look for ways to boost their retirement income. The more classical way of doing this is by remortgaging or selling part of their homes.

Some experts believe that it will take some time until derivative financial instruments offered to home owners substitute the more classical process of remortgaging. By contrast, promoters of the new instruments expect a rapid rise in market interest because tangible real estate is a very illiquid market in which deals can take months and charges reach between 6 and 8 per cent in a physical property exchange.

At least for the time being, and as long as real estate derivatives are not subject to transaction tax, real estate derivative swaps can be done without the costs of a physical deal, and evidently without many delays.

In conclusion, at least at the consumer level the market for leveraging and financialization of real estate deals, known as the "equity release market", has a potential for growth which derives from the fact that people are forced to take more responsibility for funding pensions, long-term health care and education costs for children. There is no surprise in the fact that in their more classical incarnation equity release deals are aimed at homeowners who have paid off their mortgage or have only a small amount outstanding.

9.4 Leveraged trading and wealth creation are opposing concepts

Real estate derivatives are trading instruments. In the commercial real estate market they provide an opportunity for traders, investors and speculators to take a synthetic exposure to the market rather than buying properties. International swaps make it feasible to bet amongst London offices, New York apartment buildings or Tokyo warehouses, as well as to proceed with a more complex deal adding to real estate exposure risk and reward derived from:

- Interest rates;
- Currencies;
- Other commodities, like energy.

As most novelty in finance is concentrated around derivatives, the day is not too far away when a swarm of new real-estate-oriented financial instruments will be able to adapt to the idiosyncrasies of the property market. Each will create for itself a niche from which it can grow. This is good for trading, but it has no relation to creating wealth. The job is just one of switching around existing wealth while transforming it into different products. The sensation of new wealth, if there is one, comes from leveraging; but it is a Fata Morgana.

The professionals say that derivative financial instruments will rejuvenate the real estate market. The 2007 descent towards the abyss with securitized subprimes and Alt-As[11] deeply contradicts this argument. By means of overleveraging, oversecuritizing and overtrading, banks and speculators destroyed the residential real estate market and left it lying low for more years than the trough of previous real estate crises.

Evidence is provided by the fact that by 2011, four years after the beginning of the deep economic, banking and real estate crisis, the figures from America's property market were unremittingly gloomy. The National Association of Realtors reckoned that the median house price fell to a nearly nine-year low; and year-on-year sales of new houses plunged by 28 per cent to an annual rate of 250,000 – the lowest on record.[12]

Trading in highly leveraged "assets" destroys wealth rather than creates it. From being intermediaries in financial transactions, bankers turned into speculators, with bigger-and-bigger bonuses being paid for the demolition work. Several big banks drove themselves to the tip of the precipice and were saved at the twelfth hour by the sovereign's lavish spending of taxpayers' money. The capitalist economy has been shaken to its roots by tsunami after tsunami of bankruptcies engineered by lust, greed and leveraging, which increased greatly the volatility of assets and pseudo-assets. A good example of asset volatility in normal times, and profit opportunities associated with it, is the Rockefeller Center dealings. Between 1989 and 1991, the Rockefeller family sold 80 per cent of the Rockefeller Center to Mitsubishi Estate, Japan's second-biggest property group, for $1.4 billion. As far as the investor is concerned, shortly thereafter the commercial property slump turned the deal on its head.

The Rockefeller Group, through which Mitsubishi bought its stake, had hoped that soaring rents would pay the $1.3 billion mortgage on the property. That was an over-optimistic estimate as annual mortgage payments on the complex outstripped rental income by a margin. However, the Rockefeller family, which still held a 20 per cent stake in the Rockefeller Group, hardly lost out. Mitsubishi was the loser with red ink running to more than $500 million.

That was big money at the time and a material loss for Mitsubishi Estate, but it was not an outsized one because it was not leveraged. Non-leveraged deals are not accompanied by widespread wealth destruction when they unravel.

Here is another example using old-fashioned leverage, as contrasted with that of derivatives. During the third quarter of 1994, in Britain, directors and bankers of the debt-burdened Wembley Company were studying different scenarios for refinancing. This stadium and leisure company was only a small player on the British corporate field but its exposure was significant. Its debts exceeded £100 million ($160 million under the current exchange rate, though in 1994 money), and a market value of £29 million made it a star in negative equity.

After over-expanding in the 1980s Wembley found itself in a sea of red ink from borrowing – a wrong-way risk many firms willingly take. Moves to revive the company began after it reported a near-doubling of pre-tax losses in 1993. Lenders demanded large debt repayments and the leveraged company was unable to oblige.

Wembley's debt-funded acquisitions strategy led to write-offs and hefty interest payments, which ripped through the profit and loss account – even if its core venue management and greyhound track activities remained profitable. In the period between 1988 and 1991, Wembley had spent more than £130 million to expand from a London-based venue business into an international leisure group. It bought lots of unrelated businesses, such as:

- Five US greyhound tracks;
- A disco and hospitality company;
- Catering interests;
- A film distributor;
- Ticketing operations;
- Overseas betting equipment manufacturers.

It also invested heavily in improving its flagship assets: the north London soccer stadium, a conference centre and exhibition halls. Then a combination of rising interest rates and recession began to undermine the ill-conceived expansion strategy, hitting the company's weak balance sheet like a 100-mile-an-hour wind.

By the end of December 1993, net borrowings stood at £125 million, equivalent to almost three times the shareholders' funds. Under that debt burden, the balance sheet proved too weak to absorb large property write-downs, which Wembley made in 1994, following its first valuation in three years.

The results were disastrous. The value on its net assets tumbled from £175 million to £63 million forcing the company to put a £48 million loss through its profit and loss account, as an exceptional charge. Management then embarked on a round of disposals to meet bank demands for a £40 million debt repayment. It took a near-miracle to turn the company around.

Not without reason, the reader will probably say that Wembley deserved its plight since it was leveraged at 300 per cent. That was true in 1993–94. Two decades down the line, however, 300 per cent is taken as a rather conservative exposure (though personally I would never buy equity in a company whose debts are higher than 50 per cent of its equity) – banks, hedge funds and other go-go market players not infrequently leverage themselves by 3,000 per cent and the top gamblers by 5,000 per cent.[13]

The freedom to fail is the good old capitalist principle. Deals which find themselves in turbulence, because of mismanagement, absence of limits, lack of a strategic plan or simply throwing money to the wind, should be free to fail – but such failures are usually a blip on the screen. They do not bring to its knees the American economy, as happened with the highly geared, derivatives-based and globalized subprimes scam of 2007.

Real-estate routs come and go, but as long as they are not super-leveraged they are not widely destructive. Foreclosures on unrented apartments, houses and empty office buildings are only local gut punches. Slightly more fortunate are ventures with properties whose net worth and cash flow may be negative, but which are at least still in operation.

Under classical capitalism, turbulence in the real estate industry may smash local property values, but if there is no great gearing and deals have not been globalized, then the way to bet is that the net effect will be limited. Leveraging and globalization aside, big failures happen when investments and business plans are made on a fad, without fully studying the many "ifs" and in the absence of a risk control system which sets limits and anticipates possible turns of the market. Dismal failures also happen when creditworthiness is absent and loans are made against all good sense.

In the late 1980s/early 1990s, and prior to that timeframe, banks were using creditworthiness criteria with cash flow lending. They divided borrowers into "good" and "bad" depending on their ability to repay; and they examined corporate borrowings inter alia in regard to the quality of management – because time and again good governance is instrumental in upholding the quality of a company's assets.

True enough, this system had its weaknesses. Sometimes bankers and other businessmen were too confident that the client would use the money as promised and that it would generate the income necessary to pay for the loan. Things which are expected to happen don't really happen as a matter of course. But the damage was limited because it was local, not global, and the lack of high gearing saw to it that losses were contained and taken care of by loan reserves.

This is precisely the difference between *then* and *now*. In the land of the blind everything goes. There are no limits because these work against runaway businesses and fat bonuses. Loans are no more an objective but a raw material to be securitized and sold away at a profit (and, often enough, at heavy loss). Creditworthiness matters little or nothing as long as there are blind buyers of garbage, mortgage-backed securities (MBSs). Worse yet, in several cases worthless MBSs qualify as Tier 1 and Tier 2 capital in some credit institutions.

9.5 The problem is mismanagement and subdued ethics

Good old capitalism has gone absent, while at least in some countries democracy has turned into cleptocracy. This has led to a widespread conviction that bankers who take inordinate bets and care for their bonuses more than for society constitute a protected class who enjoy special privileges – which are poorly related or totally unrelated to performance and which go up even when profits fall or red ink becomes a substitute for profits.

In former times, many banks hit by heavy losses in real estate loans considered the alternative of simply writing off the loans and dumping them, provided they had enough reserves for doing so. This is not done today because the losses are huge compared to the core capital and, moreover, because of inventiveness. The more recent "solution" is to create a separate institution to handle the dirty work, a "special purpose vehicle",[14] or so-called "bad bank", which is expected to hold on and ride out the real estate recession.

To this has been added the fact that sovereigns, who are themselves overindebted, are using lavish amounts of taxpayer money to salvage self-wounded big banks. An important difference with previous real estate debacles, for instance in the early 1990s, is that then sovereigns were not ready to throw massive public money at private banks to pull them up. Financial institutions had to find their own way out of the mess.

First Chicago, for example, dealt with this problem with a mixture of stock sales and accounting gimmickry.[15] The bank offset a $625 million write-off in the third quarter of 1992 with a $300 million gain, by marking up the value of its venture-capital portfolio to its market value. In addition, to bolster its capital further, it put on the block some $600 million of preferred stock.

As for the "bad bank" idea, this was still confined to a single institution which was inventive. An early pioneer of the bad bank, in

1988 the Mellon Bank set up Grant Street National Bank to which it sold $500 million of bad real estate loans. To do so, it had to:

- Mark down the loans to about 41 cents on the dollar;
- Float $500 million in debt;
- Raise $175 million from a private investor.

Grant Street then put those marked-down real-estate loans up for sale, unloading all but $5 million of them, but not without unpleasant consequences. Mellon and Grant Street have been sued by several former borrowers whose loans ended up in Grant Street's portfolio. Some critics said that the bad bank was not an ethical solution, and should not be expected from senior bankers. In 1988 the bad bank was still an exceptional case. But two decades later it became the easy and painless way out for mismanaged banks – and the taxpayer pays for it all.

Back in the 1990s other banks favoured the auction block. In August 1992 Jones Lang Wootton USA, an arm of the British development company, tried to auction off $500 million in commercial real estate, much of it foreclosed bank property. The result was far from fulfilling expectations. Even though bidders from the US, Europe and the Pacific Rim crowded the Century Plaza Hotel in Los Angeles, barely half the properties sold and those that did fetched less than half their original value. Worse yet, several buildings sold for less than their published minimum prices.

This is a telling example of how mismanagement can severely damage a financial institution. In September 1992, Shawmut National Corporation entertained offers for a parcel of loans with a face value of about $100 million. The bidding from institutional investors started at 55 to 60 cents on the dollar, but at short notice 50 per cent "haircuts" prevailed as the auction turned in favour of the buy side. There was no real lack of capital. The issue was pricing; and cash carried the day. Could this rescue-by-haircut be expected to continue? The answer is "Yes!" if no gearing upsets the scales, and "No!" if the weight of losses becomes unsupportable and turns investors away.

Take Spain as an example. In January 2012 the new government's finance minister, himself a former banker, reckoned the country's banks, which had leveraged real estate financing in a big way, needed to set aside another €50 billion ($65 billion) in provisions for bad property loans. What was not publicly stated was the level of mismanagement which created that gaping hole.

The Bank of Spain said that there were €176 billion ($229 billion) of non-performing real-estate loans and foreclosed assets. This represents a cool 52 per cent of the banking system's total property book. Spanish banks have already set aside provisions to cover a third of these bad assets – but it may not be enough. According to Morgan Stanley's estimates, if the Spanish sovereign plays *deus ex machina*, then it would need to purchase the assets and recapitalize the banks to the tune of more than 10 per cent of GDP.[16]

Taxpayers, not only Spanish taxpayers, are not at the end of their pains. Bad rescue policies with plenty of moral hazard (instituted in 2008) die hard. At the time, a friend of mine remarked that giving the banks absolution of their sins in the years preceding their descent towards the abyss is like giving monkeys the freedom to reproduce as they please. And reproduce they did.

On 1 January 2012, in Britain, there was an estimated £280–293 billion ($448–469 billion) of debt secured against commercial property. A very large slice of this huge amount, if not already in breach of financial covenants, is at loan-to-value ratios that would be near impossible to refinance.

"A lot of loans have no covenants built in, but are impossible to refinance so they go into distress at maturity", said one senior property banker. "There isn't a chance in hell you are going to be able to refinance it. If you want to take a catastrophic view of the world, then anything above 60 per cent loan to value (LTV) is effectively distressed or distressed in waiting."[17]

This statement was made at a time of worsening sentiment about the future prospects of the real estate sector, a situation already causing institutions to pull back from property lending. Regulatory rules aimed at preventing a new real estate catastrophe, along with market psychology, have made it harder to find cash to buy the swarm of non-performing loans.

Mismanaged banks who thought that, given the links between banks and governments, sovereigns would rush to their rescue have lived to regret it. It looks as if times have changed. During the 2008 crisis, governments propped up their banks; but by 2012 governments are leaning on banks to keep buying their bonds.

This, too, is a policy which can only come out of a second-rate public administration: banks buy non-investment-level, sovereign bonds; then the sovereign uses taxpayers' money to save the banks from bankruptcy – because these banks find it hard to borrow from other institutions or from investors. According to learned opinion, the bond-buyers' strike afflicting banks is more worrying than that associated with sovereign bonds and loans.

Even the classical source of funding by borrowing through short-term interbank markets or tapping money markets is drying up. In the second half of 2011 American money-market funds, which were a big source of dollars for the European banking system, have reduced loans by more than 40 per cent – and for good reason. Banks are reluctant to lend to one another, except for the shortest possible time, usually overnight.

Because of the mismanagement of Western economies, savers have lost faith in banks and sovereigns. Greek depositors have been allegedly shifting their money to the tune of €65 billion ($84 billion). Citizens in Italy and Spain are starting to do the same. For their part, large corporations, which know how to shift deposits early, are seeking relative safety further afield.

In conclusion, after years of second-class management at the sovereign level as well as in high finance, practically all assets are suspect. As of early 2012, fund managers privately confess that they wish they could move entirely into cash and sit out the market turmoil. Vulnerabilities are present all over the financial industry. The nightmare scenario is that deposits leaking from banks in peripheral countries will turn into a full-flood bank run.

9.6 Questioning whether a steady financial innovation is useful to society

The world of assets could be described as existing along a continuum running from strictly *real* assets to strictly *virtual* assets (financial instruments including paper money). In this clarification, the *really* real assets are either fixed in supply or grow slowly. According to Marrinner Eccles, Chairman of the US Federal Reserve in the Franklin Roosevelt Administration, our productive capacity is limited, while there is no limit to the expansion of the money supply (the virtual assets).[18]

Expectations and preferences can have dramatic influences on the price of real assets, and their worth is also strongly affected by the rate at which the currency is depreciating (the inflation rate). However, with the exception of hyperinflation, the price volatility of real assets tends to stay within certain bounds.

At the opposite end of this spectrum are the strictly virtual assets whose purchasing power is subject to a much higher volatility, and therefore to opportunity and risk. In addition, it follows that the greater is the leveraging factor, the more a virtual asset is thought to be worth – until the bubble is burst. Beyond that point, the virtual asset's worth can fall away to hell.

Derivative financial instruments[19] are the virtual assets of virtual assets. When marked-to-market they easily turn from assets to liabilities and vice versa, creating a gap which at times demolishes the centuries-old concept of the "balance sheet", originally established by Luca Pacciolo, a contemporary and friend of Leonardo da Vinci.

In contrast to the years prior to World War II (and, to a significant degree, prior to the 1970s and 1980s), when banking was about deposit-taking and lending, today's bankers engage in complex trading deals which do not necessarily fit the old established principles of being financial intermediaries. *Off-balance sheet* financial reporting, and the practices which go along with it, are an example of big profits and losses. Financial innovation created an accounting challenge, and the origin of off-balance sheet practices is in itself instructive.

In the mid-1980s when derivatives deals started to become a certain size a question came up regarding the way derivatives transactions should be written in banking books. The answer was not self-evident because when marked-to-market the value of these instruments moved from the left side of the balance sheet (assets) to the right side (liabilities) and vice-versa. American banks asked their regulators where to write derivative transactions and the answer they got has been: write them off the balance sheet.

Little thought was given to the fact that what was then treated as an exception might become a mammoth in the financial industry and so cast its shadow on the banks' balance sheets. Neither have the events which took place afterwards rung any alarm bells, for instance, the intensity of derivatives exposure in certain financial centres. By the early 1990s the market where the largest risks were taking place was New York. A study done at the time found that

Australian banks had more derivatives exposure in New York than in Melbourne or Sydney.

As a rule the control of exposure lags way behind financial innovation. If the organization, sophistication and technology of risk control was commensurate to those characteristic of financial innovation, then the Western world's banking industry would not have melted down the way it did in 2008 and in subsequent years. Furthermore, if ethics had reigned supreme, then banks would not have shown a disregard in the management of their customers' fortunes.

Fiduciary obligation, too, has become a casualty of deregulation. If added evidence is needed that at the level of financial institutions risk control is an irrelevance and a bother – while shareholder value and client attention are fake slogans – then all one needs to do is to look at the record of the 2 February 2012 investigation of the MF Global scam by the US Congress.

MF Global bet $6.3 billion on European sovereign debt. This was the wrong gamble and it went bust. (There has also been a scam involving money missing from its clients' accounts.) Congressmen asked whether MF Global had exercised prudential and rigorous risk control, and in their testimony their former and current chief risk officers gave the impression that "intramural" it was known that their company was dancing its way to the precipice.

On 2 February 2012 Michael Roseman, the former chief risk officer (from 2008 to January 2011), said before the House investigations subcommittee that during his period in office he expressed his increasing concerns (with regard to the potential capital risk) to MF Global's CEO Jon Corzine (a former US senator, state governor and boss of Goldman Sachs). His risk scenarios were however challenged, and in the end he was dismissed. As for his successor to MF Global's top risk management job, his deposition did not express any regret. What he said was: "I would like to wait for the final chapter to be written"(!).[20]

One of the main reasons regulators have no clue about exposure assumed by banks with their derivatives gambling is that about 80 per cent of derivatives trades are done over the counter (OTC) and banks keep them close to their chest.[21] To make matters worse, up to 95 per cent of OTC off-balance-sheet deals are bank-to-bank. They are not made on behalf of the banks' clients, whether corporates or other entities, but as a hazardous speculation "for profits".

Whoever says "profits" also means "bonuses", and the wheeling and dealings are closely kept secrets. Some of these secrets, however, eventually hit the public eye and end in court. On 2 February 2012 Milan's chief prosecutor asked for Alessandro Profumo (the former CEO of UniCredit, Italy's largest bank), three Barclays employees and 16 other people to stand trial for alleged tax fraud set up by the British bank and used by the Italian one.

This Milan trial request comes at a bad time for Barclays as it also faces questions in America over cross-border finance deals and whether they resulted in abusive tax avoidance. The Internal Revenue Service (IRS), the US tax authority, is in court with four American banks over more than $1 billion in disallowed foreign tax credits that came from those deals; and so on and so forth.

While Barclays is not a party in the aforementioned cases, it is portrayed as a pivotal promoter in deals dubbed "stars" (structured trust advantaged repackaged securities) that exploited existing asymmetries in tax systems. The core issue is whether these private deals by banks were legitimate business and whether it complied with taxation laws in America and in England – or were designed specifically to generate improper American tax credits.

This and other similar cases are one more documentation – if one is needed – of the wisdom and importance of the US Volcker Rule which is part of the Dodd-Frank Act and, up to a point, prohibits banks from going overboard and into proprietary trading. Whoever says "no speculation" also means "smaller bonuses"; therefore American banks, asset managers as well as foreign governments have mounted a well-financed campaign against the Volcker Rule on the ridiculous claim that "it could harm markets" (a more truthful claim would be "it would harm pockets").

* * *

Is financial innovation a *poisoned gift*? No less an expert than Adair Turner, head of the British Financial Services Authority, thinks that many parts of the banking business had grown beyond a socially reasonable size. On 28 January 2012 in Davos, Switzerland, Turner participated in a panel discussion about the banking industry, which also included: Jean-Claude Trichet, former European Central Bank president; Nouriel Roubini, New York University professor of economics; Peter Sands, CEO of Standard Chartered bank; Guillermo

Ortiz, former Mexican central bank governor; and Luc Frieden, Luxembourg Finance Minister.

The panel has been debating the progress of regulators in taming risk in the financial system after years of crises. Particular attention was paid to financial innovation and to high-frequency trading[22] where banks and other financial entities use computer-driven algorithms to place hundreds of trades a second. (This now accounts for more than half the US stock trading volume, according to data compiled by Bloomberg.)

"Before the crisis, there was a very strong belief within the economics profession that this was good," Turner said of high-frequency trading. "But once you've got a reasonably active, liquid market, is there any real value? I think it's quite reasonable of us to ask searching questions in a way we didn't before the crisis on whether this is limitlessly good."

Other panelists, too, criticized high-frequency trading as a source of systemic risk. Guillermo Ortiz pointed out that "we must be questioning whether all financial innovation is useful". Peter Sands said that "we never really know which banks are systematically important". And Jean-Claude Trichet added that "central banks can only reduce the intensity of bank collapse".

"We should be more cautious than before the crisis in allowing processes like high-frequency trading," Turner stated. "Banks should have internal ring-fencing. Anybody who after dividing commercial from investment banking forgets about investment bank supervision has forgotten Lehman."

"I'm comfortable if a hedge fund takes risk on behalf of its own investors and if they do well they do well, if they fail they fail", said Nouriel Roubini. "I'm less comfortable with using taxpayers' money." Roubini has been in favour of breaking up large banks and of restoring the Glass-Steagall Act.

Another key issue which attracted the panel's attention is that trading volumes in foreign exchange and credit have exploded in recent years, as improvements in technology enable companies to place more trades more quickly in more asset classes. "It is an incredible intellectual exercise to try to catch up with these new tools that are permanently putting into question the wisdom of our own regulation", Trichet said. "We have to be prepared for even more dramatic changes in the functioning of IT and therefore the functioning of markets."

"The acid test here is to ask yourself whether new (financial) products and innovation is something that benefits directly or indirectly the real sector of the economy, the households", concluded Ortiz. "Does it help to better allocate resources, does it help distribute risk better, or are we just talking about bets that are being taken in the financial sector and have nothing to do with the real economy?"

Notes

Introduction

1. John Kenneth Galbraith, *The Affluent Society*, Penguin Books, London, 1970.
2. Not to be confused with George W. Bush's devil.
3. André Maurois, *Ariel, ou la Vie de Shelley*, Bernard Grasset, Paris, 1972.
4. See D.N. Chorafas, *Basel III, the Devil and Global Banking*, Palgrave Macmillan, London, 2012.
5. Liaquat Ahamed, *Lords of Finance*, Windmill, London, 2010.
6. UBS, *Wealth Management Research*, 29 March 2012.
7. D.N. Chorafas, *Risk Pricing*, Harriman House, London, 2010.
8. Paul A. Samuelson, *Economics*, McGraw-Hill, New York, 1948.
9. Though this cannot be exactly stated of Leon Walras, also of the late nineteenth century.
10. A third, though quite different, reason is that in all likelihood before too long colleges and universities will be teaching twenty-first-century household economics and finance. It is hard to imagine that we educate physicists, chemists, engineers, medical doctors, as well as business managers and other professionals, on how to run their laboratories, their offices or their firms, but provide them with no knowledge on how to be in charge of their families' finances.
11. Milton and Rose Friedman, *Free to Choose*, Harcourt, Orlando, FL, 1980.
12. CNN, 3 April 2012.
13. The Bible, for instance, is full of metaphors. Paul, the Apostle, loved them and for good reason.
14. My advice is not to use them because paper houses will take most people for a ride and lead to huge abuses.
15. Luciano Biancardi, *Garibaldi*, Mondatori, Milan, 1972.
16. John P. Kotter, *Matsushita Leadership*, The Free Press, New York, 1997.

1 Our Society Has to Review its Business Model

1. This was President Johnson's theory that the US could afford Medicaid, Medicare and other services while the war in Vietnam was in high gear.
2. All macroeconomic models are wrong, but some are useful.
3. *The Economist*, 9 December 2006.
4. *Financial Times*, 14/15 January 2012.
5. *The Economist*, 22 January 2011.
6. *Bloomberg News*, 13 April 2012.

7. The large majority of ordinary citizens (99 per cent) might not know that, whether they belong to the left or the right, those who govern always lie in the top 1 percent of income earners. And if they don't do so when they enter government, their membership is assured when they leave. François Hollande, the French president who led the Socialist party in the April/May 2012 elections was earning a cool €30,000 per month before he entered the Elysée Palace – all public money from different political posts. With €360,000 ($475,000) per year the Socialist party candidate for the presidency fully met the definition by *The Economist* and US Congressional Budget Office of belonging to the top 1 percent of income earners.
8. There were 1,100 billionaires world-wide in 2007 prior to the deep economic and financial crisis. In 2009 their number dipped to 800, but rose to nearly 1,000 in 2010.
9. Wealth serves as a fallback in times of crisis, and in the longer run it is worth what its owner is doing with it. Is he or she managing it right?
10. Even if, according to the *Los Angeles Times*, six Wal-Mart heirs are wealthier than the entire bottom 30 per cent of the US population (*Financial Times*, 3 January 2012).
11. *Financial Times*, 3 January 2012.
12. *Financial Times*, 30 March 2012.
13. *Bloomberg News*, 6 April 2012.
14. This figure includes unemployment benefits, health care and lost tax revenue.
15. *Fortune*, 4 March 1996.
16. The way economists describe "rent seeking" includes all the efforts made to influence political decisions in regard to handouts. A rent seeker is any group (or individual person) that depends on government favours – whether engineered by special interests or by the populist ballot.
17. D.N. Chorafas, *Education and Employment in the European Union: The Social Cost of Business*, Gower, London, 2011.
18. *Bloomberg News*, 27 October 2011.
19. Participants in the movement prefer the park's original name to that of Zucotti.
20. Some of the fruits of the Russian Revolution, particularly the leaders who came to power in 1917, were wiped out. Zinoviev fell so low as to lick the boots of his guards just prior to being shot.
21. This has been repeatedly tested in France and in Britain – under Tony Blair with the label "The Third Way" – without any success.
22. Margaret Macmillan, *Paris 1919*, Random House, New York, 2001.
23. Deutsche Bundesbank, Monthly Report, January 2012.
24. European Central Bank, Monthly Bulletin, January 2009.
25. Daniel Amman, *The Secret Lives of Marc Rich*, St Martin's Griffin, New York, 2009.
26. See D.N. Chorafas, *Financial Boom and Gloom: The Credit and Banking Crisis of 2007–2009 and Beyond*, Palgrave Macmillan, London, 2009.

27. D.N. Chorafas, *Globalization's Limits: Conflicting National Interests in Trade and Finance*, Gower, London, 2009.
28. One can export democracy if one finds it difficult to export goods, but this does not solve the trilemma's problem.
29. China has copied the industrialization blueprint of nineteenth-century Germany. The British had Sheffield, the Germans Solingen; Solingen produced the same things Sheffield did but much more cheaply. What the Chinese government has probably failed to notice in Germany's case is that this led straight into World War I – because industrial competition and preservation of British dominance in the industrial market wanted it that way.
30. *The Economist*, 29 October 2011.
31. One example Suskind brings up is that in early 2009 Geithner deliberately ignored Obama's instructions and the advice of Larry Summers, former treasury secretary and former president of Harvard University, and Christine Romer, former chair of the economic advisors to President Obama, to develop a plan to wind up, rather than bail out, Citigroup (Ron Suskind, *Confidence Men: Wall Street, Washington, and the Education of a President*, Harper, New York, 2011.
32. The ECB's equivalent to quantitative easing has been the Long Term Refinancing Operation.
33. While by 2011 American manufacturing activity had started to pick up, few new jobs have been created. To compete in a globalized manufacturing environment, where every penny in cost counts, companies use automation as far as they can and they look at every cost dollar like an eagle.
34. Edith Hamilton, *The Greek Way*, W.W. Norton, New York, 1930.

2 Entitlements

1. *Financial Times*, 3 January 2012.
2. John Kenneth Galbraith, *The Affluent Society*, Penguin Books, London, 1970.
3. Ibid.
4. See D.N. Chorafas, *Financial Boom and Gloom: The Credit and Banking Crisis of 2007–2009 and Beyond*, Palgrave Macmillan, London, 2009.
5. Jobs then were scarce in Brazil, though the situation was better than in neighbouring countries. In Guatemala the Minister of Education had said that a young fellow had three career opportunities: he could become unemployed, a pimp in the city or a guerrilla in the countryside. Think of that if you are against birth control.
6. *Financial Times*, 13/14 August 2011.
7. *Financial Times*, 21 December 2011.
8. Contrary to the British "middle class" definition, in America skilled blue-collar workers are part of the middle class.
9. *International Herald Tribune*, 23 November 2009.

10. *The Economist*, 10 September 2011, Carlo Ponzi was an Italian–American who, for a period of time, successfully used the swindle of paying new investors exorbitant interest with the money of those already in the game, until the whole system collapsed.
11. *The Economist*, 15 October 2011.
12. *Financial Times*, 3 January 2012.
13. *The Economist*, 6 December 2010.
14. Data from a panel discussion on CNBC, 22 November 2011.
15. *Bloomberg News*, 2 May 2012.
16. *Bloomberg News*, 29 June 2011, Notice that Coburn's 3 to 1 ratio for Medicare becomes 9 to 1 when applied to the wider US population because of Medicaid's impact.
17. Ibid.
18. *Le Figaro Magazine*, 5 March 2011.
19. Ibid.
20. The unofficial but more realistic rate of US unemployment gravitates between 20 and 25 per cent, including part-time workers, those who think long term, and others. Statistics depend on which school one believes.
21. *The Economist*, 2 April 2011.

3 Jobs and Education

1. *The Economist*, 19 November 2011, If young people in full-time education are excluded, Britain's youth unemployment rate is estimated to be about 22 per cent, below that of countries like France, Italy and Spain.
2. "Learn how to learn" was the advice that Andrei Gromyko (long-time foreign minister then president of the Soviet Union) gave to parents asking him what was the best policy for their children.
3. William W. Davenport, *Gyro! The Life and Times of Lawrence Sperry*, Charles Scribner's, New York, 1916. This reference talks volumes both about Lawrence Sperry's eagerness to learn and about the richest man in the world teaching at Sunday school to help shape the next generation.
4. Apprenticeship is still widely practised in Germany and Switzerland, and it is considered to be a reason why in both countries the level of unemployment is low compared to France and the US.
5. *Canard Enchainé*, 27 June 2012.
6. Quite informative is the old question, "What's the difference between a piece of wood and a bureaucrat?", the answer being that wood works.
7. Henry Adams, *The Education of Henry Adams*, The Modern Library, New York, 1931.
8. This does not mean that for higher education there should be no fees. There should be, but for parents and students this is a problem they need to address.
9. *Bloomberg News*, 16 February 2012.

10. Social networks are making matters worse by offering bank accounts to teenagers as young as 14. There is talk that Facebook will lower that age and in a sample of parents interviewed on this absurdity three out of four had no negative opinion.
11. *L'Express*, 3 August 2011.
12. *Bloomberg News*, 2 July 2012.
13. About 50 per cent of the world's disk drives are nowadays made in Thailand. PCs, desk top boxes and other equipment create a huge demand for disk drives, and the interruption of the supply chain, because of persistent floods in Thailand, has created a global shortage of millions of units (CNBC, 13 December 2011).
14. *The Economist*, 11 June 2011.
15. *Financial Times*, 16/17 July 2011.
16. By watering down or nullifying entry exams the states have de facto spoiled a large part of their investment in university education.
17. *Le Figaro*, 13 June 2012.
18. There is a similar scheme in Britain, but of smaller dimensions, and the authorities already estimate that one-third of student loans will never be repaid.
19. *Financial Times*, 17 June 2012.
20. *Bloomberg News*, 25 July 2012.
21. John Kenneth Galbraith, *The Affluent Society*, Penguin Books, London, 1970.
22. Télévision Suisse Romande, 28 October 2012.
23. *The Economist*, 10 September 2011.
24. Ibid.
25. The well-known French socialist leader at the beginning of the twentieth century.
26. Peter Drucker, *The Effective Executive*, Heinemann, London, 1967.

4 The IOU Abyss

1. A government organization, like the Federal Deposits Insurance Corporation (FDIC) in the US, guarantees (up to a certain level) the money in depositors' accounts. There exist different schemes of deposit insurance.
2. In December 2011, Commerzbank, Germany's second largest bank, had to raise €5.3 billion ($6.9 billion) to satisfy the regulator's request for new capital. This sum equalled 80 per cent of Commerzbank's market value, at a time when investors were risk averse. Hence, the need for resorting to government help.
3. Lendol Calder, *Financing the American Dream: A Cultural History of Consumer Credit*, Princeton University Press, Princeton, 1999.
4. R. Christopher Whalen, *Inflated*, Wiley, New York, 2011.
5. *Financial Times*, 17 November 2011.
6. Golda Meir, *My Life*, G.P. Putnam's Sons, New York, 1975.
7. *The Economist*, 10 April 2010.

8. CNBC, 11 November 2011.
9. It is very bad policy to imprint on the mind of the new generation the leveraging one can get through credit cards. Several banks are now offering a rebate on fees to make teenagers into credit card addicts. "Ma Premiere Carte" by Crédit Agricole, in France, is an example.
10. *The Economist,* 1 December 2007.
11. Durable goods bought by consumers tend to last and can be used repeatedly. Their longer service means that they have some of the attributes of assets, though their price decreases rapidly as they are used.
12. *Executive Intelligence Review,* 25 January 2008, my emphasis.
13. www.automotivedesign.eu.com
14. The two global non-financial companies confronted by the largest amount of debt are General Electric (GE) and Toyota. GE's market capitalization is about $180 billion; its debt stands at $420 billion – 233 per cent of its capitalization. Toyota's capitalization is $130 billion, and the corresponding debt is $150 billion, well over equity.

5 Households and the Value of Money

1. Golda Meir, *My Life,* G.P. Putnam's Sons, New York, 1975.
2. Up to and including World War II most families first earned and then spent money. This has radically changed due to easy credit. The best policy today is to watch out carefully for *net debt.*
3. See D.N. Chorafas, *Basel III, the Devil and Global Banking,* Palgrave Macmillan, London, 2012.
4. In East and South East Asia in 1997 and 1998 the so-called "Tigers" fell into the same trap – and were criticized by Westerners, who went on to repeat the same mistakes.
5. Merrill Lynch, "Global Economics", 28 November 2007.
6. Margaret Heffernan, *Willful Blindness,* Simon & Schuster, New York, 2011.
7. Jeffrey Sachs, *The Price of Civilization: Reawakening American Virtue and Prosperity,* Random House, New York, 2011.
8. See D.N. Chorafas, *Globalization's Limits: Conflicting National Interests in Trade and Finance,* Gower, London, 2009.
9. *M6,* 23 March 2010.
10. For two reasons. A larger sample is better; it is easier to calculate the average of past years by summing up, doubling the addition and dividing by 10.
11. *The Economist,* 30 May 2009.
12. See D.N. Chorafas, *Wealth Management: Private Banking, Investment Decisions and Structured Financial Products,* Butterworth-Heinemann, London and Boston, 2005.
13. Even better would be a rolling three-month period, so that the household finances have better visibility, thereby avoiding the mismatch of assets and liabilities.

6 Managing Family Wealth

1. See D.N. Chorafas, *Alternative Investments and the Mismanagement of Risk*, Palgrave Macmillan, London, 2003.
2. It is no less true that in practice small shareholders don't have much say on the way a company is run.
3. Convertibles are derivative instruments at the border between stocks and bonds. Initially issued as bonds, they are convertible to equity, but with a catch. The issuer's redemption right may also have an impact on the investor's ability to sell his or her bonds as the redemption date approaches.
4. In a broad sense the OTC market used to include distribution of new securities to investors through underwriting operations, as well as through other means, such as providing a direct, off-exchange market for securities that are already outstanding. Nowadays, however, by far the biggest OTC trades are in derivatives – which are not the retail investor's business in the first place.
5. This is an example of trading through derivatives, not of investing. We will discuss the difference later on.
6. See D.N. Chorafas, *An Introduction to Derivative Financial Instruments*, McGraw-Hill, New York, 2008.
7. *Global Economic Weekly*, 12 June 2009.
8. *The Economist*, 9 July 2011.
9. *Bloomberg News*, 7 January 2012.

7 The Market Does not Crawl: It Jumps

1. See D.N. Chorafas, *Managing Risk in the New Economy*, New York Institute of Finance, New York, 2001.
2. Retirees whose pensions exceed the PBGC's cap would see their benefits drop.
3. In 2011 even hedge funds believed to have the clout to manipulate the market lost plenty of money. In the month of December the hedge fund Flash Return was down 0.54 per cent (Bank of America Merrill Lynch, Hedge Fund Monitor, 27 December 2011).
4. This was a pity, because, while she was a poor gambler, she was a first-class baker. Under the ownership of the man who subsequently acquired her bakery, quality drifted and customers ceased to patronize it.
5. Bernard Baruch, *My Own Story*, Buccaneer Books, Cutchogue, NY, 1957.
6. Ron Chernow, *The House of Morgan*, Touchstone, New York, 1990.
7. What is relevant is not the so-called "core inflation rate", which does not consider energy and food prices, but the actual cost of living of private households shown through "headline inflation".
8. Bob Woodward, *Bush at War*, Simon & Schuster, New York, 2002.
9. Along this line of thinking, Brandon Davies, when he became the treasurer of UK operations at Barclays Bank, charged his assistants with

studying 200 years of British economic and financial history to uncover the ways and means through which financial crises built up.
10. *The Economist*, 19 June 2004.
11. UBS, Wealth Management Research, 9 December 2011.
12. A central principle of Keynesianism is that the alignment between savings and investments is not always automatic, and that misalignment can have serious consequences.
13. *Financial Times*, 11 August 2011.
14. See D.N. Chorafas, *Alternative Investments and the Mismanagement of Risk*, Palgrave Macmillan, London, 2003.
15. *The Economist*, 5 March 2011.
16. *Nice Matin*, 29 October 2011.
17. See D.N. Chorafas, *Financial Boom and Gloom: The Credit and Banking Crisis of 2007–2009 and Beyond*, Palgrave Macmillan, London, 2009.
18. *The Oxford Companion to Family and Local History* is a most helpful guide in this area. In Britain there is a "Land Registry" where anyone can inspect details of land with the buildings on it; but that does not guarantee that a piece of land and the buildings thereon is listed. In theory it should be, but in fact many properties only get measured and detailed when ownership changes and that can be after many generations. It is a long, tangled story but "cadaster land register" does not quite fit in a UK context.
19. The first significant real estate swap materialized in January 2005 with a £40 million ($64 million) contract. Since then there has been a torrent of such deals.
20. Roger Lowenstein, *Buffett, the Making of an American Capitalist*, Weidenfeld & Nicolson, London, 1996.

8 Home Ownership: Shelter or Burden?

1. By the end of the first quarter of 2009, a year and a half after the bust, 14 million American households (27 per cent of mortgage holders) owed more than their homes were worth, according to estimates by financial analysts.
2. *Financial Times*, 13 January 2011.
3. The value of American homeowners' equity in their own houses had slumped by over 50 per cent by 2011 from a peak of $12.5 trillion in 2005, destabilizing family finances.
4. The Federal National Mortgage Association (Fannie Mae) dates from the New Deal of the 1930s; the Federal Home Loan Mortgage Corporation (Freddie Mac) was instituted in the early 1970s by the Nixon Administration. Both have been government-sponsored enterprises which, by the time of their bankruptcy (and takeover by the US government), guaranteed about $5.4 trillion worth of US home mortgages.
5. Bank of America Merrill Lynch, Global Economic Weekly, 18 March 2011.

6. *Financial Times*, 13 January 2011.
7. And left taxpayers holding the bag to the tune of $150 billion, compared with the $25 billion asserted in Congress when they were taken over by the government.
8. Subprime mortgages are typically granted to people who simply cannot afford them. These home buyers were used as raw material for what became the biggest financial scam in history. We will see the reasons for this.
9. See D.N. Chorafas, *Financial Boom and Gloom: The Credit and Banking Crisis of 2007–2009 and Beyond*, Palgrave Macmillan, London, 2009.
10. Countrywide, conceivably the most aggressive player in the subprimes market, went bankrupt. Its remains were acquired by Bank of America, which is still paying for Countrywide's misdeeds.
11. Lawrence G. McDonald and Patrick Robinson, *A Colossal Failure of Common Sense*, Crown Business, New York, 2009.
12. Ibid.
13. Lehman Brothers had been forced to drop the price, selling CDOs at 95 cents to the dollar: a $100 million loss.
14. Citigroup and Bank of America were said to be the biggest buyers of subprime securities. Yet it is not unreasonable to expect that two of the largest banks in the world should have known what they were doing.
15. This is an estimate because the cadaster is neither updated nor precise.
16. ECB, "Financial Stability Review", June 2005.
17. Maxim Gorky, *Fragments from My Diary*, Allen Lane, The Penguin Press, London, 1940.
18. In spite of all the talk that alternative energies are the future.
19. *EIR*, 22 July 2005.
20. According to transcripts of meetings released in January 2012.
21. *Financial Times*, 13 January 2012. The first sentence in Bernanke's statement is correct. As a prognostication, the second sentence missed the mark by 180 degrees concerning what did happen after the house bubble.
22. Luciano Bianciardi, *Garibaldi*, Mondatori, Milano, 1972.

9 A Chapter on the Blind for the Benefit of Those Who Can See

1. UBS, Wealth Management Research, 13 January 2012.
2. The Hungarian government also announced an option for borrowers, if they could come up with the cash, to repay their mortgage at the favourable rate of 180 and let banks assume the corresponding loss.
3. In the last week of October 2011, for example, the Japanese yen hit a post-World War II high against the US dollar, prompting the Bank of Japan to engage in intervention in an effort to weaken their currency and support domestic exporters.
4. "Going long" and "going short" are terms used with equity investments. When an investor is long on securities, it means that he holds the assets he bought for the longer term. By contrast, by going short he is selling

the assets that he does not possess, typically by borrowing them from somebody else. In the case of "naked shorting" he may be selling assets without even having borrowed them.

5. See D.N. Chorafas, *Alternative Investments and the Mismanagement of Risk*, Palgrave Macmillan, London, 2003.
6. Arthur Andersen was one of the half-dozen, big, global auditors that turned a blind eye on accounting irregularities of the firms they audited. Its demise came after the Enron scandal.
7. Derivative financial instruments are typically based on an "underlying" which may be an interest rate, a currency exchange rate, the securitization of a pool of mortgages or another commodity.
8. See also in section 6.4 the discussion on derivative financial instruments and the advice that households should abstain from using them for investment purposes.
9. Such a practice amounts to a conflict of interest. The dice is cast against the investor.
10. This contract for difference was arranged by Deutsche Bank and Eurohypo, the German specialist real estate bank.
11. See D.N. Chorafas, *Financial Boom and Gloom: The Credit and Banking Crisis of 2007–2009 and Beyond*, Palgrave Macmillan, London, 2009.
12. *The Economist*, 26 March 2011.
13. This 5,000 per cent mark was set in 1998 by the practically bankrupt Long Term Capital Management, though it took a number of years before it became more generalized. See D.N. Chorafas, *Managing Risk in the New Economy*, New York Institute of Finance, New York, 2001.
14. See D.N. Chorafas, *Financial Boom and Gloom: The Credit and Banking Crisis of 2007–2009 and Beyond*, Palgrave Macmillan, London, 2009.
15. *Business Week*, 5 October 1992.
16. *The Economist*, 7 January 2012.
17. *Financial Times*, 6 January 2012.
18. William Greider, *Secrets of the Temple: How the Federal Reserve Runs the Country*, Simon & Schuster, New York, 1989.
19. See D.N. Chorafas, *Outsourcing, Insourcing and IT for Enterprise Management*, Palgrave Macmillan, London, 2003; and D.N. Chorafas, *Alternative Investments and the Mismanagement of Risk*, Palgrave Macmillan, London, 2003.
20. *Financial Times*, 3 February 2012.
21. Only recently an effort by the International Securities Dealers Association (ISDA) aimed to make such deals OTC-traded, but so far the results, in risk management terms, are rather limited.
22. In October 2011 the European Union announced a plan to curb high-frequency trading following the "flash crash" in May 2011, during which the Dow Jones Industrial Average briefly lost almost 1,000 points.

Index